Social Democracy in the Austrian
Provinces 1918-1934: Beyond Red Vienna

Social Democracy in the Austrian Provinces 1918-1934: Beyond Red Vienna

Charlie Jeffery

Leicester University Press
LONDON

Fairleigh Dickinson University Press
MADISON • TEANECK

LEICESTER UNIVERSITY PRESS
A Cassell imprint
Wellington House, 125 Strand, London WC2R 0BB, England
and **Associated University Presses**
440 Forsgate Drive, Cranbury, NJ 08512, USA

First published in 1995

British Library Cataloguing-in-Publication Data
A catalogue record for this book is available from the British Library

ISBN 0–7185–1398–3 (Leicester University Press)
ISBN 0–8386–3629–2 (Fairleigh Dickinson)

Library of Congress Cataloging-in-Publication Data
Jeffery, Charlie.
  Social democracy in the Austrian Provinces, 1918–1934 : beyond Red
Vienna / Charlie Jeffery.
    p. cm.
  Includes bibliographical references and index.
  ISBN 0–8386–3629–2 (alk. paper)
  1. Sozialdemokratische Arbeiterpartei Deutschösterreichs—History.
2. Austria—Politics and government—1918–1938. I. Title.
JN2031.S58J46   1996
324.2436'038'09041—dc20   95–33956
                                                            CIP

Printed and bound in Great Britain by Biddles Ltd, Guildford and King's Lynn

Contents

List of Tables

List of Abbreviations

AMG	Alpine Montangesellschaft
AVABKA	Allgemeines Verwaltungsarchiv, Bundeskanzleramt
AZ	*Arbeiter-Zeitung*
BCA	Boden-Credit-Anstalt
CSP	Christian Social Party
DÖW	Dokumentationsarchiv des Österreichischen Widerstands
FTU	Free Trade Union
IFZ	Institut für Zeitgeschichte, Vienna
KPÖ	Kommunistische Partei Österreichs
LTP	*Linzer Tagespost*
LVB	*Linzer Volksblatt*
LVSt	*Linzer Volksstimme*
MAV	Metallarbeiterverband
NSDAP	Nationalsozialistische Deutsche Arbeiterpartei
ÖMA	*Der Österreichische Metallarbeiter*
OÖAZ	*Oberösterreichische Arbeiterzeitung*
OÖLA	Oberösterreichisches Landesarchiv
OÖTZ	*Oberösterreichische Tageszeitung*
ÖVP	Österreichische Volkspartei
ÖVW	*Der Österreichische Volkswirt*
SAJ	Sozialistische Arbeiterjugend
SDAP	Sozialdemokratische Arbeiterpartei
SPÖ	Sozialistische Partei Österreichs
STB	*Steyrer Tagblatt*
SZ	*Steyrer Zeitung*
VGA	Verein für Geschichte der Arbeiterbewegung

Preface

This study has grown out of my doctoral thesis, *The Social Democratic Movement in Steyr, Austria, 1927-1934* (Loughborough University of Technology, 1990). Working on the doctoral thesis exposed me to the crude Vienna-centrism which has traditionally dominated research into Austrian Social Democracy. It produced a commitment to write a wider work on the Social Democratic movement in the Austrian provinces which would consciously look beyond and, where appropriate, qualify and reject the distortions of a Vienna-centred received wisdom. Such is the aim of this book. While retaining the empirical core of the doctoral thesis, the book also provides as comprehensive as possible a survey and analysis of Social Democracy throughout the Austrian provinces, and of the relationship between Viennese 'core' and provincial 'periphery' in the Social Democratic movement. It shows that Social Democracy outside Vienna was a weak and fragmented force, thrown on the defensive directly after the First World War by a front of hostile and far more powerful forces which included the parties of the Right, the Catholic Church and the fascist *Heimwehr*. It also shows that the Social Democratic 'citadel' in Vienna was too consumed in the grandeur of its project of 'socialism in one city' to generate strategies which might have been capable of lending support to the embattled provincial movement. This neglect of the periphery allowed the anti-socialist front in most cases to erode the power bases and morale of Social Democracy in the provinces well before the end of the 1920s, and long before 'Red Vienna' itself came under threat in the early 1930s. This is the central message of the book, for without a sturdy provincial backbone to draw support from, even the Viennese citadel found itself forced to succumb to the diktats, and finally the artillery, of the Austrian Right in 1934.

Neither this book, nor the doctoral thesis which inspired it, could have appeared without the robust research supervision and friendly support of Stephen Padgett or the advice of my surrogate *Doktorvater* during my initial research visits to Austria, Joe Weidenholzer. And my research visits to Austria would have been far less fruitful and much less enjoyable without the help, congenial atmosphere and, to all intents and purposes, second home provided by, among others, Andrea Tippe, Edith Jakob, Franz Turek, Christa Orthofer, Johanna Klammer, Günther Spatzenegger, Gerhard Lörenz and Erwin Lunger. Back in the UK I have been lucky to have had the support of a small but vibrant community of Austrianists, above all Jill Lewis and Robert Knight, whose ongoing commitment, provocative debate and critical suggestions have enriched my ideas, and Richard Luther, whose encouragement spurred on this project from the early stages. A particular debt is owed to the patience of Alec McAulay and Nicola Viinikka at Leicester University Press during my persistent overshooting of submission deadlines. Finally, the environments provided by colleagues in the Department of European Studies at Loughborough University of Technology, the Department of Politics at Leicester University, the Institute für Gesellschaftspolitik and Moderne und Zeitgeschichte at the Johannes-Kepler-Universität Linz, and more recently the Institute for German Studies at Birmingham University have helped to make the rather protracted work on this book a pleasure.

The research for the book was carried out in the Oberösterreichische Studienbibliothek and the Oberösterreichisches Landesarchiv in Linz, the Magistrat der Stadt and the Museum Industrielle Arbeitswelt in Steyr, and the Allgemeines Verwaltungsarchiv, the Dokumentationsarchiv des Österreichischen Widerstands, the Verein für Geschichte der Arbeiterbewegung and the Arbeiterkammer in Vienna, in all of which the staff were uncommonly helpful. A particular pleasure was to talk and correspond with a number of First Republic Social Democrats - above all Josef 'Pips' Mayrhofer, Alois Zehetner and Peter Kammerstätter - who could tell me far more than any library or archive about what being a Social Democrat meant in such a fraught era of political history. Lastly, of course, those bodies which helped to fund the research also need to be thanked for their generous support: the Economic and Social Research Council, the Österreichischer Gewerkschaftsbund, the Bundesministerium für Wissenschaft und Forschung der Republik Österreich, and the Research Boards of Leicester University.

Charlie Jeffery
Birmingham, 1995

Introduction:
Looking Beyond 'Red Vienna'

Back in 1990 one of Austria's leading historians, Gerhard Botz, made the telling plea: 'Why not a new history?'[1] Botz' plea was inspired by some of the problems, particularly of methodology and political partisanship, which have beset and frustrated the development of contemporary historiography in Austria. Post-war historical research in Austria has been heavily constrained by the sensitive legacies left by Austria's turbulent experience of the 20th century: the transition from vast empire to 'dwarf-state' at the end of the First World War; the Civil War of 1934 and the subsequent entrenchment of 'clerico-fascist' dictatorship; the absorption of the 'dwarf-state' into the Third Reich between 1938 and 1945; and the reestablishment of an independent Austrian state against the background of four-power occupation in the years 1945-1955. Botz' plea, written under the impression of the events of 1989 in Eastern Europe, was that it was now time for these constraints to be thrown off and for historical research in Austria to enter, like the East Europeans, a brave, new and liberated era.

This plea for a 'new history' is immediately understandable to anyone who, as I did, began research in the mid-1980s on Social Democracy in the Austrian First Republic. At that time the existing literature presented a distorted and romanticised vision of the Social Democratic movement. It was largely restricted to the 'high' politics of the Social Democratic Party (SDAP) in Vienna - to the party's national-level leaders, their ideas, and the policies they developed both for the national stage and for their municipal power base in 'Red' Vienna itself. It was also highly partisan and uncritically sympathetic towards the Social Democrats, and in particular towards the politics of Red Vienna.

Only in more recent years has there emerged a more balanced literature which has begun to look beyond Social Democratic high politics and Red Vienna and to present a more critical and detached assessment - and a better understanding - of the Social Democratic movement in Austria as a whole.[2] The purpose of this book is to offer a further contribution to this process of reassessment. It seeks to investigate the issues which confronted, and shaped the character of, Social Democracy in the Austrian provinces 'beyond Red Vienna', and to discuss the findings of this investigation in the light of 'traditional' perceptions of the Social Democratic movement. The aims, approach and content of the book are presented in more depth below. First, however, the context for the study is set out in a discussion of the ways

1

in which, and the reasons why, the established vision of Social Democracy in the First Republic has been so distorted.

Looking Through the Viennese Prism

In some ways the tendency to view the history of the Social Democratic movement through the 'prism' provided by the high politics of the SDAP in Vienna is understandable and justified. Firstly, as capital city and seat of federal government, Vienna was the centre stage of national politics in Austria. As such it naturally provided the arena and focal point for Social Democratic party politics at the national level: Vienna was the site of the National Secretariat and Executive of the SDAP, the forum for intensive theoretical and strategic debate between the leading protagonists of 'Austro-Marxism', and the setting for high-profile parliamentary conflicts between the Social Democrats and their political opponents.

Secondly, Vienna was also an important political stage for the SDAP in its own right. As the largest industrial centre in Austria, it was home to a dense concentration of SDAP supporters. Vienna accounted, for example, for some 59.46% of the party's national membership in 1930 and 46.36% of its all-Austrian vote in the national election of that year.[3] This concentrated support provided the party with a clear majority in the Viennese city council throughout the First Republic. In addition, the city council enjoyed the extensive budgetary and policy autonomy of a federal *Land*. From these twin bases of concentrated party strength and constitutional autonomy emerged the 'socialism in one city'[4] of Red Vienna. Red Vienna was an innovative, internationally renowned and thoroughly unique experiment in social engineering, comprising not just a radically redistributive programme of municipal socialism, but also an attempt to mould, educationally and culturally, the supporters of Social Democracy into the 'new human beings' fit to populate the socialist society of the future.[5]

Thirdly, and bridging the above two points, this Viennese experiment came to dominate the strategic vision of the national party leadership in the course of the 1920s. The SDAP was guided by the theoretical commitment of Otto Bauer, its most influential top-rank leader, to a peaceful, evolutionary transition to socialism within the framework of the post-war democratic state. Initial progress was made on this reformist project during the SDAP's short period in federal government between 1918 and 1920. With its return to opposition, however, the party was forced to retreat to a 'fall-back' position of generating the electoral majority in Austria which would enable the 'transition to socialism' to be resumed. Red Vienna took on central importance in this electoral strategy. Its achievements were styled as an electoral 'beacon' which would attract and win over enough support in the Austrian provinces to supplement the party's strength in Vienna and secure a majority of the national vote. Although this strategy was not a success, it served to lift Red Vienna onto a pedestal as a shorthand symbol for the politics and aspirations of the Social Democratic movement as a whole.

The national and municipal politics of the SDAP in Vienna are, for these reasons, clearly of fundamental importance in the study of Austrian Social Democracy. That importance has, though, tended to be overstated in much of the work on the subject. It has, for example, even led one author to consider it legitimate to use 'the terms "Red Vienna" and "Austro Marxists" or "Social Democracy" *without any distinction'.*[6] This is clearly going too far. The importance of high party politics in Vienna was by no means all-encompassing and needs to be qualified in at least three in part overlapping respects. Firstly, as is clear from the figures quoted above, around half of the party's electoral support and some two-fifths of its membership were located outside Vienna. The SDAP in the provinces faced circumstances vastly different from those which existed in Vienna. Beyond Red Vienna there were very few large and integrated industrial areas in Austria. Industrial communities - the centres of strength of the SDAP - were more often than not isolated enclaves situated amid the broad swathes of the country dominated and governed by the various right-wing opponents of Social Democracy. The narrow geographical research focus on Vienna has meant - despite the repeated urgings of Helmut Konrad[7] - that far too little attention has been paid to the characteristics of the SDAP in these enclaves or to the significance - if any - of the high politics of Social Democracy in Vienna to the Social Democratic grass roots in the provinces.

Secondly, the emphasis on high politics implicitly assumes that the preoccupations of the party's leaders acted as a guideline and inspiration for Social Democratic activities at all levels of the party. This emphasis deflects serious attention away from the 'low' politics of the party both in and outside Vienna: from the party's rank and file supporters, their immediate, everyday concerns, their self-perceptions as Social Democrats, their roles in the party's organisation, their views on the party strategy, their attitudes towards 'socialism in one city' and so on. In this way the literature delivers a simplistic and skewed picture of the party as a kind of puppet theatre, with Otto Bauer and the party executive pulling the strings, and the party activists and ordinary members dancing jerkily across the stage of history towards the final curtain of the Austrian Civil War of 1934.[8]

Thirdly, the persistent research emphasis on the party politics of Social Democracy in Vienna has served to prevent a full recognition of the different concerns of, and problems faced by, other Social Democratic organisations and their members, particularly the trade unions, but also the myriad auxiliary - mainly educational and recreational - organisations which were clustered around the SDAP. The Social Democratic Free Trade Union movement was, in numerical terms at least, stronger than the SDAP throughout the years 1920-1929[9] and enjoyed a relationship with the SDAP which was closer than, for example, that in Germany. Little attempt has, however, yet been made to delve consistently or in any critical depth into the history of the trade unions and their members either in or outside Vienna, or to investigate the nature of the relationship between unions and party.[10] Quite remarkably, the major work on the First Republic trade unions remains, in the 1990s, Fritz Klenner's monumental, but essentially narrative two-volume magnum opus from the early 1950s, which has unrivalled value as a reference work, but which never shakes off its somewhat anodyne character as an official history of the union movement.[11] Equally, work on the auxiliary organisations of the Social Democratic movement has rarely been distinguished by genuinely critical analysis; nor has it been tempted to venture very far from a limited Viennese focus.[12]

For these reasons, the historical depiction of the Social Democratic movement in the First Republic has tended to a spurious homogenisation, fixed on the top echelons of the party in Vienna and neglectful of the provinces, the party rank and file and the non-party components of the movement. In a sense, though, such a one-dimensional depiction is not entirely out of place in post-war historical writing. Similar tendencies to view history in general, and the labour movement in particular, from 'above', through the prism of high (party) politics, have also been predominant elsewhere in western Europe. This was, for example, certainly the case for many years in research into perhaps the nearest equivalent of the SDAP, the German SPD of the Wilhelmine and Weimar eras.[13] It seems hardly surprising that there have been similar trends in Austria as well, especially when one considers two characteristic features of the SDAP in the First Republic: on the one hand the SDAP leaders themselves were deeply preoccupied with their immediate Viennese environment and remote from the 'outside world' of the rest of the Social Democratic movement; and on the other, this preoccupation was shielded from sustained challenge from other elements in the movement by the highly undemocratic internal structures of the party.[14] The party leaders were therefore able, as it were, to set an unchallenged, Vienna-dominated agenda which pervades the historical sources they left behind: the party press, the minutes of party executive and conference proceedings, biographical material and so on. This agenda, has, it seems, come to be reproduced by historians who, in later eras, have approached their subject from 'above'.[15]

Elsewhere in western Europe, though, methodological innovations emerged, particularly in the field of social history, which opened up new angles of historical enquiry. These shifted the emphasis away from history from above and towards the examination of the broader context within which politics is conducted at the grass roots of society. This history from 'below' focused increasingly on everyday life, experience and culture, often shifting attention away from metropolitan centres and towards under-researched provincial locations. Over time the use of such methods contributed to the development of a more nuanced and differentiated historical analysis of West European labour movements.[16] Research in Austria, though, failed to keep pace fully with these methodological innovations. It largely failed as a result to ask the questions and provoke the debates on labour history which might otherwise have helped to supplement the inherited historical agenda and qualify established Vienna-dominated perceptions of the Social Democratic movement.

The failure to keep pace with new methodological trends in historical research is the central problem Gerhard Botz was calling attention to in his plea for 'a new history' for the 1990s. Its roots can be traced to the years immediately after the Second World War. In those years, the major parties of government in the new Austrian Second Republic, the Socialist Party (SPÖ) and the Christian Democratic People's Party (ÖVP), had to confront a complex of interlinked problems. First and foremost they had to present an image of responsibility and unity to the four occupying powers in Austria which would prevent both full retribution for Austria's part in the Third Reich and ensure that their country, unlike Germany, did not become divided as the Cold War took hold. To construct this image they had, secondly, to patch over the bitter social and political divide which had plunged their predecessors in the First Republic into Civil War, and which had smoothed the way for Austria's absorption into the Third Reich.

The means to these ends were an elaborate elite-level compact which bridged past divisions and underpinned a Grand Coalition of SPÖ and ÖVP until 1966, and an even more enduring 'social partnership' of the major economic interests which remains broadly intact today. This 'consociational'[17] compact between Left and Right fulfilled its main purpose well, succeeding by 1955 in securing Austria's international rehabilitation and the end of the occupation regime, as well as providing a stable basis for domestic political and economic reconstruction. One of the essential components of this compact was, though, to have a profound impact on post-war historical research: an understanding that neither side would dwell on and reopen the wounds of the inter-war years. This understanding found an echo in the historical writing of the period, reflecting in part a generalised, post-war aversion towards open discussion of the past, but also the extension of a key element of consociationalism - proportional party-political patronage - into the historical profession.[18] The result was the so-called 'coalition history' of the 1950s and 1960s, a consociational compact among historians which drew a thick and forbidding line under the recent past.[19]

In these circumstances the in-depth, critical study of contemporary, twentieth century history came late to Austria. It could only commence, falteringly, as the perceived post-war need to tread carefully with the past became gradually less pressing. Accordingly, the country's first university institute of contemporary history was not founded (in Vienna) until 1966, some fifteen years after its pioneering German counterpart in Munich,[20] and the appearance of the first Austrian journal of contemporary history, *Zeitgeschichte*, did not follow until 1972. As a result the period of soul-searching which contemporary historians underwent elsewhere in the *Aufbruchstimmung* of the late 1960s, and which opened up new and fruitful methodological avenues, largely passed Austria by. Since then, Austrian historiography has been playing 'catch-up'. And despite advances in the last two decades it has still not yet been fully able to cast off the 'quality of provincialism'[21] caused by political-historical sensitivities about the previous half-century of extraordinary upheaval.

In Search of a Heroic History

This 'quality of provincialism' helps explain the methodological limitations which have restricted the *scope* of the research questions asked about Social Democracy in the First Republic. It does not, however, obviously account for the overt *friendliness* of many of the questions asked of the Social Democratic movement. Much of the research on the movement has been pervaded by an undisguised, partisan commitment to the Social Democratic cause. An unfortunate by-product of such partisanship has been the tendency to play up the virtuous, to play down the unflattering, and thus to contrive a 'heroic' depiction of the movement which often approximates more to mythology than to reasoned historical debate.

The mythologisation of the Social Democratic movement has been most clearly evident in a series of officially sponsored and romantically titled 'histories' of local Social Democratic organisations. These present bland chronicles of the unstoppable rise of the movement from its origins in the late 19th century, against all the odds and via a vast array of setbacks and crises, through to the mighty organisation (in which the authors are invariably active) of today.[22] Such works of Social Democratic *Heimatkunde* are, of course, more or less explicitly designed to provide the local movement with an 'acceptable' history and have few or no pretensions to critical scholarly distance or analysis. The tendency to myhologisation has also extended less justifiably into more serious academic research on Social Democracy, particularly on Red Vienna. Immense energies have been invested in the discussion of the redistributive policies of the SDAP city council in Vienna, especially its massive council housing programme, and of the attempt to reeducate the supporters of the movement into 'new human beings' steeped in a new and selfless socialist culture. These discussions have often tended towards the openly acclamatory, presenting uncritically the scope of party aims and programmes, the institutional structures set up to carry them out and the sheer, quantitative scale of what was achieved. They have not, as Helmut Gruber has repeatedly stressed,[23] sought to look beneath the programmatic and institutional surface and examine some of the less appealing, perhaps uncomfortable implications of SDAP policies in Red Vienna.

Two examples are worth mentioning by way of illustration. The first is a consistent theme in Gruber's own work and concerns the party's quest for the cultural reeducation of its supporters. This quest was carried out in a way which was thoroughly paternalistic towards those supporters. The party's educationalists had a deep distaste, bordering on contempt, for the established forms of cultural expression of the Viennese working class and sought to sweep these away wholesale and replace them with their own (often pretentiously and narrowly intellectual) priorities.[24] Scant attempt has been made in the many monographs[25] on the various Social Democratic auxiliary organisations to examine this unabashed cultural paternalism and the way it was perceived by the culturally 'inferior' workers, although, as Gruber has shown, such an enterprise is quite possible. *Critical* investigation of the SDAP's cultural policies in Vienna has, it seems, been beyond the pale.

Beyond the pale too has been the discussion of whether the SDAP city council in Vienna used the extensive powers it held as a consciously manipulative means of *compelling* support for the party. The SDAP's successor party in the Second Republic, the SPÖ, is renowned as a party of patronage, a party which (like the ÖVP) has sought to bind supporters to it more tightly through the provision of membership-dependent material benefits.[26] It is astonishing that there has as yet been no systematic investigation of Red Vienna from this same perspective of party patronage. The Social Democratic city council in Vienna certainly had the wherewithal for an extensive patronage strategy, particularly in the allocation of council housing and of jobs in the municipal workforce. But despite occasional hints in the literature about patronage in Vienna[27] (and despite evidence that Social Democratic organisations outside Vienna, which possessed far fewer patronage resources, consciously employed political patronage as a strategy of mobilisation)[28], Red Vienna has managed to escape any depth of scrutiny in this field.

The purpose in highlighting the less *salonfähig* faces of SDAP policies is not to deny the significance of the party's achievements in Vienna. City council policies unquestionably improved the standard of living of countless Viennese. And the cultural and educational activities of the party and its auxiliary organisations clearly opened up new and often emancipatory forms of cultural and leisure activities for the party's supporters. But as long as these positive aspects of Social Democratic policies are presented without consideration of their perhaps less 'wholesome' implications, those policies risk being reconstructed as unchallengeable icons which disguise more than they reveal about the Social Democratic movement.[29]

The question of course needs to be addressed why, in these and in other[30] areas, the historiography of the Social Democratic movement came to enter the realms of iconography and mythology. A crucial factor here was the break-up of the SPÖ-ÖVP Grand Coalition in 1966 and the subsequent years initially of ÖVP (1966-70) and then of SPÖ (1970-1983) single-party government. The end of the Grand Coalition broke the 'intellectual chains'[31] which had sustained consensual 'coalition history'. It certainly did not, however, break the hold of politics over history in Austria. Even after the Grand Coalition, the historical profession retained unusually close personal and institutional links to the major political parties.[32] These close links provided the basis for the emergence of a *'Hausgeschichtsschreibung'*, a polarised 'in-house history' in which the expression of value judgements by historians close to one or the other major parties about 'their' party's past often tended to obstruct critical reflection and explanation.[33]

'In-house history' was certainly not restricted to those close to the SPÖ.[34] It did, though, emerge most strongly on the Left, particularly after the establishment of Socialist single-party government in 1970. Under the active patronage of the SPÖ in its first tenure of the Ministry for Science and Research, there emerged a 'growth industry'[35] of research into the Social Democratic movement in the First Republic. This 'growth industry', in Gruber's words, put 'the history of the movement in the service of the subject it describes'.[36] Many of its products had a more or less explicitly didactic purpose, intended in the first instance not to extend knowledge, but to provide a sense of direction for the supporters of a party which had become increasingly remote, bureaucratised and directionless in the stifling atmosphere of

Grand Coalition politics. An extreme and revealing expression of this combination of partisanship and didactic purpose was given by Helmut Konrad in 1981:

> A historiography of the labour movement which sees itself not as ivory-tower scholarship, but as *research in the service and the interests of the movement* ... must still - alongside all consideration of qualms about academic rigour, precision and the verifiability of what is written - keep in mind *the key question of whether the products of the research correspond to the needs of the potential 'consumers'*. Without wanting to go into a discussion of the dangers of a scholarship of legitimation, it has to be said that *the necessary partisanship for a historiography of the labour movement must also have didactic consequences*.[37]

To me, Konrad's statement seems quite remarkable in so explicitly reducing history to a tool of politics, in so openly prioritising partisan commitment, the needs of history's 'consumers', and the interests of the movement over any sense of critical reflection and distance. The result of such priorities is, inevitably, the 'scholarship of legitimation' he alludes to. This has been dubbed by Gruber as a unity of scholarly and practical commitment to the Social Democratic movement,[38] a commitment whose search for a usably heroic history has, in local organisational histories, in studies of Red Vienna and in other fields, marred and skewed much of the past research into the Social Democratic movement.

Why Not a New History?

It would, of course, be churlish and inaccurate to imply that the whole genre of Austrian labour history remains beset by overt partisanship and an obsession with high politics. In recent years a number of Austrian historians have begun to adopt new approaches and pose less orthodox questions, with often stimulating results.[39] There has also been a noticeable decline in the overt partisanship of scholarship, a factor which reflects in part a growing disenchantment with the established parties in Austria, but also the (related) erosion of the 'hold' of party patronage in the Austrian public sector.[40] It is in the light of these more recent historiographical trends that this work should be seen. While not seeking to deny clear sympathies with the inter-war Social Democrats in Austria, particularly at the rank and file level, this book stands aside from overt party-political partisanship. The book presents, in other words, a critical account[41] which looks past the Social Democratic mythology of the post-war era. It also looks very firmly beyond high party politics and beyond Red Vienna. Its focus is the local-level Social Democratic movement in the industrial centres of the

Austrian provinces, where 'movement' is understood to mean not just the SDAP, but also the Social Democratic trade unions and the diverse network of Social Democratic auxiliary organisations, and, perhaps most importantly, the individuals who constituted the Social Democratic membership and electorate.

In other words, this work seeks to approach the history of Austrian Social Democracy 'from below', from the perspective of the grass roots of the Social Democratic movement in the provinces. The focus on the grass roots level allows a far more nuanced approach to the study of Social Democracy which can extend beyond the more or less fixed reference points - leaders, organisational structures, ideology and policies - which dominate studies in high politics. In particular, it allows for a much closer examination of the interests, values, mentalities and social relationships which provided the fundamental stimulus and inspiration for political organisation and behaviour. The aim is to investigate the political attitudes and experiences of Social Democrats at the local level in the provinces and to analyse the impact of those attitudes and experiences on the character, activities and priorities of the local-level movement, and on the dynamics of the relationship between provincial 'periphery' and Viennese 'centre'. This approach will, it is hoped, go beyond the over-generalisations and over-simplifications inherent in histories from above and produce new insights into the central question which ultimately underlies any study of inter-war Austrian Social Democracy: How and why did this movement, which had by far the largest membership, per head of population, in the world,[42] and which stood as an unchallenged force in left-wing politics, come to disintegrate and be destroyed just fourteen years after successfully leading the transition to democratic government in Austria after the First World War?

A useful analytical starting point in approaching the history of inter-war provincial Social Democracy from below is provided in the concept of 'milieu'. The term 'milieu', as refined and employed by Ernst Hanisch,[43] points to the existence in Austria of more or less closed communities with a broadly homogenous 'environmental' background comprised of shared socio-economic interests and experiences, party-political and religious traditions (and the conflicts associated with them) and the particularistic forms of popular culture shaped by all of these. The 'classic' milieux of the Austrian provinces were, according to Hanisch, manual worker communities with strong, often vehemently anti-clericalist Social Democratic party and trade union traditions and conservative, normally staunchly anti-socialist, rural communities pervaded by the influence of the Catholic Church.[44]

Research based around the concept of milieu has hitherto focused on the role of 'environmental' background in mediating and shaping the responses of the inhabitants of these 'classic' milieux to the experience of National Socialist rule in Austria between 1938 and 1945.[45] The investigation of 'environmental' background also offers, however, two potentially useful points of departure for the study of local-level Social Democracy in the First Republic. The most obvious is the influence of the distinctive internal characteristics of manual worker milieux in shaping the political behaviour and orientations of local-level Social Democrats in the inter-war years. The second, related, but perhaps more important point of departure is the imprint left on political behaviour and orientations by the social and political conflicts which arose from the contrasts between the overwhelmingly Social Democratic manual worker milieux of the provinces and the overwhelmingly anti-Social Democratic rural milieux which typically surrounded them.

This twofold research focus was something alluded by Helmut Konrad in a manifesto he set out in 1983 for future research priorities in the field of local/regional labour history in Austria. Konrad noted firstly the 'decisive importance' which should be accorded to 'the internal conditions of the region in the emergence of the cultural and political forms of behaviour of the working class'. He then added that regional labour histories, most of which concentrate on industrial areas, must, without fail, take the structure of the (usually non-industrial) hinterland into consideration, since 'the working class and its organisations do not develop in a vacuum, but rather establish their field of activity within an environment whose character largely helps shape the possibilities and types of activity undertaken'.[46]

This work is an attempt to fulfil the manifesto 'pledges' of Konrad, to examine the 'environmental' backgrounds which shaped Social Democratic politics in the provinces. Its empirical backbone is a case study of Social Democracy in the industrial town of Steyr, an entrenched Social Democratic stronghold situated in the predominantly rural backwater of south-eastern Upper Austria, some 100 miles west of Vienna. This choice of case study does not imply that Steyr was selected for its presumed typicality among Austrian industrial towns; indeed it is doubtful whether there can be such a thing as a 'typical' town.[47] Rather, Steyr was selected for the following *extraordinary* characteristics:

• Firstly, Steyr was one of the main industrial centres in Austria, with a long tradition of metalworking industry in the armaments and, after the First World War, the automobile sectors.
• Secondly, its industrial, working class background formed the social basis of a Social Democratic movement which

was able to establish hegemonic control over local politics
for most of the First Republic.

• Thirdly, the local hegemony of the Social Democratic
movement stood in stark contrast to the situation in the
surrounding, predominantly rural area dominated by
steadfastly hostile, Catholic-conservative opponents of
Social Democracy.

• And finally, Steyr's economy in the First Republic was
dominated by one single works, the Steyr-Werke,[48] an
automobile factory whose violent fluctuations in economic
performance structured and shaped the political
'conjuncture' in the town.

In all these respects Steyr was a manifestly extreme case. But, as
David Crew has suggested, 'the extreme case can often be extremely
revealing'.[49] The milieu in which Social Democratic politics in Steyr
were located exemplified, in exaggerated form, the broader
circumstances which confronted Austrian Social Democracy as a whole:
the stark pattern of social segmentation, the deep political cleft between
the Austrian *Lager*, and the unpredictability and fragility of the inter-
war Austrian economy. The purpose of this study is to investigate the
political 'products' of these unusual and exaggerated circumstances, to
investigate what kind of Social Democratic movement emerged from
the socio-economic background and socio-political conflicts of this
extraordinary 'milieu', and to ask what new insights into the history of
the wider Austrian Social Democratic movement the experience of
Social Democracy in Steyr might offer.

Any such study must, though, remain aware that its local focal
point can offer little of wider value if treated purely in isolation. Even if
the experience of a 'Red Steyr' stood in stark contrast to an established
picture derived from Red Vienna, it would not necessarily mean much
per se. For this reason the case study of Steyr is embedded throughout
in a comparative context which draws, as far as is possible, from the
experience of the Social Democratic movement across all of the
Austrian provinces.[50] This approach allows broader patterns of
development in provincial politics, which the experience in Steyr may or
may not have reflected, to be drawn out and properly assessed in their
significance for the history of the movement as a whole.

The combination of this wider comparative context alongside the
local case study is reflected clearly in the structure of the book. Part One
focuses on the broader problems and features of provincial Social
Democratic politics. Chapter One shows that the centres of strength of
the Social Democratic movement were typically isolated industrial
enclaves surrounded and threatened by a rural socio-political

environment, or milieu, marked by a hostile conservative traditionalism. Chapter Two discusses and explains the failure of the national and provincial levels of the SDAP to offer any real sense of succour or assistance to these local enclaves in confronting the hostile political atmosphere they faced on the ground. The local level was, as it were, abandoned by the higher levels of the party to face up to the hostility of provincial conservatism on its own. Chapter Three begins by examining the pattern of response of the local level to this situation, which typically saw the local movement turn defensively in on itself and 'fortify' the enclave against the threats it faced from outside. This defensive 'fortification' in many cases succeeded, at least temporarily, in shielding the movement from external threat, but did so at the expense of a distinct narrowing of political perspective which ultimately left the movement fragmented and vulnerable to its opponents. This problem is exemplified in the later sections of Chapter Three, which outline the post-war rise and, after 1929, the precipitate fall of such a 'fortified' Social Democratic 'stronghold', or *'Hochburg'*, in Steyr.

Part Two of the book builds on these themes in a detailed examination of Social Democratic politics in Steyr. Chapters Four, Five and Six deal with the bases - and weaknesses - of 'stronghold' politics in Steyr, focusing in turn on the (for many years dominant) role of the Social Democratic Metalworkers' Union in industrial relations in the Steyr-Werke, the scope and significance of Social Democratic patronage in Steyr, and the purpose of the vast network of Social Democratic auxiliary organisations which existed in the town. Chapter Seven then assesses the impact of 'stronghold' politics on the political character of the local movement, focusing on a tendency to 'Michelsian' bureaucratisation within the SDAP, and on the ultra-cautious reformist outlook this promoted. The final chapter examines the implications of the collapse of the stronghold after 1929 and the process of organisational disintegration which followed amid deepening economic crisis and intensifying right-wing repression. Of particular significance was the emergence of a radical left-opposition in the movement which rejected the established bases of reformist politics in favour of a dynamic, if unsophisticated quasi-Bolshevik strategy which sparked and fuelled Social Democratic resistance in Steyr in the Civil War of 1934.

All the chapters in Part Two, while concentrating on the experience of Steyr, begin with a comparative analysis which illuminates the themes under discussion with insights form other local-level provincial strongholds of Social Democracy. The comparative focus of Part One is thus retained throughout the book, and provides the basis in the Conclusion for a wider evaluation of the politics of provincial Social Democracy. This returns to the considerations set out in this Introduction, above all the need to develop a 'new history' which looks beyond Red Vienna and narrow partisanship to develop new, and more balanced insights to why the Austrian Social Democratic movement came to be destroyed in 1934.

Notes

1   Gerhard Botz, '"Eine neue Welt, warum nicht eine neue Geschichte?" Österreichische Zeitgeschichte am Ende ihres Jahrhunderts, Teil I', *Österreichische Zeitschrift für Geschichtswissenschaften*, **1** (1990); 'Teil II: Die "Goldenen Jahre der Zeitgeschichte" und ihre Schattenseiten', *Österreichische Zeitschrift für Geschichtswissenschaften*, **1** (1990).

2   See e.g. Jill Lewis, *Fascism and the working class in Austria, 1918-1934. The failure of Austrian labour*, Berg, Oxford and New York (1991); Kurt Greußing (Ed.), *Die Roten am Lande. Arbeitsleben und Arbeiterbewegung im westlichen Österreich*, Museum Industrielle Arbeitswelt, Steyr (1989); Ulrike Weber-Felber, *Wege aus der Krise: Freie Gewerkschaften und Wirtschaftspolitik in der Ersten Republik*, Europaverlag, Vienna and Zurich (1990); Helmut Gruber, *Red Vienna. Experiment in working class culture 1919-1934*, Oxford University Press, New York and Oxford (1991). The first three are discussed at length in my review article 'Beyond Red Vienna: new perspectives on social democracy in the Austrian First Republic', *German History*, **11** (1993).

3   *Jahrbuch der Österreichischen Arbeiterbewegung 1930*, Verlag der Wiener Volksbuchhandlung, Vienna (1931), 111, 140-145.

4   Jill Lewis, 'Red Vienna: Socialism in one city, 1918-1927', *European Studies Review*, **13** (1983).

5   By far the best - and most refreshingly critical - analysis of 'Red Vienna' is Gruber (1991).

6   My italics. Cited in Josef Weidenholzer, 'Red Vienna: A new Atlantis?, in Anson G. Rabinbach (Ed.), *The Austrian socialist experiment: Social democracy and Austromarxism 1918-1934*, Westview Press, Boulder (1985), 198.

7   Throughout the early 1980s Konrad repeatedly pressed for the approach he had taken in his study of the emergence of the Upper Austrian labour movement in the 19th Century (Helmut Konrad, *Das Entstehen der Arbeiterklasse in Oberösterreich*, Europaverlag, Vienna (1981)) to be applied and developed further by other historians of the Austrian Left. See for example, Helmut Konrad, 'Zur Regionalgeschichtsschreibung der Arbeiterbewegung in Österreich', in *International Tagung der Historiker der Arbeiterbewegung. 17. Linzer Konferenz 1981*, Europaverlag, Vienna (1983).

8   To adapt a metaphor used elsewhere by Richard Evans. See Richard J. Evans, 'Introduction: Wilhelm II's Germany and the historians', in Richard J. Evans (Ed.), *Society and politics in Wilhelmine Germany*, Croom Helm, London (1978), 23. Evans' metaphor is itself adapted from the image used by Hans-Günter Zmarzlik, 'Das Kaiserreich in neuer Sicht?', *Historische Zeitschrift*, No.222 (1976), cited in ibid., 38 (note 56).

9   See Lewis (1991), 211-212.

10   Welcome exceptions are Weber-Felber (1990), who analyses the economic policy priorities of the unions in the First Republic and the tensions these priorities caused in union-party relations, and Lewis (1991), who highlights the

irrelevance of the SDAP's national political strategy to the needs and concerns of the trade unions in Upper Styria.

11   Fritz Klenner, *Die Österreichischen Gewerkschaften*, 2 volumes, Verlag des Österreichischen Gewerkschaftsbundes, Vienna (1951 and 1953).

12   See the discussion of 'heroic history' below and, in particular, in Chapter Six.

13   See e.g. Stephen Padgett's review article on work on the SPD in those eras: Stephen Padgett, 'Social and cultural studies in mass politics: The German Social Democratic Party', *West European Politics*, 7 (1984), esp. 193-194.

14   See Jeffery (1993), 86 and Chapter Two of this work.

15   C.f. Helmut Konrad, 'Regionale Arbeitergeschichte in Österreich: Oberösterreichs Entwicklung und die Metallarbeiter Niederösterreichs als Beispiel', in Verein für Geschichte der Arbeiterbewegung (Ed.), *Feuer - nicht Asche. Festschrift zum 25-jährigen Bestehen des Vereins für Geschichte der Arbeiterbewegung*, Vorwärts, Vienna (n.d.), 79-80.

16   For the German case, see Padgett (1984) and Evans (1978). For a broader discussion of changing trends in European historiography see also George C. Iggers, *New directions in European historiography*. Revised edition, Methuen, London (1985), esp. 175-205.

17   For an assessment of the central features of Austrian consociationalism - now under considerable challenge - see Kurt Richard Luther, Wolfgang C. Müller (Eds.), *Politics in Austria. Still a case of consociationalism?*, Frank Cass, London (1992).

18   See Botz (1990a), 54

19   Ibid., 50-64.

20   Ibid., 57.

21   Helmut Gruber, 'History of the Austrian working class: Unity of scholarship and practice', *International Labor and Working Class History*, No.24 (1983), 62. C.f. Botz' assessment of the 'state of the art' in 1990, in Botz (1990b), 85-86.

22   E.g. Josef Kaut, *Der steinige Weg. Geschichte der sozialistischen Bewegung im Lande Salzburg*, Graphia, Salzburg (1982); Siegfried Nasko, *Empor aus dumpfen Träumen. Arbeiterbewegung und Sozialdemokratie im St. Pöltener Raum*, SPÖ-Bezirksorganisation St. Pölten, Vienna and St. Pölten (1986); Walter Radmoser, *Der lange Weg. 100 Jahre Sozialdemokratie in Steyr*, Gutenberg, Linz (n.d.); SPÖ-Bezirksorganisation Vöcklabruck (Ed.), *Zeit und Zeugnis. Chronik der Sozialdemokratie im Bezirk Vöcklabruck*, Institut für Wissenschaft und Kunst Oberösterreich, Linz (1989); SPÖ Mauthausen (Ed.), *Der harte Weg. Die Geschichte der Arbeiterbewegung von Mauthausen*, Edition Geschichte der Heimat, Grünbach (1989).

23   Gruber (1983); Helmut Gruber, 'Socialist Party culture and the realities of working class life in Red Vienna', in Rabinbach (1985); Helmut Gruber, 'Working class women in Red Vienna: Socialist concepts of the "new woman" v. the reality of the triple burden', in Friedhelm Boll (Ed.), *Arbeiterkulturen zwischen Alltag und Politik. Beiträge zum europäischen Vergleich in der Zwischenkriegszeit*, Europaverlag, Vienna (1986); and most recently Gruber (1991).

24   See e.g. Gruber (1991), Chapters 4 and 5.

25   For a full list, see notes 12 to 21 in Chapter Six.

26   For a survey of party patronage in the Second Republic, see Wolfgang C. Müller, 'Patronage im österreichischen Parteiensystem: Theoretische Überlegungen und empirische Befunde', in Anton Pelinka, Franz Plasser (Eds.), *Das österreichische Parteiensystem*, Böhlau, Vienna (1988).

27   Ranging from Charles A. Gulick, *Austria from Habsburg to Hitler*, University of California Press, Berkeley and Los Angeles (1948), 454-455) to Helmut Weihsmann, *Das rote Wien. Sozialdemokratische Architektur und Kommunalpolitik 1919-1934*, Edition Spuren, Vienna (1985), 39-41.

28   See my 'Patronage, Macht und Ohnmacht: Die Sozialdemokraten in Steyr in der Ersten Republik', *Österreichische Zeitschrift für Politikwissenschaft*, 21 (1992) and Chapter Five of this book.

29   C.f. Gruber (1985), 223.

30   The tendency to mythologisation has, for example, been highlighted with regard to the Civil War of February 1934 by Gerhard Botz, and with regard to the relationship between former SDAP supporters and the Third Reich by Rudolf Ardelt. See, respectively, Gerhard Botz, 'Der Mythos vom "Februaraufstand" und von Richard Bernaschek', in Internationale Tagung der Historiker der Arbeiterbewegung. *20. Linzer Konferenz 1984*, Europaverlag, Vienna (1989), and Rudolf G. Ardelt, 'Arbeiterschaft und Nationalsozialismus - ein Thema zwischen Legende und Realität', in Rudolf G. Ardelt, Hans Hautmann (Eds.), *Arbeiterschaft und Nationalsozialismus in Österreich. In Memoriam Karl R. Stadler*, Europaverlag, Vienna (1990).

31   Botz (1990a), 65.

32   Ibid., 54.

33   Botz (1990b), 74.

34   See e.g. Botz (1989), 493.

35   Gruber (1983), 50.

36   Ibid., 60.

37   My italics. Quoted in Konrad (1983c), 420.

38   Gruber (1983), esp. 60-62.

39   E.g. Greußing (1989), Weber-Felber (1990), Ingrid Bauer, *'Tschikweiber haum's uns g'nennt ...' Frauenleben und Frauenarbeit an der 'Peripherie': Die Halleiner Zigarrenfabriksarbeiterinnen 1869 bis 1940*, Europaverlag, Vienna (1988); idem (Ed.), *Von der alten Solidarität zur neuen sozialen Frage. Ein Salzburger Bilderlesebuch*, Europaverlag, Vienna (1988). It is also worth mentioning a particularly impressive shorter work, Elisabeth Dietrich's 'Feindbilder und Ausgrenzung als Fermente der politischen Radikalisierung in Tirol zwischen 1918 und 1923', in Helmut Konrad, Karin Schmidlechner (Eds.), *Revolutionäres Potential in Europa am Ende des Ersten Weltkrieges*, Böhlau, Vienna (1991).

40   On this point see e.g. Müller (1988).

41   Which does not mean, as some present-day Social Democrats in Austria all too easily assume, that its approach is 'hostile', or has a 'conservative' hidden agenda.

42   The SDAP was able to organise upwards of 15% of the electorate as party members during the First Republic (not to mention a trade union membership which was from 1920-1929 even larger than that of the party). See further in Peter Kulemann's excellent *Am Beispiel des Austromarxismus. Sozialdemokratische*

Arbeiterbewegung in Österreich von Hainfeld bis zur Dollfuß-Diktatur, Junius, Hamburg (1979), 298-303.

[43] See Ernst Hanisch, 'Bäuerliches Milieu und Arbeitermilieu in den Alpengauen: ein historischer Vergleich', in Ardelt, Hautmann (1990).

[44] Ibid.

[45] See ibid., and Charlie Jeffery, 'Konsens und Dissens im Dritten Reich. Mit einer Fallstudie über Oberösterreich', in *Zeitgeschichte*, **19** (1992).

[46] Helmut Konrad, 'Arbeitergeschichte und Raum', in Helmut Konrad (Ed.), *Geschichte als demokratischer Auftrag*, Europaverlag, Linz (1983), 67.

[47] C.f. the comments on this point of David Crew in his study of Bochum in Germany, *Town in the Ruhr. A Social History of Bochum*, Columbia University Press, New York (1979), 7.

[48] The Steyr-Werke operated under the name Österreichische Waffenfabriksgesellschaft until February 1926. However, to avoid unnecessary confusion, the post-1926 name will be used throughout the book, even when referring to the period before 1926.

[49] Crew (1979), 7.

[50] The scale of research so far undertaken on individual provinces in the First Republic varies greatly from the extensive coverage of Upper Austria and Styria, the less comprehensive consideration of Lower Austria, Tirol, Salzburg and Vorarlberg and through to the outright neglect of Carinthia and Burgenland.

Part One

Politics in the Provincial Context

1 The 'Front-Lines' of Provincial Politics

One of the defining features of provincial politics in the conflict-ridden atmosphere of the First Republic was the deep-seated and persistent hostility displayed towards Social Democrats by non-Social Democrats. This pervasive hostility was without doubt the most severe and fundamental problem which faced provincial Social Democracy. This chapter examines the origins of this hostility in the highly segmented socio-political structure[1] of inter-war provincial Austria, and the ways in which hostility was perpetuated in an ongoing misperception of the Social Democratic movement as a revolutionary political force.

The first section of the chapter examines the pattern of socio-political segmentation, using the example of Upper Austria to show how party support tended to be concentrated in particular social groups and - as a result - in particular, clearly defined geographical contexts, or, to use Hanisch's term, milieux. Concentrations of SDAP support tended to be in the industrial communities which were specked unevenly around a countryside which was otherwise dominated by a deeply conservative, traditionalist culture. In the uncertain atmosphere which followed the end of the First World War, these concentrations of Social Democratic support were widely, exaggeratedly and erroneously perceived in that conservative culture as an 'enemy within', committed to overthrowing the established order. They consequently became focal points of the suspicion, and increasingly the antagonism, of the non-Social Democratic population. The second section of the chapter then examines how this antagonism - together with the misperceptions which fuelled it - not only endured throughout the First Republic, but also fed, over time, into the outright persecution and repression of the local-level Social Democratic movement.

Social Democracy in the Provinces: the 'Enemy Within'

The 'Inselbewegung'

The typical conditions faced by Social Democracy in the Austrian provinces were, by any standards, extremely inhospitable. This situation reflected the retarded and patchy nature of the industrialisation process in Austria. Outside Vienna, with the exception of the plain stretching from the southern boundary of the city into the northern half of Burgenland and the the south-eastern segment of

Lower Austria, there were few concentrated and integrated industrial areas. Industrial sites had sprung up unevenly at the location of transport intersections or of natural (water or mineral) resources, or had been grafted onto pre-industrial centres of trade and commerce. These irregularly distributed industrial sites, with their growing manual labour forces, evolved into the centres of strength of the Social Democratic movement.

A broad indication of the political implications of this uneven process of industrialisation is given in the tables below. Table 1.1 shows the distribution of communities[2] throughout the Austrian provinces which recorded an SDAP majority vote in the national election of April 1927. Only 10% of communities overall - and far less in some provinces - were able to record an SDAP majority. At the same time, though, the SDAP's overall share of the vote in the provinces - with the exception of Tirol and Vorarlberg, where Social Democracy was especially weak - stood between 30-40%. This gives a crude measure of the tendency for SDAP strength in the provinces to be concentrated into a limited number of enclaves. These enclaves were also - with the exception of

Table 1.1 SDAP Majority Communities in the Provinces, 1927

Land	Total number of communities	Number of SDAP majority communities	% SDAP majority communities	% overall SDAP *Land* vote
Burgenland	326	53	16.26	40.81
Carinthia	249	27	10.84	36.89
Lower Austria	1,708	200	11.71	37.62
Salzburg	157	11	7.01	32.30
Styria	1,015	96	9.46	36.39
Tirol	308	4	1.30	22.40
Upper Austria	506	18	3.36	29.54
Vorarlberg	99	1	1.01	22.22
Totals	4,368	410	9.36	34.11

Source: *Calculated from Bundesamt für Statistik (Ed.), Statistische Nachrichten. Sonderheft. 'Wahlstatistik'. Nationalratswahlen vom 24. April 1927. Einzeldarstellung nach Gemeinden und Geschlecht, Überreuter, Vienna (1927).*

the industrial plain to the south of Vienna - widely dispersed throughout the provinces. Of the 410 SDAP majority communities recorded in Table 1.1, some 149 were concentrated in the eleven administrative districts[3] which covered the industrial area south of Vienna. The other 261 were spread throughout the remaining 94 administrative districts of the provinces,[4] often, particularly in Alpine areas, physically remote from their nearest counterparts. The dispersal of Social Democratic strength left the typical SDAP majority community as an isolated outpost, more often than not heavily outnumbered in the surrounding area by the opponents of the Social Democratic movement. This can be seen more clearly in Table 1.2,which lists the communities in the province of Upper Austria which recorded an SDAP majority vote in the national election of 1927. These were all industrial communities with a substantial manual working class presence. The contrast between the levels of SDAP strength within and outside each of these communities is striking, particularly in Steyr

Table 1.2 Social Democratic 'Islands' in Upper Austria, 1927

Community	% SDAP vote (a)	Surrounding area	% SDAP vote (b)	(a) - (b)
Obertraun	83.9	Gmunden District	40.0	43.9
Ampflwang	62.1	Vöcklabruck District	29.1	33.0
Wolfsegg	60.3	Vöcklabruck District	28.8	31.5
Langenstein	54.8	Perg District	23.4	31.4
Ottnang	58.5	Vöcklabruck District	28.1	30.4
Luftenberg	53.5	Perg District	23.8	29.7
Steyr	59.9	Steyr-Land District	30.3	29.6
Hallstatt	67.3	Gmunden District	40.0	27.3
Gosau	67.3	Gmunden District	40.0	27.3
Haid	50.3	Perg District	23.6	26.7
Attnang-Puchheim	53.7	Vöcklabruck District	28.2	25.5
Puchberg	53.1	Wels District	31.2	21.9
Reichraming	51.0	Steyr-Land District	29.5	21.5
Linz	51.7	Linz and Surroundings Constituency	31.2	20.5
Ebensee	58.3	Gmunden District	37.8	20.1
Leonding	54.7	Linz-Land District	35.1	19.6
Traun	54.3	Linz-Land District	34.9	19.4
Goisern	58.5	Gmunden District	39.3	19.2
		Upper Austria	**29.3**	

Note: *The 'surrounding area' in each case is the local administrative district (Bezirk) minus the locality concerned, excepting the entry for the town of Steyr, where the surrounding, but separate administrative district of Steyr-Land is used, and that for Linz, where the 'Linz and Surroundings' electoral constituency (minus Linz) is used.*
Source: *Calculated from Bundesamt für Statistik (Ed.), Statistische Nachrichten. Sonderheft. 'Wahlstatistik'. Nationalratswahlen vom 24. April 1927. Einzeldarstellung nach Gemeinden und Geschlecht, Überreuter, Vienna (1927).*

and in the Districts of Vöcklabruck (with its coal-mining and railway communities), Gmunden (site of the mineral/chemical industry centres of the Salzkammergut) and Perg (with its quarrying villages). Industrial communities on the one hand stood out starkly as centres of SDAP strength, but were always overshadowed on the other by an equally stark non-SDAP (and as will be shown below, invariably anti-SDAP) majority[5] in the surrounding, overwhelmingly rural areas. Upper Austria thus presents a picture of a distinctively segmented society in which the social divisions created by the faltering process of industrialisation were overlain and reinforced by patterns of party-political allegiance.

This picture of social and political segmentation was repeated across provincial Austria[6] and forms a persistent theme in the literature on provincial politics in the First Republic.[7] The centres of strength of the Social Democratic movement in the provinces were typically 'red' enclaves scattered haphazardly throughout a mainly 'black' (i.e. Catholic-conservative) Austrian countryside. Provincial Social Democracy was an *'Inselbewegung'*,[8] a movement concentrated outside Vienna in small, and geographically isolated 'islands' of strength. This was not, for a variety of reasons, a promising situation for the pursuit and defence of Social Democratic interests. Firstly, and most obviously, Social Democracy was, in the absence of a more thoroughgoing industrialisation (and thus of a larger potential pool of Social Democratic voters), always a minority movement in the provinces. In stark contrast to its Viennese counterpart, it was accordingly excluded from the exercise of significant governmental power through the institutions of the Austrian federal system.[9] Secondly, the Social Democratic 'islands' frequently had poor communication links to one another, especially in Alpine areas. Communication difficulties hindered the emergence of the consolidated provincial-level structure of Social Democratic organisations which might otherwise have provided for a more effective assertion of Social Democratic interests.[10] These inherent disadvantages of an *Inselbewegung* placed provincial Social Democracy in a situation of vulnerability *vis-à-vis* its opponents. The sense of vulnerability was, thirdly, magnified by the intense hostility expressed towards the supporters of Social Democracy in the areas surrounding the Social Democratic enclaves.

Perceptions of the 'Enemy Within'

This hostility had its origin in the intrinsic suspicion shown to Social Democracy during the First Republic by an often deeply conservative, largely pre-industrial, provincial society. Provincial conservatism typically[11] combined a rigid sense of social hierarchy, an autocratic, patriarchal approach to employer-worker relations, an intense parochialism,[12] and a deep-seated allegiance to the Catholic Church. In certain areas this engrained, anti-modernist conservatism was further buttressed by distinctive traditions of provincial exceptionalism. This was the case in particular in the two westernmost provinces of Tirol and Vorarlberg whose peripheral geographical location had, over centuries, lent them a clear sense of self-reliance and separate identity. Expressed in Vorarlberg as a sense of almost tribal 'rootedness' (*Bodenständigkeit*) and in the 'holy land' of Tirol in terms of religious particularism, these identities tended - and were used - to sharpen popular perceptions of those who 'belonged' and those who did not.[13]

Seen through the lens of provincial conservatism in western Austria and elsewhere, the Social Democratic movement in the First Republic clearly did not 'belong'. It represented a new and disturbing manifestation of an accelerating socio-economic modernisation process. Moreover its novel - and, for 'traditional' provincial society, threatening - features were highlighted in exaggerated form in the stark contrast between industrial Social Democratic enclave and surrounding rural hinterland.[14] This was a densely concentrated movement with its own distinctive forms of political and cultural expression, equipped with an alien, 'imported'[15] ideology which lay down a challenge to existing visions of social hierarchy, to property rights and to the privileges of the Catholic Church. Most significantly it had, in the *Umbruch* of 1918-1919, won new rights and powers in politics and industrial relations which suggested it might be able to turn its ideas into policy practice. In these circumstances, Social Democracy was widely seen as a perfidious 'enemy within', a manifold threat to the established order which had to be marginalised or removed.[16]

The perception of the 'enemy within' generated for the non-Social Democratic population an inherent distrust of the Social Democratic movement. This sense of distrust was further intensified in the uncertain atmosphere which existed in Austria in the chaotic hiatus between the last months of the First World War and the reestablishment of administrative order in the new Republic during 1919. In this period the Social Democrats won an undeserved reputation for 'revolutionary', bolshevik radicalism which confirmed the intrinsic suspicions and fears already felt in the provinces about Social Democracy. The experiences of this 'revolutionary' era coloured provincial perceptions of Social Democracy in a way which helped to perpetuate the negative image of the 'enemy within' and thus to mark out a political 'front-line' between Social Democracy and its opponents which was to endure throughout the First Republic.

The Social Democratic reputation for revolutionary radicalism had a variety of sources. It was certainly rooted in part in the militancy displayed by parts of the industrial labour force in the strike waves of the later war years and in a series of abortive and politically naïve attempts by local Social Democratic trade unionists in Styria, Lower Austria and Salzburg to 'socialise' their factories early in 1919. The extent to which these examples of industrial militancy had any real 'revolutionary' motivation is, however, debatable. The wartime strikes generally broke out as expressions of war weariness and of dissatisfaction over food shortages and deteriorating real wages and working conditions.[17] Although the strikes were routinely channelled by the Social Democratic leadership to support demands for political 'revolution' - i.e. the formal democratisation of the Habsburg state - any further-reaching revolutionary demands, for example, for changes in property relations, always remained marginal and, moreover, marginalised by a moderate leadership.[18] Similarly, the post-war 'socialisation' experiments seem far more to be 'elemental' outbursts of protest about a standard of living which had not improved significantly since the end of the war than the 'revolutionary efforts'[19] which Karl Stocker has, perhaps rather romantically, identified. These outbursts evidently seized upon the terminology of the then current debate about socialisation[20] but demonstrated no clear ideological perception either of the concept of 'socialisation' *per se*, or of how 'socialisation' might conceivably contribute to any broader restructuring of social relations.[21] 'Socialisation' had, in this local-level, provincial context, little to do with 'revolution', but was rather an expression of unfocused and localised, albeit militant, social protest.

This distinction was, of course, academic to non-Social Democrats in the areas affected. To them the apparition of 'socialisation' undoubtedly represented a 'shocking'[22] revolutionary threat to the property rights of the existing order and served to harden anti-Social Democratic attitudes in the areas concerned.[23] In other words, a *perception* of Social Democratic revolutionary threat emerged after the war which bore little resemblance to the largely moderate *reality* of Social Democratic politics. This perception was further strengthened by two institutions which, though organisationally short-lived, helped to bequeathe a long-term antipathy towards Social Democracy in the provinces: the SDAP-dominated *Volkswehr*, which temporarily took over security functions in the new Republic until the creation of the Austrian *Bundesheer*; and the Workers' and Soldiers' Councils which sprang up across Austria in the aftermath of the war with a majority Social Democratic and a minority Communist composition. The self-perception of *Volkswehr* and Councils was clearly as forces for the upholding of law and order, particularly in the distribution of scarce food supplies. From the perspective of the non-Social Democratic population, however, they were viewed rather differently. This was not a form of 'law and order' that part of the population could easily identify with. In some Tirolean circles the *Volkswehr* was seen, for example, as the 'occupation force of an alien power',[24] an affront to Tirolean traditions of self-reliance. Further east in Upper Austria perceptions of the Workers' Councils were also negatively coloured by their involvement in rowdy and sometimes violent demonstrations on the streets of Linz, and by the overzealousness of some of their members in searching out (or, as it was seen by those affected, 'plundering') food supplies hidden on the property of the Catholic Church.[25]

More generally, and perhaps most significantly, the activities of *Volkswehr* and Councils in securing and distributing food supplies helped to sour relations between Social Democracy and the farming population.[26] During 1919 the task frequently fell to the *Volkswehr* or the Councils of requisitioning food supplies from the countryside throughout Austria on behalf of an often half-starved urban population. This was no doubt seen by the Social Democrats and their urban constituency as the justified (if not always especially orderly) requisitioning of unjustly hoarded provisions. To the farmers involved, however, it was inevitably seen somewhat differently. To them requisitioning involved the heavily symbolic invasion and occupation of the farmstead and the forced handover - often at gunpoint - of products which they felt were rightfully theirs to dispose of however they saw fit. Requisitioning was for them evidence of a blatant disrespect for, and threat to, property rights and helped to produce a bitterness towards the Social Democrats which endured throughout the First Republic.[27]

A full understanding of the predisposition in the provinces to see the revolutionary worst in the Social Democratic movement requires, finally, some consideration of the wider political background of the early post-war era. The years 1918-1920 saw immense upheaval. The new Republic was faced with a struggle to establish its authority both internally, amid widespread food shortage and the chaotic and often lawless passage of former Habsburg soldiers from the wartime front-lines to their far-flung homelands, and externally, where its borders were under threat in Tirol, Carinthia, Styria and Burgenland. The uncertainties of this situation were magnified by the apparent spread of Bolshevism after the war, especially during the existence of the short-lived Soviet Republics in neighbouring Hungary and Bavaria during 1919. The sense of Bolshevik threat in Austria at the time was, understandably, acute. It was then heightened by the passing resemblance of the Austrian Workers' and Soldiers' Councils to their Hungarian, Bavarian (and Russian) counterparts, and by the fumbling attempts of the Austrian Communists to foment unrest in Linz, Graz and Vienna in the first half of 1919.[28]

In these circumstances the perceived threats to the existing order posed in the name of an essentially moderate, reformist Social Democratic movement - industrial militancy, the 'occupation force' of the *Volkswehr*, the councils movement and requisitioning - were all too easily understood as 'Bolshevik' phenomena, part of a dreadful wave of revolutionary fervour sweeping across Europe. This enabled the provincial opponents of Social Democracy consciously to use the (often graphically constructed)[29] imagery of the 'Bolshevik threat' as an apocalyptic symbol with which to cement and focus popular opposition to the Social Democrats. The result, within a year of the establishment of the First Republic, was a marked hardening of anti-Social Democratic prejudice, with the Social Democratic movement cast and demonised as a 'fifth column' of bolshevism, a pariah movement, utterly alien to the values of, and with no legitimate place within, conservative, provincial society.

Deepening the Political Divide in the Provinces

After 1920 it was evident even to the most jaundiced provincial observer that the 'Bolshevik threat' was fading. Nevertheless, the provincial Social Democrats remained unable to divest themselves of their pariah-like status. On the contrary, the social and political cleavage between 'red' enclave and dominant culture tended, if anything, to solidify and reinforce itself. This once again had more to do with perceptions and image than political reality. Much was made, for example, of alleged Social Democratic 'terrorism'. The (grossly hyperbolic) perception of Social Democracy as a 'terroristic' movement had a variety of sources. A first concerned the closed shop arrangements set up at the behest of the Social Democratic Free Trade Unions in firms across Austria directly after the war, and defended with varying degrees of success before their final abolition by the 'Anti-Terror Law' of 1930. Such arrangements were condemned for 'terrorising' non-Social Democratic workers by forcing them to join and pay dues and political levies to Social Democratic trade unions in order to get work.[30] A second concerned the regular ceremonial parades of the Social Democratic movement, particularly on 1 May and on 12 November (the national holiday commemorating the foundation of the Republic in 1919). These were widely seen as intimidatory attempts to establish a 'dictatorship', or 'monopoly' of the streets and thus to prevent the freedom of expression of the non-Social Democratic population.[31]

These depictions of Social Democratic intimidation were not without an element of truth (although the term 'terror' stretches the point somewhat). Closed shop arrangements were used to discriminate consciously and actively against non-Social Democrats, and local Social Democratic organisations did aspire to a 'monopoly' of the streets, at least within the territorial limits of their various enclaves.[32] The point is, though, that such forms of intimidation were not the sole preserve of the Social Democratic movement. As will be shown below,

Social Democrats were themselves far more often excluded from employment because of their political allegiance than were their opponents. Moreover, various combinations of provincial authorities, police and *Heimwehr* frequently colluded to establish right-wing 'monopolies' of the streets. But what was seen as 'terror' in the hands of the Social Democrats was considered a legitimate form of self-assertion wherever non-Social Democrats were involved. This was characteristic of a bizarre form of routinised political 'double-vision' in inter-war provincial Austria which perpetuated the 'front-line' mentality of the early post-war years by persistently condemning in the Social Democrats what was lauded in one's own ranks.

Nowhere was this 'double-vision' more clearly illustrated than in the assessment of a third manifestation of Social Democratic 'terror', the perceived threat of Social Democratic insurrectionary violence, represented above all in the *Republikanischer Schutzbund*. The *Schutzbund* was established in 1923 as a Social Democratic paramilitary force committed both in a general sense to the protection of the democratic order of the First Republic and more specifically to provide security at Social Democratic parades and meetings from external disruption and internal indiscipline. Unsurprisingly, the *Schutzbund* was rarely assessed on the basis of this essentially defensive orientation by the opponents of Social Democracy. It was seen - much as the *Volkswehr* before it - as an armed and extremely dangerous threat to the established order. The perception of armed threat was inadvertently confirmed by the national-level SDAP in the wording of part of its 1926 Linz Programme. The Linz Programme was not wisely formulated. The central theme running through it was the commitment of the SDAP to use the structures and procedures of the democratic system to secure the reforms needed gradually to usher in socialism. This gradualist democratic reformism was wholly overshadowed, though, by a passage which hypothetically foresaw the use of force and of temporary dictatorial powers as a necessary means for the party to reestablish democratic government in the eventuality of a right-wing putsch.[33]

Non-Social Democrats typically did not comb through the fine print of the Linz Programme and clarify the precise, hypothetical circumstances in which the use of force might be considered. Rather they came (and were encouraged to come) to the conclusion that 'the Social Democrats had decided that violence was the only path open to them'[34] in *any* circumstances and that they thus had to be countered and faced down, above all by the main right-wing paramilitary force, the *Heimwehr*. This distorted view is clearly illustrated in the following quote, drawn from the memoirs of Heinrich Raab, a stalwart of the Christian Social Party in St. Pölten in Lower Austria:

> The *Schutzbund* in particular had terrorised the people of St. Pölten. It ... wanted to assert its dominance through parades, in which several thousand men, armed with *Ochsenziemer*, marched through the streets, and through the Linz Programme, which had called for a dictatorship of the proletariat. This Austro-Marxism inevitably strengthened the will to resist of all democrats in our home town. The *Heimwehr* ... became ever stronger as the farmers flocked to join it.[35]

The depiction of the *Heimwehr* as the saviour of 'democratic' provincial society from a 'violent' and 'dictatorial' Social Democratic movement is especially ironic given that it - in contrast to any half-realistic assessment of Social Democracy - was an explicitly and unambiguously anti-democratic, insurrectionary force committed to the forcible suppression of its opponents. Unfortunately for the Social Democrats, though, the upside-down logic of this form of depiction was given apparent confirmation in the events of July 1927.

It is not necessary here to recount the events surrounding 15 July 1927 in any depth.[36] What is important in the context of this chapter is, though, to point to the interpretation given to these events in the Austrian provinces. The militant, mainly Social Democratic protest demonstration in Vienna on 15 July, the violence which accompanied and ultimately suppressed it, and the subsequent strikes called by the national leadership of the SDAP met with a near-hysterical reception in the provinces which invoked and reproduced the imagery of the 'Bolshevik threat' of the immediate post-war era. July 1927 had seen an 'attempted putsch' (according to Catholic-conservative sources in Upper Austria), 'red terror' (Tirol), and 'Mexican and Russian atrocities'[37] (Vorarlberg). In Salzburg it was, apparently, felt that 'Social Democracy, an agency of Moscow', was 'planning the establishment of a Soviet Republic in Austria' (or, more poetically: 'The grim reaper from the north-east is pounding with his skeletal fingers on the gates of our state').[38]

This flight into fantastic hyperbole was fed in particular by the events of 16 July 1927 in the SDAP stronghold of Bruck an der Mur in Upper Styria, where a committee headed by the local Social Democratic leader, Koloman Wallisch, temporarily, illegally, and amid expressions of fairly blood-curdling rhetoric, assumed executive powers in the town. These measures were, it seems, taken - and soon revoked - by Wallisch' committee as a means of upholding law and order by appeasing a labour rank and file enraged by the events in Vienna and demanding some kind of retaliatory action.[39] Outside Bruck they were presented, though, as a 'dictatorship of the proletariat', a misrepresentation which was particularly effective since Wallisch had been a minor functionary in the short-lived Soviet Republic in Hungary in 1919: 'The Social Democrats had, at least for a few hours, taken off their mask and shown their real, truthful Soviet face'.[40]

However absurd and overblown these depictions of the events of July 1927 may have been, they clearly fell in line with - and were used to reinvigorate - established provincial perceptions of Social Democracy as an unwelcome and dangerous 'enemy within'. Moreover the renewed sense of violent and revolutionary threat conjured up in July 1927 also reinforced the status of the *Heimwehr* as the focal point and general-purpose bludgeon of the anti-Social Democratic cause. It would be wrong, though, to assume that the *Heimwehr* was the sole, or necessarily the most important weapon used in the provinces to counter the Social Democratic 'threat'. It would also, more importantly, be wrong to assume that the events of 1927 were a crucial turning point in anti-Social Democratic politics in provincial Austria. There is certainly a tendency to see July 1927 as *the* crucial turning point in the First Republic, a decisive shift in the balance of power in Austrian politics away from Social Democracy which was ultimately to culminate in the destruction of the Social Democratic movement in the Civil War of 1934.[41] This interpretation is, though, a further example Vienna-centred overgeneralisation which ignores the realities of political life in the provinces, where there had *always* been a gross imbalance of power in favour of conservative forces. Long before July 1927, in fact right from the earliest days of the First Republic, the engrained provincial antipathies towards Social Democracy discussed in this chapter had found expression in the emergence of broad-based fronts of anti-Social Democratic forces. July 1927 may have confirmed and accelerated this process; it did not start it. Moreover, these fronts consisted, above and beyond the *Heimwehr*, of various combinations of employers, the provincial authorities and police forces controlled by the Christian Social and German Nationalist Parties, the Catholic Church and its network of auxiliary organisations, and rival trade unions. The next section of the chapter examines the strategies these anti-Social Democratic forces used - before and after 1927 - in mobilising against, and closing in on, the isolated and vulnerable Social Democratic 'enemy within'.

Confronting the 'Enemy Within'

The means by which anti-Social Democrats took the 'fight' to the Social Democratic movement in the provinces can be divided into three broad (and in part overlapping) categories: first, the denial of statutory and constitutional rights, particularly at the workplace; second, outright intimidation on the streets, above all by the *Heimwehr*; and third, social ostracism at the hands of the Catholic Church.

The Erosion of Statutory and Civil Rights

The immediate post-war years in Austria saw the enactment of a series of new laws in social and employment policy. In theory this raft of legislation considerably strengthened the position of labour in industrial relations, especially the strongest, i.e. Social Democratic, trade union movement. In practice, though, the rights enshrined in post-war legislation were frequently violated or ignored, exposing Social Democrats to various forms of chicanery and repression at the workplace long before the final weakening of the Free Trade Unions during the Great Depression. Particularly widespread, for example, was the refusal of employers, above all in smaller-scale industry and commerce, to abide by the letter of the law on the length of the working day, overtime payments, holiday entitlements, the establishment of Works Councils and so on.[42] Also frequent was an unwillingness in the provinces to tolerate the right of the Social Democratic trade unions to strike. Here, employers had ready allies in provincial governments, especially in western Austria, which were all too eager to help chip away at the rights and powers of the 'alien' Social Democratic movement, in this respect by seconding police and even army units to strike-breaking duties.[43] The *Heimwehr* could also be relied upon as a solid strike-breaking weapon, as seen most notably in 1927 when 'everything which was staunchly anti-Marxist was called up',[44] at least in Vorarlberg, Styria and Tirol,[45] to face down the national Social Democratic railway strike called in protest at the violence used against demonstrators in Vienna on 15 July.

More fundamental even than denying the right to strike was the common practice throughout provincial Austria of undermining and/or preventing Social Democratic shopfloor organisation. Social Democratic influence was marginalised at the workplace through a combination of personnel policies which discriminated against Social Democratic trade unionists, and the practice of conducting negotiations on wages and conditions solely with non-Social Democratic trade unions. The beneficiaries in both cases were most frequently the Christian trade unions and their members,[46] but also, from the later 1920s, the 'Independent' Trade Union of the *Heimwehr*. The 'Independent' union emerged as a new branch of *Heimwehr* activity from 1928. Working in cahoots with like-minded employers, the *Heimwehr* union succeeded, especially against the background of mass unemployment after 1929, in fracturing even previously solid Social

Democratic union organisations, for example in the Upper Austrian coalfield[47] and the Lower Austrian industrial centres of St. Pölten and Wiener Neustadt.[48]

The heartland of 'independent' unionism was, though, Upper Styria. Upper Styria in many respects presents a special case in First Republic industrial relations, above all because of the Alpine-Montangesellschaft (AMG). The AMG, coal mining and iron and steel conglomerate and dominant employer in the region, developed the most sophisticated and enduring anti-unionist strategy seen in First Republic Austria. Drawing on the anti-socialist industrial relations philosophies of its counterparts and controlling stake-holders in German heavy industry, the AMG launched a concerted offensive against the Free Trade Unions which began in the early 1920s and continued unabated through to the demise of the unions in 1934. This offensive combined all the anti-unionist tactics pursued elsewhere in Austria with more specific forms of repression unique to its sphere of influence, ranging from attempts to propagate a sense of 'harmonious' (i.e. anti-Social Democratic) 'works community' (*Betriebsgemeinschaft*) to interventions in the electoral process designed to undermine the influence of the SDAP in Upper Styria.[49] The most destructive aspect of AMG anti-unionism was, though, undoubtedly its sponsorship of the 'Independent' Trade Union. Following its foundation in May 1928 the 'Independent' union was openly nurtured, through politicised personnel policies and other forms of intimidation, as the primary means of marginalising the influence of Social Democracy in AMG plants. The success of this strategy is clearly shown in Table 1.3 below, which records the progressive elimination of Free Trade Union representation in the annual Works Council elections at the Donawitz steelworks in Upper Styria.[50]

Table 1.3 Union Representatives Elected to the Donawitz Works Council, 1926-1932

Year	Social Democratic	Communist	Christian	Independent
1926	10	7	2	--
1927	13	4	2	--
1928	13	1	1	5
1929	10	--	--	10
1930	6	--	--	13
1931	--	--	--	All
1932	--	--	--	All

Source: *Eduard G. Staudinger, '"Unabhängige Gewerkschaft" und Arbeiterschaft in der Obersteiermark 1927 bis 1933', Geschichte und Gegenwart*, **4** (1985), 66.

The experience in Upper Styria represents something of an extreme case, but is nevertheless indicative of a more general intolerance towards, and drive to be rid of, the rights and powers exercised by the Social Democratic movement in the economic sphere in provincial Austria. The anti-Social Democratic drive also invaded the wider political arena, where Social Democrats faced restrictions on their constitutionally enshrined freedoms of expression and organisation in the provinces long before this became a fully-fledged nationwide policy in the post-1932 Dollfuss years. This was the case in particular in the deeply reactionary provinces of Tirol and Vorarlberg. In Vorarlberg, for example, official restrictions were placed on SDAP meetings and on the distribution of party campaigning material from the mid-1920s onwards.[51] Moreover, Josef Riedmann writes - in what seem to be surprisingly approving terms - of 'the gradual elimination of Social Democracy in Tirol, as successfully carried out in several stages by the legal majority in the province', suggesting quite plausibly that this provided a proven model for Dollfuss' later 'salami-tactic' of step-by-step elimination of Social Democratic rights.[52] Such open disregard by elected provincial authorities for the freedom of expression of Social Democrats was, however, a feature more or less[53] unique to these two intensely particularist westernmost provinces, at least until the emergence of the more generally repressive mood of the early 1930s. Until then central roles in restricting the broader freedom of manoeuvre of the Social Democratic movement were performed by the *Heimwehr* and the Catholic Church.

Destroying the 'Bastions of Marxist Terror'

The *Heimwehr's* origins lay in the predominantly rural 'self-defence' units which had emerged throughout Austria after the First World War. These units had been set up in part in response to external threats to the new republic's borders and to the threat to property posed by indisciplined soldiers returning waywardly home from the fronts. A subsidiary motivation for the establishment of these *'Heimwehren'*, which soon became their overriding rationale, was to counter the perceived threat to the established order posed by the Social Democratic movement.[54] In these early years the significance of what was always a regionally highly diverse movement varied greatly from province to province. In Vorarlberg, Tirol and Carinthia it was nurtured by the provincial authorities as a semi-official auxiliary police force, while in Styria the radical and activist *Heimatschutz* of Walter Pfrimer also found - at least where the Social Democratic 'threat' was concerned - the favour of the provincial government.[55] Elsewhere, though, the *Heimwehr* remained an essentially marginal force.

The great watershed for the *Heimwehr* came in 1927, when it 'distinguished' itself in helping break the Social Democratic railway strike called in response to the events of 15 July. The role it played in July 1927 subsequently acted as a major recruiting point for the *Heimwehr*, leading both to a significant expansion of its organisation throughout Austria, and to an intensification of its anti-Social Democratic activities.[56] There followed, for example, its diversification into the 'independent' trade unionism discussed above. There also followed a widespread campaign of street-level intimidation directed at the Social Democratic movement. This campaign was consciously and carefully focused on the 'red' enclaves scattered around the Austrian provinces, not just in the traditional areas of *Heimwehr* strength in the western and southern provinces, but also in Upper and Lower Austria and Burgenland, hitherto practically virgin territory for the *Heimwehr*.[57]

Although this campaign frequently flared into violent confrontation, most notably in St. Lorenzen in Upper Styria in August 1929,[58] its main aim was psychological, to intimidate the supporters of Social Democracy and to deter open expressions of allegiance to the Social Democratic cause. The aim was to create the impression of an inexorable advance of anti-Social Democratic forces by symbolically 'encircling', 'invading' and 'taking' the remaining strongholds of the Social Democratic movement one by one: Bruck and der Mur in November 1927, Wiener Neustadt and Linz in October 1928, St. Pölten in May 1929, the Upper Austrian coalfield and Steyr in August 1930[59] - and, one day, Vienna ...?

A clear illustration of this tactic was given in the campaign launched by the increasingly prominent Upper Austrian *Heimwehr* leader, Ernst Rüdiger Starhemberg, against 'red Steyr'. This began in the autumn of 1928 with the foundation of *Heimwehr* sections in the villages in the Steyr area. During 1929 these sections played host to ever larger paramilitary parades and exercises. In August 1929 a *Heimwehr* section was founded in Steyr itself, which began to hold provocative 'Sunday strolls' on Steyr's main square - hitherto an exclusive parade ground of the Social Democratic movement - from December of that year. From February 1930 the Upper Austrian *Heimwehr*'s newspaper, the modestly titled *Starhemberg-Jäger*, began a high-profile and vitriolic campaign against Social Democratic Steyr. And in April, Starhemberg felt confident enough to make his first visit to Steyr in preparation for the *coup de grace*, a full-scale, mass-attendance parade on the town square in August 1930, which was loudly heralded with the fanfare: 'The last bastion of Marxist terror destroyed'.[60]

The effect of these incursions into the local 'red stronghold' was, in Steyr as elsewhere,[61] deeply demoralising, particularly since the *Heimwehr* campaigns were generally organised with the connivance (i.e. the police protection) of the provincial authorities and - literally! - the blessing of the Catholic Church.[62] The impression was one of a relentless tightening of the front-lines drawn around a vulnerable, beleaguered, outnumbered and - increasingly - psychologically broken provincial Social Democratic movement.

Fire, Brimstone and Social Democracy

The role of the Catholic Church in supporting the anti-Social Democratic crusade of the *Heimwehr* - a role which ranged from holding 'field masses' at *Heimwehr* parades to offering monasteries for use as weapons stores[63] - should come as no surprise. Probably more consistently than any other political force in Austria, the Church mobilised its considerable weight against the provincial Social Democratic movement throughout the First Republic. The role it played was of course of a different quality than the outright persecution and intimidation of Social Democrats carried out by employers, provincial authorities and *Heimwehr*. It was, though, nevertheless instrumental in creating and perpetuating an intolerant, *Kulturkampf*-like political atmosphere which buttressed the drive to remove from provincial Social Democrats the rights they had won in the First Republic.

The Church's forte was the 'fire and brimstone' politics of moral and spiritual condemnation. Through the pastoral letters of its bishops and in the sermons of its priests it nourished the image of Social Democrats as the *'Gottseibeiuns'*, the 'Evil Ones',[64] who, given the chance, would deliver the Austrians via abortion, contraception, the corruption of children, cremation and divorce into the hell-on-earth of aetheistic bolshevism. A carefully crafted and by no means untypical[65] example of these politics of condemnation and demonisation are given in the quote below, which is drawn from the pastoral letter of Bishop Sigismund Waitz issued on the occasion of the national elections of April 1927, and passed on from the pulpits of western Austria's Catholic churches:

> Catholics! ... A decisive battle is under way in Austria between Christianity and faithlessness. For decades Austria has been losing ever more of its Christian character, but still much remains. The coming elections will decide whether this residue too will disappear. The anti-religion party [the SDAP] is looking to take power in Austria, and if it does, then it will go all the way in this battle against Christianity ... The sort of danger which threatens ... is shown by the commitment to tearing down all the barriers of

morality in marriage law, to giving free rein to immorality in all
fields of life, in education, in art and literature, in cinema and
theatre; it is shown by the desire even to remove the penalties in
law which protect human life in its earliest stage ... If [this]
bolshevism comes to power in the Austrian Parliament, then that
will be ... disastrous for the whole of Europe. The situation is like
1683, when the Turks stood before the gates of Vienna. Today it is
the advance of bolshevism which is recognised as a danger for the
whole of Europe and for Christian civilisation ...[66]

The vitriolic bombardment launched by the passionately anti-
Social Democratic Catholic establishment had two major implications
for Social Democrats in the provinces. Firstly, it helped to 'immunise'[67]
the Catholic population against the attractions of Social Democracy.
This 'immunisation' process was facilitated by the many conduits for the
transmission of Church doctrines offered in the extensive provincial
network of Catholic organisations: trade unions, youth groups, social
and leisure clubs and so on.[68] The effect was to ostracise *'die Roten'*, to
raise - in the contemporary terminology - a 'protective dyke against the
storm floods of socialism'.[69] This severely limited the potential for the
expansion of the Social Democratic movement in the provinces beyond
its 'island' strongholds and thus helped confirm and perpetuate the
isolation and beleaguerment of the Social Democratic *Inselbewegung*.

Catholic anti-socialism also had a second, more serious, albeit
rather less clear-cut function: that of justifying, in the name and
authority of Church, Pope and God, the persecution of the designated
Gottseibeiuns. The terminology of Catholic anti-Social Democratic
discourse was - as illustrated in Waitz' pastoral letter - militant and
confrontational, making use of militaristic analogies to evoke the
atmosphere of a battle of 'Good' against 'Evil'. The exact extent to
which this fed into the practices of persecution of provincial Social
Democrats discussed earlier is a matter of conjecture. There is clear
evidence, though, that Church authorities used their influence in
pushing for provincial government restrictions on the civil rights of
Social Democrats,[70] and - as noted above - that they gave their support
to the anti-Social Democratic activities of the *Heimwehr*. There is also
some, rather more impressionistic, evidence that Church
pronouncements directly incited violence against Social Democrats.[71] A
fair conclusion would seem to be that the prejudices of the Catholic
Church may well have incited and certainly, in the eyes of its flock,
legitimised the persecution of Social Democrats.

The conclusion seems clear: Social Democracy at the local level was,
from the immediate post-war months onwards, fighting a losing battle
against overwhelming odds. It was perceived by the anti-Social

Democratic majority as a threatening and alien force and was subjected to the enduring and vehement hostility, and increasingly the open repression, of forces representative of that majority. Moreover, the territorial fragmentation of the 'island' movement heightened its vulnerability to repression; the Social Democrats were 'easy prey for their opponents'.[72]

The scale of Social Democratic vulnerability and the rate at which the battle was lost were not, of course, uniform across provincial Austria. In Tirol and Vorarlberg the Social Democrats were particularly weak and were overwhelmed from the earliest days of the First Republic. In the more industrialised province of Styria a much stronger movement steadily fell victim to an unusually radical and militant coalition of anti-Social Democratic forces. In Salzburg, Upper and Lower Austria there existed a somewhat less intolerant political atmosphere which spared the Social Democrats, at least until the later 1920s, from some of the excesses experienced elsewhere. As for Carinthia and Burgenland, there exists too little evidence to make a firm judgement, although an educated guess would be that their experience approximated to that of their closest neighbours, Styria and Lower Austria respectively.

Looking aside from these differences in provincial experience, the broader point is that local Social Democracy was, at the very best, experiencing severe problems, at worst, broken and defeated some time before what are normally seen as the key events in the decline of Austrian Social Democracy: July 1927, the onset of economic depression in 1929-1930, and the appointment of Dollfuss as Chancellor in May 1932.[73] The increased momentum of conservative anti-socialism after July 1927, the debilitating effects of mass unemployment after 1929 and Dollfuss' concerted, nationwide programme of repression all of course had damaging effects on the local-level Social Democratic movement, but only, in a sense, served to deepen existing problems and exacerbate existing weaknesses. The discussion moves on now to the question of how these entrenched, long-term problems and weaknesses were acted upon, and reflected in, the politics of the Social Democratic Party at the national and provincial levels.

Notes

[1]   The terminology here is close to that of Adam Wandruszka's classic discussion of the three Austrian *Lager*: 'Österreichs politische Struktur. Die Entwicklung der Parteien und politischen Bewegungen', in Heinrich Benedikt (Ed.), *Geschichte der Republik Österreich*, Verlag für Geschichte und Politik, Vienna (1954). Wandruska's *Lager* theory has endured well and provides useful insights into the depth and persistence of the entrenched and self-reinforcing

social and political divisions which paved the way for the collapse of the First Republic, and which had to be bridged by the 'consociational compact' of SPÖ and ÖVP after 1945 to secure the stability of the fledgling Second Republic. However, it has to be remembered that the concept of *Lager* is a shorthand tool of *macropolitical* analysis, designed to cast light on national-level political trends. As such it inevitably attributes to each of the *Lager* uniform characteristics, implying that each was a cohesive and disciplined structure, marshalled and guided by its foremost national-level representatives. This they were, as the discussion in this and the following two chapters clearly shows, certainly not. The term *'Lager'* is thus avoided. For a more general criticism of the *Lager* theory, focusing on the deeply fragmented German nationalist *'Lager'*, see e.g. Ulrich Kluge, 'Krisenherde der Ersten Republik Österreich. Beiträge zur Früh- und Spätphase der innenpolitischen Entwicklung', *Neue Politische Literatur,* 29 (1984), 80-83.

2   'Community' refers here both to *Gemeinden* (one or more villages constituting a local authority) and to *Statutarstädte*, towns established by statute.

3   The *Bezirke* (the intermediate level of administration between *Land* and *Gemeinde*) of Hietzing, Mödling, Baden, Bruck an der Leitha, Wiener Neustadt and Neunkirchen and the statutory town of Wiener Neustadt in Lower Austria and the *Bezirke* of Eisenstadt, Neusiedl and Mattersburg and the *Statutarstadt* of Eisenstadt in Burgenland.

4   Calculated from Bundesamt für Statistik, *Statistische Nachrichten. Sonderheft. 'Wahlstatistik'. Nationalratswahlen vom 24. April 1927. Einzeldarstellung nach Gemeinden und Geschlecht*, Überreuter, Vienna. (1927).

5   It should perhaps be noted that the non-SDAP majority vote was usually split between a number of Catholic-conservative and German Nationalist parties, with the Christian Social Party at the forefront. These parties had, though, one crucial uniting factor: their anti-socialism.

6   Again, see the detailed figures in Bundesamt für Statistik (1927).

7   See e.g., Karl Gutkas, 'Niederösterreich', Ernst Hanisch, 'Salzburg' and Josef Riedmann, 'Tirol', all in Erika Weinzierl, Kurt Skalnik (Eds.), *Österreich 1918-1938. Geschichte der Ersten Republik*, Volume 2, Verlag Styria, Graz (1983), 845, 913 and 974 respectively; Lewis (1991), 95; Gerhard Oberkofler, *Die Tiroler Arbeiterbewegung. Von den Anfängen bis zum Ende des 2. Weltkrieges*, Second Edition, Europaverlag, Vienna (1986), 160.

8   Ingrid Bauer, 'Zu diesem Buch' in Bauer (1988b), 6.

9   The SDAP did still participate, despite its electoral weakness (see Table 1.1.), in most of Austria's *Länder* governments under the *Proporz* system. It was, however, generally kept carefully away from the most significant provincial government portfolios. This theme is addressed in more depth in the following chapter.

10   The nature and implications of local-level insularity in the Social Democratic movement is examined in Chapter Three.

11   See e.g. Hanisch, (1990), esp. 584-585.

12   This was based, especially in rural areas, in long-standing family traditions of land ownership and the low levels of social and geographical mobility this encouraged.

[13]   See Markus Barnay, '"Echte Vorarlberger" und "fremde Bettler". Bildung von Landesbewußtsein und Ausgrenzung von Zuwanderern in Vorarlberg im 19. und 20. Jahrhundert', in Greußing (1989); and Dietrich (1991), esp. 157-166.
[14]   See e.g. the descriptions of the 'colonies' of coal-miners in the Upper Austrian coalfield in Hubert Hummer's excellent '"Waun heit mei Vota aufstand, der sogat, ihr hoabts den Hümmi auf der Welt. Des haum mir erkämpft ..." Ein Bericht zur politischen Sozialisation im Kohlenbergbau-Revier', in Greußing (1989), 96-97, and in Thomas Karny, *Lesebuch zur Geschichte der Oberösterreichischen Arbeiter*, Edition Geschichte der Heimat, Grünbach (1990), 198.
[15]   Hanns Haas, 'Es geht vorwärts. Die Salzburger Arbeiterbewegung von den Anfängen bis zum Ersten Weltkrieg' in Bauer (1988b), 56. The 'importation' in question points to the prominent role often played by migrants from elsewhere in the Habsburg Empire, above all from Bohemia, in the establishment and consolidation of the Social Democratic movement in (German) Austria before the First World War.
[16]   See e.g. Dietrich (1991), 161, 163-171; Barnay, (1989) 134-136; Haas, (1988), 56.
[17]   This was, for example, clearly the case in Steyr, a supposed hotbed of radicalism. A prime example was the so-called 'offal strike' (*Beuschelstreik*) which broke out in the Werndl munitions factory in May 1917. According to a contemporary account: 'The offal strike broke out in the canteen on 7 and 8 May 1917. After some time offal had once again come on the menu, but in such a foul condition, full of bristles. The displeasure grew so great that the whole labour force laid down tools.' Quoted in Hans Witzany, 'Kreigszeit und Revolution in Steyr', in 'Ein Oberösterreicher', *Oberösterreich und die Novemberrevolution*, Gutenberg, Linz (1928), 82.
[18]   See e.g. the summary and assessment of the academic debate in Karin M. Schmidlechner, 'Arbeiterbewegung und revolutionäres Potential in Europa am Ende des Ersten Weltkriegs: Die Situation in Österreich', in: Konrad, Schmidlechner (1991).
[19]   Karl Stocker, '"Trotz völliger Lockerung der Mannszucht ..." Soziale Konflikte in der Österreichisch-Alpinen Montangesellschaft 1917-1919', in: Konrad, Schmidlechner (1991), 123.
[20]   For the most comprehensive account of the socialisation debate, see Erwin Weissel, *Die Ohnmacht des Sieges. Arbeiterschaft und Sozialisierung nach dem Ersten Weltkrieg in Österreich*, Europaverlag, Vienna (1976).
[21]   See Stocker (1991), 120-126; Ingrid Bauer, '"Uns das Bißchen nackte Leben erhalten ..." Die Jahre 1918 bis 1920', in Bauer (1988b), 86-87, esp. 95-96.
[22]   Gerhard Pferschy, 'Steiermark', in Weinzierl, Skalnik (1983), 948.
[23]   In this respect it is worth noting that the socialisation episodes in Salzburg and Styria acted as catalysts for the formation of anti-Social Democratic 'self-defence' units which subsequently evolved into the paramilitary *bête-noire* of inter-war Social Democracy, the *Heimwehr*. See Bauer (1988d), 86-87; Pferschy (1983), 948-949.
[24]   According to Richard Steidle, who subsequently became leader of the Tirolean *Heimwehr*, in August 1919. Quoted in Oberkofler (1986), 198.
[25]   See e.g. Josef Weidenholzer, 'Ein Jahrhundert Sozialdemokratie in Linz', in SPÖ-Bezirksorganisation Linz-Stadt (Ed.), *Die Bewegung lebt. 100 Jahre Linzer Sozialdemokratie*, Gutenberg, Linz (1988), 34-36; Harry Slapnicka,

'Oberösterreich', in Weinzierl, Skalnik (1983), 889; Felix Kern, *Der Oberösterreichische Bauern- und Kleinhäuslerbund*, Volume 2, Oberösterreichischer Landesverlag, Ried (n.d.), 92-95.

26   See e.g. Gutkas (1983), 848; Hanisch (1983), 878; Pferschy (1983), 946; Dietrich (1991), 158-159, 166-168; Bauer (1988d), 85-86.

27   This issue was another which inspired the formation of anti-Social Democratic 'self-defence' units in the provinces. See e.g. Lewis (1991), 91-93; Dietrich (1991), 167-168.

28   See e.g. Gulick (1948), 69-84.

29   The 'fear of bolshevism' produced, apparently, the need to take precautions against the 'possible rape of Salzburg by a minority', and the 'bolshevik danger' was used in Tirol to unsettle the population in the same way one would 'frighten children with the bogeyman'. Even in Vorarlberg, where the SDAP was a tiny and impotent force, the Social Democrats were described as '90% Muscovites', a dire threat to the Vorarlbergian identity which had to be confronted 'if necessary by armed force'. See respectively Bauer (1988d), 86-87; Dietrich (1991), 156; and Barnay (1989), 136.

30   See e.g. Gutkas (1983), 860; Eduard G. Staudinger, '"Unabhängige Gewerkschaft" und Arbeiterschaft in der Steiermark 1927 bis 1933', *Geschichte und Gegenwart*, 4 (1985), 72-73. Particularly instructive in this respect is Wilhelm Salzer, *Geschichte der christlichen Arbeiterbewegung Oberösterreichs*, Oberösterreichischer Landesverlag, Linz (1963), 154, 161-164. Salzer's work is an official and highly partisan history of an Upper Austrian Christian labour movement which periodically fell foul of such closed shop arrangements, and gives a characteristic and vividly bombastic rendition of the 'dreadful terrors' seen in this respect by the Catholic population in the Social Democratic movement.

31   See e.g. Pferschy (1983), 947; Riedmann (1983), 982-983; Harry Slapnicka, *Oberösterreich - Zwischen Bürgerkrieg und Anschluß (1927-1938)*, Oberösterreichischer Landesverlag, Linz (1975), 25.

32   See further in Chapters Four and Five.

33   See Klaus Berchthold (Ed.), *Österreichische Parteiprogramme 1868-1966*, Oldenbourg, Munich (1967), 251-253.

34   Quoted in Lewis (1991), 138. The quote is from an anti-SDAP leaflet distributed in Bruck an der Mur in Upper Styria in the spring of 1927.

35   Quoted in Nasko (1986), 168-169.

36   Despite its now advanced age, Charles Gulick's account of July 1927 remains one of the best introductory sources on the topic. See Gulick (1948), Chapter 20.

37   The quotes are from, respectively: Karny, (1990), 135; Riedmann (1983), 983; Gerhard Wanner, 'Vorarlberg', in Weinzierl, Skalnik (1983), 1026.

38   Hanisch (1983), 924.

39   R. Hinteregger, K. Schmidlechner, E. Staudinger, 'Koloman Wallisch', in R. Hinteregger, K. Müller, E. Staudinger (Eds.), *Auf dem Weg in die Freiheit (Anstöße zu einer steirischen Zeitgeschichte)*, Leykam, Graz (1984), 201-202.

40   Ibid., 203.

41   See e.g. Kulemann (1979), 356; Hans Hautmann, Rudolf Kropf, *Die österreichische Arbeiterbewegung vom Vormärz bis 1945. Sozialökonomische Ursprünge ihrer Ideologie und Politik*, Europaverag, Vienna (1974), 152-153; Norbert Leser, *Zwischen Reformismus und Bolschewismus. Der*

Austromarxismus als Theorie und Praxis, Europaverlag, Vienna (1968), 412-417; Melanie Sully, *Continuity and Change in Austrian Socialism. The Eternal Quest for the Third Way*, Columbia University Press, New York (1982), 54-56.

[42]   See e.g. the catalogue of infringements noted and documented in the province of Salzburg by Ingrid Bauer in Bauer (1988d), 113-124.

[43]   On Vorarlberg, where strikes were characteristically seen as 'harbingers of revolution and bolshevism', see Wanner (1983), 1021 and Dreier (1984), 177, 208. On Tirol, see Oberkofler (1986), 186-187.

[44]   Dreier (1984), 208.

[45]   See respectively ibid.; Lewis (1991), 141-144; Gerhard Oberkofler, *Der 15. Juli 1927 in Tirol. Regionale Bürokratie und Arbeiterbewegung*, Europaverlag, Vienna (1982). The latter is a fascinating collection of documents which show how the railway strike was defeated in Tirol through the carefully coordinated actions of provincial government, army, police, *Heimwehr* and local authorities.

[46]   See e.g. Oberkofler (1986), 186; Nasko (1986), 249; Andreas Resch, '"Rotes Gsott" und christlichsoziale Bauern. Der Steyrer Landarbeiterstreik im Jahre 1922', in Greußing (1989), 82-83; Günther Grabner, Reinhold Hangler, Christian Hawle, Peter Kammerstätter, *"An die Wand mit ihnen". Zu den Ereignissen des Februar 1934 im Bezirk Vöcklabruck. Eine Dokumentation*, Selbstverlag, Vöcklabruck (1984), 11-12.

[47]   See Hummer (1989), 96-97.

[48]   See respectively Nasko (1986), 258; Karl Flanner, *Geschichte der Wiener Neustädter Gewerkschaftsbewegung 1889-1945*, Volume 1, Gutenberg, Wiener Neustadt (n.d.), 361, 365-366.

[49]   On the AMG's anti-unionist strategy see. P.G. Fischer, 'The Österreichisch-Alpine Montangesellschaft, 1918-1938', in P.L. Cottrell, A. Teichova (Eds.), *International business and Central Europe 1918-1939*, Leicester, Leicester University Press (1983); Otto Hwaletz, Helmut Lackner, Josef Mayer, Stefan Riesenfellner, Ingrid Spörk, Karl Stocker, Peter Teibenbacher, Ilse Wieser, *Bergmann oder Werkssoldat. Eisenerz als Fallbeispiel industrieller Politik. Dokumente und Analysen über die Österreichisch-Alpine Montangesellschaft in der Zwischenkriegszeit*, Strahelm, Graz (1984), passim; Lewis (1991), passim; Staudinger (1985); K. Stocker, 'Akkumulationszwang und Arbeiterinteresse. Beiträge über die Umsetzung von Verwertungsinteressen in soziale Tatsachen am Beispiel der ÖAMG', in Hinteregger, Müller, Staudinger (1984).

[50]   Although Free Trade Union representation was nowhere else completely wiped out in the AMG empire in Upper Styria, its previous domination of Works Councils was at the very least heavily challenged and in most cases overturned by the *Heimwehr* union. See the various Works Council election results discussed in Staudinger (1985), 67-69.

[51]   See Dreier (1984), 207-208; Wanner (1983), 1028.

[52]   Riedmann (1983), 979.

[53]   Although the authorities in Styria were also no laggards at least in sanctioning, if not officially decreeing, the persecution of Social Democrats. An example would be the provincial government role in the breaking of a Social Democratic strike in Judenburg in 1922, as recounted in Lewis (1991), 95-97.

[54]   See notes 17, 18 and 21 above.

[55]   See e.g. Dreier (1984), 176; Riedmann (1983), 970-971, 982; Erwin Steinböck, 'Kärnten', in Weinzierl, Skalnik (1983), 811-812; Pferschy (1983), 948-949.

[56] See e.g. C. Earl Edmondson, *The Heimwehr and Austrian Politics, 1918-1936,* University of Georgia Press, Athens (1978), 49-69.

[57] On the latter, see Gerald Schlag, 'Burgenland', in Weinzierl, Skalnik (1983), 781. On the others see below and the sources in the footnote 59.

[58] See Lewis (1991), 162-164.

[59] See respectively Staudinger (1985), 59; Flanner (n.d.), 99-100; STB, 16-10-1928, 1-2; Nasko (1986), 181; AVA, Sozialdemokratische Parteistellen, Karton 54; STB, 2-9-1930, 2-3.

[60] The campaign against 'Red Steyr' is fully documented in Chapter Five. The quote is the headline in the Christian Social-oriented Steyr newspaper, the *Steyrer Zeitung*. See SZ, 2-9-1930, 1.

[61] See e.g. Barry McLoughlin, 'Die Organisation des Wiener Neustädter Schutzbundes', *Zeitgeschichte,* **11** (1983-1984), 135, 142-143.

[62] In the case of Steyr, see Jeffery (1992a), 214; STB, 1.10.1929, 7.

[63] See e.g. ibid.; Oberkofler (1986), 183.

[64] Bauer, '"Und das Bißchen nackte Leben erhalten ..."' (1988), 88.

[65] C.f. the examples of vehement clerical anti-socialism recorded in Vorarlberg by Dreier (1984), 204-207, and in Upper Austria by Richard Kutschera, *Johannes Maria Gföllner. Bischof dreier Zeitenwenden*, Oberösterreichischer Landesverlag, Linz (1972), 47-56.

[66] Quoted in Oberkofler (1986), 203-204.

[67] Haas (1988), 39.

[68] Bernhard Natter, 'Ein "Schutzdamm gegen die Sturmersfluten des Sozialismus". Zur politischen Funktion der Bildungs- und Kulturarbeit der katholischen Arbeiterbewegung in Tirol vor 1934', in Greußing (1989).

[69] Ibid.

[70] See e.g. Dreier (1984), 207.

[71] A case in point would be the attack by a group of Catholic youths on meeting of Social Democratic, anti-clericalist Free Thinkers in Dornbirn, Vorarlberg in September 1926. The attack provoked the following comment by the Christian Social Provincial Governor, Otto Ender: 'What happened recently in Dornbirn was nothing other than an outbreak of healthy popular sentiment, because we in the province of Vorarlberg do not tolerate godlessness on a public stage'. Quoted in ibid., 205-207.

[72] Lewis (1991), 97.

[73] The Dollfuss era coincided with a further problem for the Social Democrats - the emergence of the National Socialists as a serious, militant, and highly dynamic anti-Social Democratic force.

2 Abandoning the Periphery:
The Local Level in the
Politics of the SDAP

The SDAP in the First Republic had a relatively straightforward, democratic party structure. There were (in slightly simplified terms)[1] three levels of party organisation - local, provincial and national - and each level was, in theory, democratically accountable to and open to the influence of the levels beneath it. This chapter focuses, though, on the *practice* of intra-party democracy in the SDAP, examining both the extent to which the local level was able to articulate its interests through the party's internal structures and the related question of whether local-level problems - such as those identified in the previous chapter - were addressed by the party at its national and provincial levels. Its central theme is that the problems of the local level were *not* addressed by either of these higher levels of the party. It argues that both the national and the provincial levels of the SDAP were so intensely preoccupied with their own immediate fields of political activity during the First Republic that they lost the wider vision necessary to confront and respond to the problems the party faced on the ground. In addition, the internal structures of the SDAP failed to provide opportunities for effective lower-level input into determining the strategic priorities of the party. The local level was thus, as it were, not only neglected, even abandoned, in the priority-setting of the higher levels of the SDAP, but was also shut out from the internal party debates which might have been able to modify higher-level priorities in its interests.

The Viennese Chimera: the Preoccupations of the SDAP at the National Level

These problems are most clearly illustrated in the relationship between 'centre' and 'periphery' in the Social Democratic movement, between its Viennese heartland and its isolated provincial outposts. The examination of this relationship has traditionally been neglected in a literature which has concentrated on the 'high politics' of Social Democracy in Vienna. As a result, and with the partial exception of work on the period 1932-1934, when the progressive disintegration of the SDAP into militant and accommodationist wings came in part to be expressed by local-level party functionaries,[2] the reader would be hard-pressed to find any evidence of significant input from the local level into internal party debates. The conclusion all too easily implied

42

from this is that the Social Democratic movement was a well-oiled, tightly organised, cohesive and disciplined structure, with the centre and periphery acting together in service of a clearly defined, uniform Social Democratic cause.[3]

This 'conclusion' has come under challenge in recent years as the focus of research has increasingly shifted away from the Social Democratic centre and towards the movement in the provinces. The results of this new research have been instructive. While confirming the impression that the input from the local level was negligble, they have at the same time undermined any notion of a well-oiled party structure. Rather, they have suggested that the relationship between national and local levels in Social Democratic politics was at best deeply flawed, at worst effectively a non-relationship in which the problems and needs of the local level in the provinces remained unrecognised and unaddressed by the movement's leadership in Vienna.[4] Drawing on this research, this section of the chapter aims to account for the flaws in this relationship, examining why the national SDAP leadership proved unable to recognise and articulate the needs of the local level or - as a result - to develop strategies attuned to local-level conditions in the provinces.

An initial pointer in discussing these issues has already been given in the Introduction to this book, which suggested that the thoughts and strategies of national party leadership were tightly bound up in the unrepresentative conditions which existed in its immediate, Viennese environment. This was seen most obviously in the electoral strategy developed after the SDAP left national government in 1920, a strategy which styled the achievements of Red Vienna - municipal socialism and cultural re-education - as an electoral beacon which was supposed to attract voters across Austria to the Social Democratic cause, and in this way to secure the party's return to government. This Vienna-centred strategy was, as Jill Lewis' path-breaking work on Styrian Social Democracy has made clear, a wholesale failure.[5] While the SDAP's vote share rose at its peak in the national elections of 1927 to an impressive 60% in Vienna, it never succeeded in gathering any more than around a third of the provincial vote or - therefore - in even approaching an overall, national majority.

The failure of this 'Viennese road' to electoral success is, in view of the themes discussed in the previous chapter, hardly surprising. Vienna was Austria's industrial heartland, a highly integrated, modern industrial conurbation in which a numerically predominant SDAP was in a position to disregard the venom and hostility of its opponents and get on with mobilising the extensive powers of the City Council and the sense of community of its densely concentrated supporters to redefine Viennese politics. Red Vienna was in other words based in conditions which were unique and non-transferable, 'dependent on factors which were specific to Viennese life and which could not be reproduced outside'.[6] The contrast with the situation facing the Social Democratic movement in the provinces could not have been more stark. It is hard to imagine what relevance, if any, a Vienna-based electoral message had in a provincial setting where Social Democrats were excluded from the levers of power, and where they were confronted daily with the concerted hostility of employers, the provincial authorities, the *Heimwehr* and the Catholic establishment. In this context the 'Viennese road' could offer at best a nebulous, symbolic vision of what life might be like in a distant Social Democratic future. It was not, though, able to offer concrete, practical solutions to the manifold problems which provincial Social Democrats faced in the present. An electoral message evoking the glories of Red Vienna may even have made matters worse in some areas, particularly in western Austria, where traditional anti-Vienna sentiments, reinforced by anti-Social Democratic (and anti-Semitic) prejudice, helped to produce a picture of First Republic Vienna as a latterday Sodom.[7] In such circumstances the Viennese model was not a promising formula for electoral expansion.

The question remains why no strategy supplementary to the 'Viennese road' and more clearly attuned to the needs of the provinces was developed. The answer would seem to lie in the internal structure of the SDAP, the intra-party relationship between centre and periphery. The best analysis hitherto of the party structure remains that of Peter Kulemann.[8] Kulemann's work draws strongly from the work of Robert Michels',[9] whose prediction of the inevitability of bureaucratic and oligarchical rule in large-scale party organisations is clearly borne out in the context of the inter-war SDAP. Kulemann presents a convincing Michelsian examination of a highly centralised party structure dominated by a National Executive Committee which discouraged any genuine debate and dissension over strategy and tactics at the lower levels of the party (and which largely succeeded in doing so until the party began to disintegrate in the early 1930s). There was limited ongoing contact or dialogue between the centre and the provinces, and little indication that the national leadership sought to keep in touch with the concerns and needs of representatives of the party on the ground;[10] in intra-party terms, the sub-units of the party in the provinces were scarcely more than passive recipients of instructions and ideas passed down from above. A particularly apt example of this one-way relationship (and indeed of the rituals through which it was conducted) was given in a local authority report of the 'discussion' which followed a lecture given by Otto Bauer to the SDAP in Bregenz, Vorarlberg, prior to local Chamber of Labour elections in 1926:

Landesrat Prieß opened the discussion and *Bundesrat* Lindner took the floor, *declaring that any discussion was unnecessary* after a speech as splendid as that given by comrade M.P. Dr Otto Bauer, and calling upon those present to stand and to vow to uphold the cause of socialism, and only to vote for the Social Democratic list in the Chamber of Labour elections. At this point the meeting was closed at 10.30pm by *Landesrat* Prieß. After singing the workers' anthem, the participants of the meeting left.[11]

The party leadership thus assumed for itself the role of the sole fount of wisdom in intra-party affairs. It also displayed an extraordinary level of continuity in its composition. The only ways to leave the National Executive were normally either to die in office or, at the very least, to fall into severe ill-health. This was a party leadership which, in Kulemann's words, 'for years and for decades on end almost single-handedly managed the fate of the party in all decisive matters'.[12] A crucial supplementary point which Kulemann does not directly make, is that this ultra-ossified leadership was almost exclusively resident in Vienna, had been for many years, and was deeply involved in shaping and running the policies of 'the socialism in one city' of Red Vienna. Only in 1928 was a provincial functionary, Oskar Helmer from Lower Austria, elected to the Executive, to be followed after 1930 by another Lower Austrian, Heinrich Schneidmadl, and the Styrian Koloman Wallisch.

The continuity and dominant intra-party position of a Vienna-based elite hints at the reasons for the Viennese orientation of the party strategy and the inability of the party to modify its direction to meet the needs of its local-level components in the provinces. As Helmer himself noted in a biting criticism of the 'outdated and unwieldy' party structure shortly before his (perhaps not coincidental) elevation to the Executive Committee, there was minimal opportunity for interaction between Executive and provinces, aside from the formalities of the annual, carefully stage-managed party conference.[13] That Helmer should make these comments is particularly significant. His Lower Austrian party had its organisational base in Vienna, which functioned as capital city of Lower Austria, and had especially close contacts to one of the more prominent party leaders, Karl Renner.[14] In these two respects it was easily the best-placed among the provincial parties to make its views felt at the level of the Party Executive. Bearing this in mind, Helmer's critique stresses all the more that the SDAP leadership, secure in its Viennese 'citadel',[15] had become irretrievably detached from the practical problems faced by Social Democrats outside the capital, 'to whom [it] rarely listened and whom it seldom understood'.[16] Further weight is added to this conclusion by the unusually candid comment of a delegate from the small Salzburg town of Zell am See to the 1920 party conference:

> I do not want to underestimate the Viennese, but still I feel justified in making the point on our behalves that our work in the provinces cannot be compared with that in Vienna. *The [Viennese] comrades have no idea* what kind of terror tactics are used in the provinces.[17]

The failure of the 'Viennese comrades' to listen to and understand the problems faced by their provincial peers was perhaps most crassly illustrated in the period after 1930 when the quest for electoral success was of necessity shelved by the SDAP leadership in favour of the more fundamental defence of the movement and the democratic constitution against the burgeoning attacks of emerging 'Austro-Fascism'. Once again the party leadership's reference point for this now defensive strategy - even in a period when it was confronted with growing expressions of dissatisfaction from the provinces[18] - was Vienna. This was seen most clearly in the 'four points' of September 1933 which set out the conditions under which active resistance would be undertaken against an increasingly repressive central government: the dissolution of the Free Trade Unions; the dissolution of the SDAP; the introduction of a fascist constitution; and the deposition of the SDAP-run Vienna City Council.

These 'four points' were indisputably *Vienna-centred* points 'which had little or even no relevance to the problems of the provinces',[19] which displayed 'no idea' of political realities in the provinces. This applied not only to the point concerning the deposition of the Viennese City Council, but also to the other three: By September 1933 party, trade union and broader constitutional rights, although formally not yet abolished, had - as the previous chapter showed - long since ceased to exist in any recognisable form in Styria, Tirol and Vorarlberg, and were severely circumscribed elsewhere in the provinces. The party leadership was committing itself to the defence of the democratic 'rules of the game' long after the rules had already been changed in the provinces As the left-wing SDAP activist, Ernst Fischer, remarked of the case of Styria some eighteen months before the publication of the 'four points': 'Styria is a fascist province; in this eastern part of the republic, the constitution is a scrap of paper, fascism is a reality'.[20]

The inability of the SDAP leadership to look beyond its Viennese backyard and confront these uncomfortable realities of provincial politics is indicative of a key and fateful failing in its outlook: it had lost its sense of political perspective and become deeply absorbed in, and consumed by, the narrow and unique context of the metropolitan politics of Vienna.[21] To put it more bluntly, the preoccupation with Red

Vienna in the electoral strategy of the 1920s and the defensive strategy of the 1930s was little more than a chimerical obsession, whose single-mindedness left the movement in the provinces invitingly exposed to the gamut of anti-socialist forces which dominated provincial politics, economy and society.

In Search of Consociation: Social Democracy at the Provincial Level

The SDAP at the provincial level was, in two ways at least, in an ostensibly better position to address the needs of the party on the ground. First and foremost, it was, compared to the national/Viennese party, physically closer to the local level and thus, in theory, more likely to be sensitive to its concerns. Second, and unlike its national-level counterpart, which remained in steadfast parliamentary opposition from 1920 onwards, the provincial SDAP was deeply committed to parliamentary and governmental cooperation with its party-political opponents. This cooperative strategy brought the provincial SDAP close to the levers of governmental power in the provinces, and put it, potentially at least, in a position to use such power in the interests of the local level. The commitment to this strategy has also raised questions for a number of authors about the possible establishment of 'consociational'[22] arrangements in the provinces in the First Republic, i.e. the attempt to manage deep-seated political divisions through mutual accommodation and power-sharing at the elite level. If the cooperative strategy of the provincial-level SDAP had been successful in managing and ameliorating political conflict on the ground - as a number of these authors have suggested it was - it would clearly have had far more direct relevance to the local-level problems of Social Democracy than the Vienna-dominated strategies of the national level. This section therefore begins by examining the case for the existence of a form of consociationalism at the provincial level in the First Republic. It then moves on to assess the intra-party relations of the provincial and local level. The broad argument is that despite greater proximity to the local level, and despite greater access to governmental powers, the provincial level proved no more effective in addressing the interests of Social Democrats on the ground than the national SDAP.

Consociationalism and the Provinces

It has become conventional for political scientists to examine the politics of divided societies against the model of consociationalism. This has applied in particular in the case of the Austrian Second Republic which, at least for the first twenty or so years of its existence,[23] was generally seen to display all the paradigmatic features of a consociational democracy: it was a segmented society in which party-political divisions overlay and reinforced social divisions to create mutually hostile 'sub-cultures' (or, to redeploy Hanisch's term, 'milieux'); there was a willingness among party-political elites to ameliorate the effects of segmentation by employing cooperative, power-sharing arrangements to 'bridge' the social and political divide; and these elites had the capacity to 'deliver' their side of the bargain by maintaining a high degree of cohesion and discipline within their respective sub-cultures.

Given that the social and party-political divisions, and in part the political élites, of the first twenty years of the Second Republic were very much those which had existed in the First Republic, it is perhaps surprising that relatively few attempts have been made to examine the First Republic against the consociational model. There have, though, been exceptions in two areas. First, Ulrike Weber-Felber has pointed to the quest by the Social Democratic Free Trade Unions in the First Republic for the establishment of what would today be termed corporatist mechanisms of 'social partnership' between unions, employers and government (mechanisms which came to be central to the power-sharing modus vivendi set up in the Second Republic)[24]. The unions' quest, as Weber-Felber clearly shows, was quite hopeless, foundering with considerable monotony on the unwillingness of employers and (right-wing) national government to pay anything more than the most meagre lip-service to the notion of cooperation.[25] A more promising case for the existence of cooperative and accommodative, potentially consociational arrangements has though been made in regard to the conduct of elite-level provincial politics during the First Republic.

The most explicit references to the model of consociationalism in work on First Republic provincial politics have been made by Ernst Hanisch and Evan Bukey. In his work on the province of Salzburg Hanisch has suggested that 'even in the First Republic a model of democracy based on consensus was established', while Bukey, focusing on Upper Austria, has proposed that a 'moderate political culture' underlay a 'consociational or concordant democracy' between 1918 and 1934.[26] These assertions are then backed up by an impressive array of examples of substantive policy agreements between the two leading party-political forces, the Christian Social Party (CSP) and the SDAP, and of an abidingly consensual mode of procedure in the Salzburg and Upper Austrian *Landtage* which endured through to the bitter end of the democratic constitution in 1934.[27]

Similar pictures of cross-party cooperation in provincial-level, parliamentary politics are frequently given elsewhere in the literature: on Lower Austria, where prominent figures on Left and Right have long been noted for their pragmatic, consensual orientation;[28] on Carinthia, where the cooperative spirit was fostered by the early post-war *Abwehrkampf* (defensive battle) against the territorial demands of the emergent Yugoslav state;[29] and on Burgenland, whose *Landtag* was a veritable smoke-filled room of frenetic inter-party horse-trading.[30] In addition, even Styria, site of the most bitter conflicts in provincial politics, and Tirol and Vorarlberg, the most deeply reactionary strongholds of provincial conservatism, saw provincial-level parliamentary politics conducted for long periods in a relatively consensual, conflict-free atmosphere.[31]

This apparently ubiquitous cooperative behaviour among provincial party-political elites raises intriguing questions, particularly given the established perception of the inter-war years as an inherently conflictual era in Austrian history. As Richard Luther and Wolfgang Müller put it in a work focused on Second Republic consociationalism, it suggests 'an alternative perspective on the development of the First Republic, namely, to see it as an ultimately unsuccessful attempt at cooperation, rather than as an exclusively confrontational episode in Austria'a political history.'[32] This is certainly the argument of Hanisch and Bukey. Their discussions of provincial politics in Salzburg and Upper Austria are based explicitly on orthodox consociational frameworks[33] characterised by elite-level 'concordance' superimposed on - and by implication mediating - the conflictual relations which typically existed at the 'basis' of provincial politics. Such findings seem to me to be trying a little too hard to 'squeeze' the First Republic into a consociational framework. They certainly require further consideration, above all concerning the nature and effectiveness of the elite-level relationship: Was this really a genuine commitment to power-sharing which was made in the interests of - and which was capable of - bridging and ameliorating the intense, everyday conflicts of political life in Salzburg, Upper Austria and indeed elsewhere in provincial Austria?

The Façade of Cooperation

A first point to make about the nature of elite-level cooperation is that it was, in most cases, a constitutional obligation. With the exception of Vienna, all the provincial governments were originally (re-)constituted after the First World War on the basis of *Proporz*, i.e. their composition was proportionate to party strengths in the respective provincial parliaments (if the parties received sufficient votes to cross a designated threshhold for *Proporz* arrangements). Provincial party elites were, in other words, *obliged* to work together - at times it seems against their better judgement, as indicated by the abandonment of *Proporz* in Vorarlberg in 1923 and Tirol in 1927 and the expression of dissatisfaction about *Proporz* in Styria and Carinthia during the 1920s.[34] This is not to say that cooperation was necessarily undertaken unwillingly. The practice of proportional government was often supported by an apparently genuine commitment to cooperation. This commitment was typically based in the perceived need to generate all-party consensus in dealing with pressing problems of public order, for example the distribution of limited food supplies in the immediate aftermath of the First World War, the Carinthian *Abwehrkampf*, the uncertainties which followed 15 July 1927 or the 1931 Pfrimer Putsch, or the challenges posed by the increasing popularity of the National Socialists after 1932.[35] Cooperation was also facilitated by the moderate and conciliatory nature of the major parliamentary parties of both Left and Right in some of the provinces, most notably in Upper and Lower Austria, Carinthia and Salzburg.

This ostensibly impressive display of cooperative spirit can, though, be misleading. It disguises the fact that the practice of proportional government was generally limited to cooperation in the exercise of *responsibility*, rarely of real *power*. Whatever the constitutional situation, the parties in proportional government were, of course, by no means equal partners. The senior partner - almost always the CSP - was generally able to shape the affairs of provincial government to suit its own ends. This applied not only to legislative matters, but also, and perhaps more crucially, to powers of patronage. The most important ministerial portfolios were, for example, kept carefully out of the hands of the SDAP.[36] Moreover, these powers of patronage were used, even in the supposedly cooperative bastion of Salzburg, to entrench non-Social Democratic influence in the administrative agencies of provincial government.[37] The institutionalisation of one-sided staffing arrangements in the executive authorities of a deeply divided society would hardly seem either to demonstrate a genuine commitment to cooperation on the part of the non-Social Democratic parties or to facilitate effective conflict management. As Ingrid Bauer has drily noted about cooperation in Salzburg politics, it was here, in the distribution of the spoils of office, that 'the willingness of the bourgeois parties to seek "consensus" had its unmistakable limits'.[38]

To put it more bluntly, the Social Democrats represented in provincial government were frequently little more than 'stooges', sharing in the responsibility for policies perhaps unpopular among their supporters, but without being granted a full input into the decision-making process or a real opportunity to pursue any alternative agenda.[39] As the Social Democratic Deputy Provincial Governor of Salzburg bitterly stated in 1920, having just worked conscientiously with his political opponents to preserve law and order in the tense months directly after the First World War for no tangible reward, the Social Democrats in provincial government were only there 'for show' (*zur Parade*), not to exercise the governmental rights supposedly due to them. They were, in the words of his Vorarlberg counterpart, little more than 'convenient lightning conductors' for popular discontent who were subsequently 'passed over where important decisions were concerned'.[40]

The above tends to confirm what Weber-Felber has already shown in the case of the Free Trade Unions, namely that a genuine willingness on the part of the Social Democrats to enter meaningful cooperation had little chance of realisation in the context of the First Republic. Although this willingness was not, as in the case of the trade unions, blithely ignored in provincial party politics, it was more or less cynically exploited by opponents who were happy to foster the appearance of cooperation without sharing out its fruits - with, perhaps, one exception: Upper Austria.

Only in the case of Upper Austria does there appear to be clear evidence that the commitment of Social Democrats to cooperation was matched by that of the parties of the Right. This emerges especially clearly from the reports made by Josef Gruber, SDAP Deputy Provincial Governor in Upper Austria from 1919-1930, to the national SDAP leadership on parliamentary politics in Upper Austria. Even a brief consultation of these reports leaves no doubt about the extraordinarily good and genuinely cooperative working relationship which existed between Social Democratic and Christian Social Parties in the *Landtag*, and between Gruber and the successive Christian Social Provincial Governors, Johann Nepomuk Hauser and Josef Schlegel.[41] This might seem to add weight at least to Bukey's arguments about provincial-level consociationalism in Upper Austria in the First Republic.

It should be stressed, though, that sincere parliamentary cooperation between opposed forces does not necessarily provide for effective conflict management outside parliament. A further condition necessary to support the consociational model would be the existence of a high level of cohesion between elite and basis within the 'sub-cultures' of provincial politics. Sub-cultural cohesion is a crucial element of any putative consociational arrangement as a guarantee of the ability of power-sharing elites to 'make stick' the decisions they cooperatively arrive at. Bukey asserts that this element too existed in Upper Austria: 'A final factor encouraging collaborative politics in Upper Austria was tight party discipline, especially in the Christian Social and Social Democratic movements.'[42] This seems doubtful in the extreme. As the next chapter shows, the Social Democratic movement was far from being a cohesive organisational entity in Upper Austria or anywhere else in the provinces. Nor can the Catholic-conservative sub-culture, which the CSP sought to represent, be seen as a cohesive force. The CSP lacked a clearly defined party structure, and was consequently subject throughout the provinces to the centrifugal forces of rival leadership claims, and of the competing priorities of functionally and ideologically divergent groups and factions. These centrifugal forces were *especially* evident in Upper Austria, where a moderate and conciliatory parliamentary leadership was in more or less constant - and ultimately losing - conflict with the extra-parliamentary forces of a 'hawkish', reactionary Bishop, Johannes Maria Gföllner, and, after 1927, Starhemberg's militant, nominally Catholic-conservative, Upper Austrian *Heimwehr*.[43] In other words, even where provincial-level cooperation had led to effective *parliamentary* power-sharing, the respective provincial party elites were by no means in a position to 'discipline' their constituencies into accepting its results *on the ground*. Despite the best efforts of parliamentary elites, little changed in the everyday experience of Social Democrats as a result of parliamentary cooperation.

These conclusions inevitably leave the consociational model proposed by Hanisch and Bukey, and implied by other writers on provincial Austria, in serious difficulties. On closer examination the case for the existence of some form of 'proto'-consociationalism in the provinces in the First Republic, which 'prefigured'[44] the consociational arrangements of the Second Republic, is a flawed one. There existed only a façade of power-sharing in the First Republic, which concealed either an unwillingness, at least on the Right, to seek accommodative solutions to Austria's problems, or an inability to ensure cooperative arrangements could have an accommodative impact on the ground. As a result everyday social and political divisions remained, behind this façade, unbridged and perhaps became - for example through party patronage in the provincial bureaucracies - even more deeply entrenched, institutionalised and ultimately destructive.[45]

Provincial-Local Relations in the SDAP

This conclusion raises important questions about the relationship between the SDAP at the provincial level and its counterparts at the local level. The energies invested by the provincial-level SDAP into a typically fruitless quest for a share of power clearly did not bridge, control and mediate the front-lines of political conflict which were drawn tightly around the local-level enclaves of Social Democracy. Local-level Social Democrats remained exposed and vulnerable to the hostility and antagonism of representatives of the same forces with which the provincial-level SDAP was trying to work constructively in the various provincial parliaments. The remainder of this chapter examines the implications this had for the nature of provincial-local relations in the SDAP?

These implications cannot be tied down with any great precision. Too little research has been conducted on provincial-local relations in the SDAP to do much more than offer tentative pointers. It does though seem doubtful whether local-level Social Democrats either fully understood or entirely approved of the parliamentary work and cooperative strategies of the provincial-level party elites. This is not to say that SDAP members of provincial parliaments and governments achieved nothing in their work. As far as the scope of their portfolios allowed them, they worked conscientiously and, it would seem, indefatigably to defend the interests of their voters. Much of this work was, though, attritional, unspectacular and 'painstakingly detailed',[46] unlikely to have much resonance outside the parliamentary arena. Much more publicly prominent - and in intra-party terms problematic - were the periodic appeals for restraint the provincial elite made in harness with their political opponents in times of crisis. As noted above, it was such appeals in particular which cast the SDAP elite in the role of stooges, for they received little in the way of a *quid pro quo*. Indeed, in some cases their commitment to compromise was perversely 'rewarded' by the collusion of the provincial governments in which they supposedly had a proportionate say in the outright repression of their supporters. The crassest example of this was, as Gerhard Oberkofler has diligently documented,[47] the deep involvement of the Tirolean provincial authorities in the suppression of the Social Democratic railway strike of July 1927, an involvement which could still occur even though a Social Democrat held the office of Deputy Provincial Governor until the end of that year.[48] The commitment of Social Democrats to institutions over which they had limited, and in some cases evidently no, control presented something of an image problem *vis-à-vis* the Social Democratic rank and file. This was something even Josef Gruber, the SDAP Deputy Provincial Governor in the far less conflictual province of Upper Austria, was forced to admit in 1930:

> This [cooperative] policy of ours can very easily lead to misunderstandings. If one looks at the matter only on a superficial level, one could come to the conclusion that we, the representatives of the party, are far too accommodating and perhaps even forsake the interests of the proletariat.[49]

Gruber's statement both implies a certain difficulty in making the rationale and results of *Landtag* work clear to the party outside the *Landtag* and points more broadly to a gulf between the perspectives and priorities of provincial and local levels. This gulf was widened by a standard problem of Social Democratic politics in Austria: the absence of intra-party mechanisms capable of maintaining ongoing contact and dialogue between different levels of the party. Just as at the national, and indeed the local,[50] levels, the provincial-level SDAP was a highly oligarchical, 'Michelsian' party. It was typically dominated by a small, long-serving, more or less closed leadership elite which was not subject to effective control by the local level of the party. There existed at the provincial level three elected party bodies, a 'core' Executive, an 'extended' Executive and a Control Commission. The core Executive was the most important body and generally brought together the luminaries of *Landtag* politics, along with other important party functionaries, usually including the leading figures in the city council of the provincial capital and the editors of the provincial party press.[51] The core Executive was consequently a body in which the clear majority of members were active in one way or another in the politics of the provincial capital. Representatives from outside the capital were, in contrast, more fully represented in the less important extended Executive and Control Commission.[52]

The focus on the provincial capital - and, by implication, the marginalisation of the local level in intra-party affairs - was further reinforced by a highly limited turnover of the membership of the core Executive. While not reaching the extreme level of ossification displayed by the National Executive, provincial core Executives rarely saw significant infusions of new blood.[53] This tendency to leadership immobilism was promoted (again as at the national and local levels) by the function and ethos of the party's internal structures. The party organisation was not intended to be a debating forum designed to seek out and discuss competing views from its members, but was rather a mechanism through which to report on and legitimise the actions of its leaders. This could be seen most clearly in the nature of the provincial party conference. The proceedings of the conference, at least as far as sources from Salzburg and Upper Austria[54] indicate, were highly ritualistic, comprising dry and uncritical reports from various Social Democratic organisations, set-piece speeches by the provincial party leader and by an invited national figure, short debates which focused almost exclusively on organisational matters and the generally unanimous (re-)election of the provincial Executive. There is certainly no evidence of genuine strategic and policy discussion in the case of Upper Austria until the 1933 conference, when, for the first time, open dissatisfaction was expressed at the inability of the party to combat the nationwide wave of repression then being conducted by the Dollfuss regime.[55]

The above presents a picture of the provincial-level SDAP as a 'capital-city' party, remote from the party's ordinary members. It was wrapped up in an earnest, tireless, but generally unsuccessful pursuit of the interests of its supporters through parliamentary channels. It was consequently - and, as it became more and more ossified, increasingly - detached from the experience of the day-to-day problems of those supporters. It was also shielded from those problems being fully aired by the party's oligarchical internal structures. These findings raise clear parallels to the situation at the national level, where a detached and ossified national party elite had become too absorbed in the opportunities presented in its immediate, Viennese political environment to address the everyday needs of Social Democrats in the provinces; the provincial level too was absorbed in its immediate environment of *Landtag* politics and politicking.

In other words, local-level Social Democrats were not only 'abandoned' by the national-level Social Democratic leadership, they were also ill-served by, and unable to help reshape, the well-meaning but ineffectual strategies of their provincial leaderships. The net result of these intra-party deficiencies was that local-level Social Democrats were effectively left on their own to confront the grass roots hostilities of provincial politics which were outlined in the previous chapter. Surprisingly, perhaps, this intra-party isolation provoked relatively few examples of open dissatisfaction at the local level, at least until the party began to fall apart in the early 1930s. This may have reflected in part the ritual deference to the principle of party unity which dominated the party from its foundation in 1889 right through to the early 1930s. It may also have reflected decades of intra-party conditioning to accept the accumulated 'wisdom' of the higher levels of the party hierarchy without dispute. It certainly did not, though, reflect a passive willingness on the part of the local level to leave its fate in the hands of provincial and national party elites. On the contrary, where local conditions allowed, Social Democrats embarked actively and independently on strategies to 'defend' themselves against the isolation and hostility they faced. These strategies are the subject of the next chapter.

Notes

[1]   More precisely, the sub-provincial level consisted of district-level (*Bezirksorganisation*) and local-level (*Ortsgruppe* or *Sektion*) party organisations. In Lower Austria, where there existed the biggest party organisation outside Vienna, there was also an intermediate *Kreis* level between district and province. See Weidenholzer (1981), 33-34. For the purposes of this chapter, the whole sub-provincial organisation is deemed to be 'local'.

2   See for example Anson G. Rabinbach, *The Crisis of Austrian Socialism. From Red Vienna to civil war 1927-1934*, University of Chicago Press, London (1983), esp. 128-180.

3   This is an inherent assumption of the *'Lager'* theory of Austrian politics. See note 1 of Chapter One.

4   This theme has been expressed most explicitly in Jill Lewis' work on Upper Styria. See Lewis, (1991), passim.

5   Ibid., 88.

6   Ibid., 84.

7   See e.g. Dietrich (1991), 156-157, 162-163; Oberkofler (1986), 204; Riedmann (1983), 964, 968.

8   Kulemann (1979), 307-318.

9   Robert Michels, *Political Parties. A Sociological Study of the Oligarchical Tendencies of Modern Democracy*, Dover, New York (1959). For a fuller discussion of the work of Michels on party organisational structures, see Chapter Seven.

10   This question has never been fully investigated in the literature. A partial exception is the work of Joe Weidenholzer on the influence of the party's central educational network outside Vienna. This shows that the penetration of the party into the provinces was, with the exception of Vienna's immediate environs in Lower Austria, at best extremely limited, and became more and more negligible the further away from Vienna one looks. See Weidenholzer (1981), 242-273. Weidenholzer's findings are backed up by my own research on Steyr - culled from reports in the party press - which suggests that national party leaders came to the provinces only to deliver election campaign addresses or to speak at provincial party conferences, and never actually to *consult* and *listen* to provincial Social Democrats. See e.g. reports of lectures by Max Adler, Wilhelm Ellenbogen, Otto Bauer and Josef Luitpold Stern in, respectively, STB 30-11-1928, 7; 12-9-1929, 9; 15-3-1930, 8; 26-9-1931, 9.

11   My italics. Quoted in Dreier (1984), 202. *Landesrat* Prieß was a member of the Vorarlberg provincial government and *Bundesrat* Lindner a member of the federal (i.e. second) chamber of the national parliament.

12   Ibid., 313-314.

13   Oskar Helmer, 'Wien und die Länder. Organisatorische Parteiprobleme', *Der Kampf,* **22** (1929), 458-460.

14   See e.g. Gutkas (1983), 851; Rabinbach (1983), 88.

15   Lewis (1991), 13.

16   Ibid., 207.

17   My italics. Quoted in Ernst Glaser, 'Über die Organisationsstrukturen im sozialdemokratischen Lager', in Erich Fröschl, Maria Mesner, Helge Zoitl (Eds.), *Die Bewegung. Hundert Jahre Sozialdemokratie in Österreich*, Passagen, Vienna (1990), 401.

18   Most notably in the angry interventions of numerous local-level delegates at the extraordinary national party conference called in April 1933. See the minutes of the conference in Verein für Geschichte der Arbeiterbewegung, Parteiarchiv, Mappe 65.

19   Slapnicka (1975), 128.
20   Quoted in Ernst Fischer, 'Österreich vor dem Bürgerkrieg', *Die Weltbühne*, 5-1-1932.
21   Recent research has also suggested that this Viennese fixation may also have been detrimental to the trade union arm of the Social Democratic movement. See Weber-Felber (1990) and the discussion of Weber-Felber's book in Jeffery (1993), 86-92.
22   Originally popularised in political science debate in Arend Lijphart, 'Typologies of democratic systems', *Comparative Political Studies*, 1 (1968), the concept of 'consociational' democracy has since spawned an immense literature. For a useful introduction see S. Halpern, 'The disorderly universe of consociational democracy', *West European Politics*, 10 (1987).
23   The question of whether the Second Republic is 'still a case of consociationalism' is addressed in depth in Luther, Müller (1992a).
24   For a brief overview of Second Republic corporatism see Peter Gerlich, 'A farewell to corporatism', in Luther, Müller (1992a). For a more in-depth treatment see P. Gerlich, E. Grande, W.C. Müller (Eds.), *Sozialpartnerschaft in der Krise. Leistungen und Grenzen des Neokorporatismus in Österreich*, Böhlau, Vienna (1985).
25   See Weber-Felber (1990) and Jeffery (1993), 88-89.
26   Quoted respectively in Ernst Hanisch 'Die sozialdemokratische Fraktion im Salzburger Landtag, 1918-1934', in Gerhard Botz, Hans Hautmann, Helmut Konrad, Josef Weidenholzer (Eds.) (1978), *Bewegung und Klasse. Studien zur österreich-ischen Arbeitergeschichte*, Europaverlag, Vienna (1978), 247; and Evan Burr Bukey, *Hitler's Hometown. Linz, Austria 1908-1945*, Indiana University Press, Bloomington and Indianapolis (1986), 39, 59.
27   Hanisch (1978), 257-265; Bukey (1986), esp. 39-74. Bukey's views are echoed by a variety of (Left- and Right-leaning) Upper Austrian historians who have somewhat proudly pointed to a highly cooperative approach to provincial government in Upper Austria which was exemplified in an *Arbeitsgemeinschaft*, a 'team-orientation' of all the major parties. See e.g. Harry Slapnicka, *Von Hauser bis Eigruber. Eine Zeitgeschichte Oberösterreichs Band 1. 1918-1927*, Oberösterreichischer Landesverlag, Linz (1974) 132-137; Josef Weidenholzer, 'Bedeutung und Hintergrund des 12. Februar 1934', in Karl R. Stadler (Ed.), *"Es wird nicht mehr verhandelt ..." Der 12. Februar 1934 in Oberösterreich*, Gutenberg, Linz (1984), 19-22.
28   See e.g. Rabinbach (1983), 147; Gutkas (1983), 851, 862; Nasko (1986), 180, 200.
29   Steinböck (1983), 810-811, 817-818.
30   Schlag (1983), passim.
31   See on Styria Pferschy (1983), 942-947; on Tirol Riedmann (1983), 967-968 and Oberkofler (1986), 221; and on Vorarlberg Wanner (1983), 1019,1025, 1028.
32   Quoted in Kurt Richard Luther, Wolfgang C. Müller, 'Consociationalism and the Austrian political system', in Luther, Müller (1992a), 8.
33   Hanisch (1978), 248; Bukey (1986), 59-60.
34   Slapnicka, (1975), 88; Wanner (1983), 1025.

35   See e.g. Pferschy (1983), 942-943; Steinböck (1983), 810-811, 817-818; Slapnicka (1983), 893; Hanisch (1978), 257-265;

36   See e.g. Riedmann (1983), 977.

37   Bauer, (1988d), 88.

38   Ibid.

39   See e.g. Wanner (1983), 1028. The latter point is also admitted even in the otherwise positive report of Josef Gruber, the Social Democratic Deputy Provincial Governor (*Landeshauptmann*) of Upper Austria, on the SDAP's work in the Upper Austrian *Landtag*, which he delivered to the national SDAP leadership in 1927. See *Jahrbuch der österreichischen Arbeiterbewegung 1927*, 140-143.

40   Quoted respectively in Bauer (1988d), 88, and Dreier (1984), 198.

41   See *Jahrbuch der österreichischen Arbeiterbewegung 1927*, 140-144; 1928, 199-201; 1929, 234-236; 1930, 255-258. See also Bukey (1986) passim; Slapnicka (1974), 132-137.

42   Bukey (1986), 60.

43   On Gföllner, see Kutschera (1972), 45-56. See also Weidenholzer (1984), 20-21; Slapnicka (1975), 111-126; and in particular (and paradoxically) Bukey (1986), esp. 48-54 and 75-86, who gives clear insights into the strains which existed within 'a heterogenous, highly diversified group that found shelter under the umbrella of Roman Catholicism' (p.48). Similar problems existed for Christian Social Party leaderships elsewhere: e.g. in Styria, where Walther Pfrimer's *Heimatschutz* veered off quite radically into an extreme German Nationalism during the 1920s; and in Salzburg, where the paramilitary confrontation of the *Heimwehr* met with open disapproval in the parliamentary CSP. See respectively, Bruce Pauley, *Hahnenschwanz und Hakenkreuz. Steirischer Heimatschutz und österreichischer Nationalsozialismus 1918-1934*, Europaverlag, Vienna, 1972; Hanisch (1978), 261-263.

44   Bukey (1986), 39.

45   This conclusion supports a more orthodox view of the relationship between the politics of the First and Second Republics, i.e. that sub-cultural divisions only became bridgeable in a consociational democracy in the Second Republic because of a recognition of the implications of the inability of political actors to bridge those divisions in the First: deepening political polarisation, civil war and the scuppering, after 1934, of any potential, united Austrian front which might have been willing and able to resist the National Socialist quest for *Anschluss*.

46   Hanisch (1978), 266. Clear examples of this 'painstaking, detailed work' are given in the long lists of *Landtag* responsibilities and activities undertaken by the SDAP and outlined in annual reports presented to the national party conference. These reports are reprinted in *Jahrbuch der österreichischen Arbeiterbewegung 1926-1932*.

47   Oberkofler (1982).

48   Riedmann (1983), 977.

49   From his speech at the 1930 Upper Austrian Annual SDAP Conference. Quoted in STB, 18-3-1930, 3.

50   See Chapter Seven of this book.

51 There was often a considerable overlapping accumulation of functions here. Especially noteworthy are: Robert Preussler, city councillor in Salzburg and Deputy Provincial Governor in Salzburg between 1918 and 1934 (not to mention his membership of both national chambers of parliament!); Johan Resel, editor of the Graz newspaper *Arbeiterwille* and member of the Styrian provincial government between 1918 and 1930; and Josef Gruber, who gave up the Deputy Provincial Governorship in Upper Austria in 1930 to become Mayor of Linz.

52 In the case of Upper Austria see STB 31-5-1927, 3; 18-3-1930, 5.

53 See e.g. Kaut (1982), passim and *Sozialdemokratische Partei Oberösterreichs, Tätigkeitsbericht*, 1923-1932 editions, Gutenberg, Linz (1924-1933). Especially instructive is Schiffer (1984), 276-277, who records the vain attempt by the Social Democratic youth organisations in Styria to bring new blood onto the provincial party executive in 1933.

54 Some indication of the situation in Salzburg is given in Kaut (1982), especially 87, 117, 136; Fuller records of Upper Austrian conferences are recorded in STB, 31-5-1927; 1-6-1927; 18-3-1930; 3-3-1931 and 18-6-1933.

55 See STB, 18-6-1933, 2.

3 Building the 'Strongholds' of Provincial Social Democracy

The previous discussion has shown that Social Democracy at the local level was a multiply isolated movement. In the most obvious sense it was an *Inselbewegung* which was geographically isolated within the deeply segmented society of the Austrian provinces. This geographical isolation was, in addition, overlain with the political isolation experienced by an 'enemy within' a hostile, overwhelmingly conservative environment. And finally, local-level Social Democracy faced a *de facto* intra-party isolation from the higher levels of the SDAP. The remainder of the book examines the character of a movement faced by what was clearly an extraordinarily difficult situation, concentrating in particular on a case study of the Social Democratic movement in Steyr, Upper Austria, arguably the most clearly defined centre of Social Democratic strength in provincial Austria. Since Steyr - as the introductory chapter of the book made clear - was, however, in many senses an extreme case in Social Democratic politics, the findings of the case study of Social Democracy in Steyr need to be kept in their proper perspective. Accordingly they are discussed throughout in the comparative context provided by local-level Social Democratic politics elsewhere in the provinces.

This is the approach taken in this chapter, which returns to the 'front-lines' of provincial politics. These were initially discussed in Chapter One from the perspective of the conservative forces which dominated in the provinces. Here, they are examined from the perspective of the local-level Social Democratic movement. The aim is to ascertain how the movement at the local level, devoid of effective support from the provincial and national levels of the SDAP, responded to, and came to terms with, the front-lines drawn around it by the suspicions and antipathies of the non-Social Democratic majority in provincial politics.

The emphasis is on the 'red islands' of Social Democracy in the provinces, the majority Social Democratic communities dotted around the Austrian countryside, and on the means used by Social Democrats in these communities to 'defend' themselves against the isolation and hostility they faced. The first section of the chapter identifies general patterns in the defensive orientation of these 'red islands', focusing on the attempt to build up local 'strongholds', 'fortified' against the hostility of the 'outside world' of provincial conservatism. Section two introduces for the first time the case study of Social Democracy in Steyr, setting out the dimensions of the 'stronghold' established by the Social

Democratic movement in the town in the 1920s. Drawing from the experience in Steyr and elsewhere, the third and final section then points to some of the wider problems and implications of defensive, 'stronghold' politics, above all the deeply insular political orientation they helped to produce. Taken as a whole the chapter is intended more broadly to introduce the key themes which are subsequently addressed in much greater depth in Part Two of the book.

The Social Democratic *Hochburg*

A useful starting point in discussing the defensive orientation of Social Democrats in the provinces is the term 'Hochburg', or 'stronghold', a term ritually applied both in the literature and the contemporary political discourse of the First Republic to the enclaves of Social Democracy in the provinces.[1] The frequency with which this term has - at times fairly indiscriminately - been used suggests its meaning should be examined more closely. The dictionary definitions of 'stronghold' are especially apposite here: 'a place dominated by a specific group'; 'a place of refuge or safety'; and 'a fortified place'. The first of these points to the most immediate, electoral meaning of 'Hochburg'. Social Democratic 'Hochburgen' were - more or less self-evidently - industrial towns and villages dominated electorally by the SDAP. This can be seen in Table 3.1 below, which gives a broad overview of the socio-political composition of the Social Democratic communities referred to in this chapter. Although of varying size - from the village of Schattendorf in Burgenland to Lower Austrian Wiener Neustadt, one of Austria's major urban centres - all were communities with a strongly industrial background, in which the SDAP stood out as the dominant political party.

This work argues, though, that the term 'Hochburg' signifies much more than just the achievement of a majority vote. It points to a perception on the part of the adherents of the Social Democratic movement that their enclaves were exclusive Social Democratic 'territories' which served as 'shields' against the antagonism and isolation they faced in what - as the final column of Table 3.1 indicates - was normally a strongly anti-Social Democratic political environment. In this sense, 'Hochburg' politics were territorial politics. They were a form of political self-assertion, expressed through the Social Democratic movement, which was rooted in a territorially based form of social identity. This supplementary meaning of 'Hochburg' reflects much more the latter two dictionary definitions given above: 'Hochburgen' were places of Social Democratic refuge and safety,

Table 3.1 Selected Social Democratic *Hochburgen* in the Provinces, 1927[2] (in %)

Hochburg	Land	Population from an industrial occupational background	SDAP vote	SDAP vote in the surrounding area
Bischofshofen	Salzburg	31.3	61.5	28.0
Bruck a. d. Mur	Styria	52.0	58.4	53.7
Ebensee	Upper Austria	52.7	58.2	37.8
Fohnsdorf	Styria	54.4	72.6	47.0
Hallein	Salzburg	46.0	58.8	20.3
Gnigl-Itzling	Salzburg	36.1	70.5	26.5
Marienthal	Lower Austria	51.6	69.6	49.7
Mauthausen	Upper Austria	46.9	49.5	23.0
Schattendorf	Burgenland	47.3	61.5	48.6
Steyr	**Upper Austria**	**69.6**	**59.9**	**30.3**
Wiener Neustadt	Lower Austria	52.5	62.4	45.3
Wolfsegg	Upper Austria	44.6	60.2	28.8
Wörgl	Tirol	33.4	52.1	22.9

Sources: Calculated from Bundesamt für Statistik (Ed.), Statistische Nachrichten. Sonderheft. 'Wahlstatistik'. Nationalratswahlen vom 24. April 1927. Einzeldarstellung nach Gemeinden und Geschlecht, Überreuter, Vienna (1927) and idem, Die Ergebnisse der österreichischen Volkszählung vom 22. März 1934. Bundesstaat Textheft, Verlag der Österreichischen Staatsdruckerei, Vienna (1935).

'*Schutzgemeinschaften*' ('protective communities') 'fortified' against the intrusions of an antagonistic 'outside' world.[3]

This protective-defensive function of the *Hochburg* is indicative of the insularity which pervaded local level Social Democratic politics in Austria. It was reflected above all in a drive for organisational penetration and control within the confines of the *Hochburg*. This drive is examined below under two complementary headings: first '*Integration nach innen*', the development of a strong, integrative organisational momentum designed to strengthen the collective identity and solidarity of the Social Democratic community within the enclave; and second, '*Abgrenzung nach außen*', a vehement and often militant mobilisation of the Social Democratic movement in defence of the boundaries of the enclave against the hostile forces which surrounded it.[4]

Integration nach innen

As Table 3.1 confirms, provincial society in Austria was deeply segmented, often providing for a clear, physical separation between Social Democratic and non-Social Democratic communities. A characteristic feature of *Hochburg* politics was a quest to consolidate and deepen this physical separation through 'Integration nach innen', or 'inward integration'. 'Integration nach innen' was the attempt to 'close ranks' and strengthen the cohesion which linked the supporters of Social Democracy within the Hochburg, and which separated and distanced them and 'their' territory from the wider political environment in the provinces.

The drive for inward integration usually had promising foundations to build upon. The tendency towards social segmentation in the provinces often meant that the manual worker constituency of Social Democracy lived in what were potentially extremely solidaristic community environments. Even in Hochburgen of widely varying size, manual workers generally grouped together in relatively compact neighbourhoods. This was true for example in Social Democratic villages such as Marienthal in Lower Austria, where an SDAP-dominated factory village, with its uniform, company-built, one-storey flats and 'barracks' stood across an unofficial, but clearly visible 'border' from the grander houses of the neighbouring, non-industrial village of Gramatneusiedl.[5] It was equally true of working class suburbs of otherwise 'bourgeois' towns, like the railway community of Gnigl-Itzling just to the east of Salzburg,[6] and of larger industrial towns like Wiener Neustadt, where the supporters of the Social Democratic movement tended to be concentrated in large working class housing estates built around major industrial sites.[7]

These were the classic manual worker milieux identified by Ernst Hanisch. They were relatively closed and socially homogenous, their inhabitants bound together by shared background, culture and interests. The myriad interpersonal contacts and shared experiences inherent in such closed milieux facilitated the development among their inhabitants of a sense of common interest, aspiration and need, in short, a shared social identity. This was especially so since these shared experiences were frequently of a negative kind, typically combining meagre standards of living, poor working conditions, the hostility of employers to labour organisation at the workplace, and the invasive proselytising of the Catholic Church. Such conditions helped cement a largely defensive and highly solidaristic form of community identity which initially provided the basis for the emergence of Social Democracy as a political force in the late nineteenth century, and which later, in the First Republic, represented, as it were, the 'raw material' for the 'inward integration' central to Hochburg politics. An extraordinarily vivid impression of the sense - and strength - of community identity which emerged in manual worker milieux is given in Hubert Hummer's work on the villages of the Upper Austrian coalfield. Through interviews with members of successive generations of miners' families he reconstructs a picture of intense social solidarity which was borne on the one hand of the *Kameradschaft* generated by the hazardous nature of the miners' work and the semi-communal living conditions of the miners' 'colonies', and which was deepened on the other by the chicaneries of the mines management and local catholic priests, the latter focused invidiously on the miners' children.[8]

In such circumstances, the Social Democratic movement at the local level acted as a conduit through which such traditions of solidarity and identity could be expressed, mobilised and deepened to provide the sense of 'refuge' and protection from the 'outside world' discussed above. It served as the political expression of a territorially defined social identity rooted in classic manual worker milieux. Its function as a conduit for the expression of identity can be seen in two main ways, both of which exemplify the drive for organisational penetration and control noted above: first the harnessing of the political power available to Social Democratic organisations within the *Hochburg* in the interests of the movement's supporters; and second the establishment of a comprehensive network of auxiliary organisations in which Social Democrats could express their solidarity and common identity beyond - and against - the influence of 'outside' forces.

It should be noted at the outset that the powers available to Social Democracy at the local level were not extensive. They were, however, often of considerable significance in two areas: municipal administration and industrial relations. Both were fields of activity which, from the Social Democratic perspective, offered new opportunities after the First World War. The introduction of universal suffrage in municipal elections after the war gave the SDAP access for the first time to powers in municipal administration commensurate to its numerical strength in industrial communities. Although these powers were generally extremely modest and often expended in technical matters such as infrastructural maintenance, they were also employed as far as possible to provide improved services for the less well-off in the communities concerned (i.e. above all the working class electorate of the SDAP). These ranged across the fields of housing, education, health, welfare, employment, cultural and transport policy.[9]

Given the severe constraints which existed on the financial resources of local councils, the real impact of such policies on the lives of the supporters of Social Democracy was inevitably somewhat limited. Their main significance was perhaps more symbolic than real, a symbolism captured in the flying of the SDAP's red flag over town halls from whose executive offices Social Democrats had previously been excluded. The mere fact that this was *Social Democratic* municipal administration, whatever its practical limitations, promoted the feeling that, for the first time, at least *something* could be done on behalf of, and by, the working class community and its representatives. In the words of a Social Democrat from Hallein in Salzburg: 'At the time it was really only the Social Democrats who were committed to the workers' cause',[10] a sentiment echoed elsewhere, for example, in the pride with which the 'commendable' achievements of 'our fraction' in the council of Upper Austrian Mauthausen, a village of 1,800 inhabitants with negligible municipal autonomy, were ceremoniously listed in the local party press.[11]

The feeling that workers' interests were being conscientiously addressed by the Social Democratic movement was experienced more consistently and concretely in the field of industrial relations. Here too the First Republic saw a new era, with the employment legislation which was passed after the First World War giving the Social Democratic Free Trade Unions a range of new, statutory powers at the workplace. Although these powers began to be attacked and eroded almost immediately by anti-unionist employers, local unions were able, if only temporarily, to secure genuine improvements in pay and working conditions.[12] These improvements, as exemplified by the recollections gathered together by Ingrid Bauer of former tobacco industry workers from Hallein near Salzburg, helped to cement loyalties to the local Social Democratic movement.[13] An apt example is given in Ingrid Bauer's interview with a former farmworker who saw her subsequent employment in the Hallein tobacco factory as:

> ... a better life! [Better] in that I was protected by the union, in that I was paid my wages, and if there was anything wrong with the wages or whatever, then it was all sorted out. Compared to that nothing was handled in a proper way on the farm. No-one, no-one at all bothered about you there. And if you didn't get your money, and if you were simply thrown out, then no-on cared ... And then it really impressed me when I went to the factory that you had somebody, if you were ill or whatever, who looked out for you.[14]

A further factor which helped to entrench loyalties to Social Democracy in at least some *Hochburgen* were the powers of patronage trade unions held under the surprising number of closed shop arrangements which existed throughout provincial Austria.[15] As Chapter Four shows, closed shops were in some cases openly exploited to provide jobs for established supporters of Social Democracy. Similarly, there is some indication, discussed further in Chapter Five, that the powers and resources of local Social Democratic councils could also be manipulated in a discriminatory way to grant political favours to members and organisations of the Social Democratic movement.[16]

There are some difficulties in assessing the significance of these powers of patronage. For example, it should be stressed that any powers of patronage available to the Social Democratic movement were of a modest scale, and in no way comparable to the extensive practice of political patronage in the Second Republic. It should also be stressed that the use of patronage as a tool of political mobilisation is, as Chapter Five confirms, by no means always unproblematic for the patronising organisation. Despite these caveats, though, it would seem reasonable to conclude that the practice of dispensing favours helped - alongside the more orthodox activities of municipal administration and trade unions - to establish the Social Democratic movement with a reputation of 'looking after its own'. The perception that the Social Democratic movement was 'doing something' about, and 'looking after' the material interests of its supporters, however modestly, was central to the territorial nature of *Hochburg* politics. It delineated the various *Hochburgen* starkly from the situation of anti-Social Democratic hostility which otherwise reigned in the provinces, and deepened the community identity and solidarity from which the movement drew its strength. Social Democratic *Hochburgen* consequently stood out as 'safe havens', as territorial entities in which the 'rules of the game' were different from those which applied elsewhere.

A further underpinning of the Social Democratic community was provided through the extensive networks of auxiliary organisations which existed alongside party and trade union even in the smallest *Hochburgen*. These networks are examined in depth in Chapter Six.[17] At this stage of the discussion, it is necessary only to point to their primary function in the provinces.[18] They provided what Erika Thurner has called a form of mutual 'moral support' (*Rückenstärkung*)[19] among Social Democrats. They established an organisational framework for everyday activities free of the otherwise pervasive influence of the opponents of Social Democracy in provincial politics, above all the Catholic Church. This function is quite starkly illustrated in the recollections of a Social Democrat, Karl Steinocher, of the highly politicised everyday life of the railway community of Bischofshofen in Salzburg during the First Republic:

> Back then there was something like a mental Berlin Wall [in Bischofshofen]. Ideologically a real wall between the bourgeoisie and us workers, us so-called proletarians. It even extended into playing sport and went so far that we weren't allowed to go to the Christian or German sports ground. We were of course 'the young proles', 'the workers' kids', 'the railwaymens' boys'. Even when we just wanted to watch a game, we were chased away, often with a thick ear. That was often difficult to take. Even in school it had its effect: There were often arguments and fights because social barriers were so strictly drawn and it was nearly impossible to get along with the others. It affected many, many areas, right into everyday life. For these reasons something like an alternative movement grew up, a

Social Democratic alternative movement. You have to have experienced it, this feeling of being a 'second-class person'. But this feeling was completely offset by the movement, by our community. It was something like a *Heimat* that we had there, and that had a profound influence on me.[20]

It is especially significant that Steinocher describes this 'alternative movement' (i.e. of auxiliary organisations) with the word *'Heimat'*, the German term for 'home area' or 'homeland', which conveys not just simple geographical origin but also a clearly defined sense of social identity and belonging. Social Democratic auxiliary organisations set up a sphere of everyday autonomy in which a Social Democratic sense of identity and belonging could be expressed, reaffirmed and consolidated without hindrance. In this sense too, Social Democratic *Hochburgen* functioned as 'safe havens', secure areas which guaranteed an individual and collective freedom of expression which was severely circumscribed elsewhere in provincial Austria.

'Abgrenzung nach außen'

Any attempt to maintain a safe haven requires effective policing. It is in this respect, in the defence of the safe haven of the *Hochburg* from its 'enemies', that the most striking expressions of territoriality in local-level Social Democratic politics were seen in the First Republic. *Hochburgen* were regarded as sacrosanct territory on which the Social Democrats aspired to a sole right to demonstrate their political identity publicly, to a 'monopoly' of the streets. This is what is meant by *'Abgrenzung nach außen'*, the marking out of the *Hochburgen* as inviolable, almost, as it were, 'sovereign territories' of the Social Democratic movement.

A key form of *'Abgrenzung'* was seen in the major Social Democratic festivals of 1 May (labour day) and 12 November (the anniversary of the foundation of the Republic in 1918), whose highpoints were as vast as possible a procession of all local Social Democratic organisations, at their forefront the paramilitary *Schutzbund*, through the town or village, including its 'bourgeois' districts, followed by a set-piece rally on the main square. Although these festivals ritually invoked their original and formal inspirations - the ideal of socialist internationalism and the transition from monarchy to democracy - their functions in provincial *Hochburgen* were far more immediate: to underline publicly and symbolically the community solidarity and identity expressed through the Social Democratic movement, to celebrate the movement's 'monopoly' over the local territory, and to deter challenges to that monopoly.[21]

This claim to monopoly was also reflected in the hostility displayed by Social Democrats to open expressions of non-Social Democratic political allegiance within the *Hochburg*. Such expressions were regarded as an affront to the local Social Democratic community and met, above all where the paramilitary Right, especially the *Heimwehr*, was concerned, with concerted and often militant opposition. *Heimwehr* shopkeepers and market traders were known, for example, to fall foul of the collective (female) consumer power of the Social Democratic rank and file, perhaps most memorably when 300-400 *Arbeiterfrauen* in Ebensee, Upper Austria, launched a protest which led to the revocation of local *Heimwehr* leader's market license in 1929.[22] Organised consumer boycotts of opponents' businesses were also conducted by Social Democrats elsewhere in Upper and Lower Austria.[23] This openly intimidatory monopolisation of the freedom of expression by Social Democrats was even able to establish some parts of the larger *Hochburgen* as virtual 'no-go areas' for the *Heimwehr*, such as Wiener Neustadt, 'a red *Hochburg* which had the respect of its opponents and where the *Heimwehr* for a long time did not dare ... to tread'.[24]

The vehemence of this claim to territorial sacrosanctity played a key role in perpetuating the 'front lines' of conflict in the provinces which were discussed earlier in Chapter One. The quest for monopoly represented on the one hand a defensive response to the hostility shown to Social Democrats by their opponents. On the other, though, it was perceived by those opponents as a form of 'terrorism' against the non-Social Democratic population which had to be broken. The response was, as outlined in Chapter One, the attempt particularly by the paramilitary Right, to 'take on' the Social Democratic movement on its *Hochburg* home ground and 'reclaim' the streets for non-Social Democrats. This, of course, merely hardened the resolve of the Social Democrats to 'hold' those streets against the external threat and fed further into the cycle of conflict.

The result was, especially in the later 1920s, an intensifying competition for territorial control in the industrial centres of the provinces. This competition produced some of the key incidents in the degeneration of First Republic politics into violent confrontation,[25] three of which in particular are worth recalling. The first was the clash between the monarchist paramilitary veterans' organisation, the *Frontkämpfer*, and the *Schutzbund* in the 'red *Hochburg*'[26] of Schattendorf, Burgenland, in January 1927. Confrontation arose here from the *Schutzbund's* attempt to face down the challenge to its 'territory' represented by a *Frontkämpfer* meeting in Schattendorf. This sparked an armed confrontation which left two Social Democrats dead and which led, via a trial in which the *Frontkämpfer* defendants were acquitted of murder, to the events - and eighty-nine deaths - of 15 July 1927 in Vienna.[27] The second was the temporary assumption of executive power by the Social Democratic movement in Bruck an der Mur, Upper Styria, on 16 July 1927. This measure, ostensibly taken as a means of preserving law and order in the uncertain atmosphere which followed the events of 15 July, also acted as a public expression of Social Democratic hegemony in the town. Perceived as a short-lived, local 'dictatorship of the proletariat', the events in Bruck helped perhaps more than anything else to whip up the anti-Social Democratic fervour displayed, increasingly violently, by the *Heimwehr* in Upper Styria and elsewhere in the following years.[28] The third, finally, was an incident which brought home the danger of Austria falling into full-blown civil war: the parade of some 14,000 *Heimwehr* members in Wiener Neustadt in October 1928. In finally 'daring' to try and open up the 'right to the street'[29] in the town, the *Heimwehr* parade provoked a counter-parade on the same day of 35,000 Social Democrats, including around 16,000 *Schutzbündler*. The result was a day of extraordinary tension, both locally and nationally, in which the peace was kept only by the deployment of police, gendarmerie and military units.[30]

All these incidents took on *national* significance in the increasingly charged political atmosphere of the late 1920s, with each making an important contribution to the degeneration of democratic politics and the descent into civil war. It is important to remember, though, that they all had *local* origins in the separate, defensive responses of Social Democrats to external challenges to the various *Hochburgen* they had carved out for themselves at the local level. These incidents exemplify the narrowness and inherent insularity of the political frame of reference of the local-level Social Democratic movement in the provinces. Local-level movements were absorbed in maintaining each individual enclave as a 'safe haven' for its inhabitants, and lacked a wider sense of perspective either on the problems each enclave had in common with its counterparts elsewhere or on the impact of local actions in the broader, national political arena. The narrow, territorial focus of this frame of reference is of central importance to this work and is taken up further below. First, though, it is necessary to set out the dimensions of the Social Democratic *Hochburg* in Steyr.

The Dimensions of the Social Democratic *Hochburg* in Steyr

Steyr is one of those towns which is often referred to in passing in works on inter-war Social Democracy in Austria, above all because of its status as a centre of active Social Democratic resistance in the Civil War of 1934.[31] In a literature focused on Vienna, however, such passing references are all that one will find. This is unfortunate since Steyr was in many respects a paradigmatic case among the *Hochburgen* of the Social Democratic in the provinces and offers especially clear insights into the nature, problems, strengths and weaknesses of the movement at the local level.

The Bases of the Hochburg

Steyr, a medium-sized town of just over 20,000 inhabitants in the west of Upper Austria, was unequivocally an *Arbeiterstadt*, a town dominated by the industrial working class. Table 3.1 above shows, for example, that 69.6% of the overall population of the town had an occupational background in 'industry' according to the population census of 1934. This figure is slightly misleading in that it includes the (comparatively small number of) owners, managers and white-collar workers who shared an industrial background. Taking these away these some 63.2% of the (employed) population were manual workers according to more detailed figures from the industrial census 1930.[32] Moreover, a centuries-long tradition in metal-working in the town meant that this manual workforce consisted primarily of skilled workers.[33] Skilled metalworkers were traditionally at the forefront of labour movement organisation in Austria,[34] and had, since the late 1880s, been the mainstay of the Social Democratic movement in Steyr.[35]

The metalworking tradition was continued into the First Republic by the Steyr-Werke, a long-established local firm which successfully made a transition from arms to large-scale car production at the end of the First World War. The Steyr car works was by far the dominant employer in the local economy. Between 1928 and late 1929, for example, some 78% of the local employed industrial workforce was employed there; this share, moreover, never dipped below a level of 53%, recorded at the economic lowpoint of the works during the Great Depression.[36] It was this workforce at the Steyr-Werke, building on the tradition of skilled, organised labour in the town, which formed the core of an unusually strong Social Democratic movement in Steyr during the First Republic.

An indication of the popular strength of Social Democracy in Steyr is given in Table 3.2 below, which sets out the results of the four elections to the town's Municipal Council in the First Republic. With the exception of the first post-war ballot in 1919, when a limited range of parties stood for election, the results show a consistent pattern, with a stable left-wing vote of 63-64%, shared between a dominant SDAP and a marginal Communist Party, and a stable right-wing vote of 36-37% split between the CSP, the German Nationalist Party and the National Socialist Party and - in 1931 only - the *Heimwehr* (with the lion's share

Table 3.2 Results of Elections to the Municipal Council in Steyr in the First Republic (in %)

Year	Social Democrats	Christian Socials	German Nationalists	Communists	National Socialists
1919	68.3	21.4	10.3	--	--
1923	57.6	32.4[a]	--	6.1	3.8
1927	60.6	26.7	9.9[b]	3.1	--
1931	57.6	23.0	8.6[c]	5.8	5.0

Notes:
a) *'Einheitsliste'* - *Christian Socials and German Nationalists*
b) *'Völkischer Wirtschaftsblock'* - *German Nationalists and National Socialists*
c) *'Deutsche Wahlgemeinschaft'* - *German Nationalists and Heimwehr*
Sources: *STB 26-4-1927, 1; 4-5-1927, 8; 21-4-1931, 11-12; 23-5-1931, 8.*

taken on each occasion by the CSP). In electoral terms, the SDAP therefore stood out clearly as a predominant force, confronted only by a fragmented and weak local opposition.

The Social Democratic movement in Steyr was also able to mobilise a substantial proportion of the local population as members of its various organisations. Although no exact figures are available, an informed estimate would suggest that the membership of the SDAP peaked at around 5,000 - almost one quarter of the local population or around 40% of the electorate - in 1928-1929. At the same time, the membership of the major Social Democratic trade union, the metalworkers (Metallarbeiterverband, or MAV), peaked at around 6,000.[37] In addition, the various Social Democratic auxiliary organisations in Steyr could muster an aggregate of over 20,000 members (including, of course, many overlapping memberships) in the later 1920s.[38]

These figures clearly illustrate Steyr's status as an especially dense concentration of Social Democratic support and organisational strength. The immediate surrounding area (in the Districts of Steyr-Land in Upper Austria and Amstetten in Lower Austria), though, had almost mirror image characteristics: it was largely rural, with around 50% of the population engaged in farming or forestry, and typically recorded an overwhelming non- and anti-Social Democratic vote of around 70%, which was won - in a devoutly Catholic region - largely by the CSP.[39] Steyr consequently stood out starkly as a 'red island' in a 'black', Catholic-conservative, rural backwater. As such it equally stood out as a target for the anti-Social Democratic antipathies which pervaded provincial politics and society. As any survey of the contemporary, local and regional conservative press will show Steyr was perceived and portrayed as an especially pernicious 'bulwark' of 'Marxist terror' (on the shopfloor and on the streets), large-scale Social Democratic corruption and, last but not least, all-round godlessness.[40]

Before outlining the response of Steyr's Social Democratic movement to the environment which surrounded it, consideration needs first to be taken of the local economic cycle and its implications. Steyr's economic development, as already indicated in the employment figures mentioned above, was dominated by the business performance of the Steyr-Werke. A broad overview of this performance, as represented in production and employment figures at the works, is given in Table 3.3 below. The trends pointed to in Table 3.3 were closely mirrored in the conjunctural development of the town as a whole, with the vagaries of the Steyr-Werke not only having direct employment effects of immense local significance, but also important knock-on effects both for local parts suppliers and for the general level of local purchasing power. This applied, for example, to the wider effects in the town of the post-inflationary stabilisation crisis of 1922-1924 at the Steyr-Werke (a crisis extended locally into 1925 by a major industrial

Table 3.3 Production and Employment at the Steyr-Werke, 1920-1933

Year	Total Vehicles Production	Employment[a]
1920-22	1719	6436[b]
1923	1035	4520
1924	1492	4070
1925	2363	3408
1926	2524	4662
1927	4621	4332
1928	5555	6018
1929	6005	6648
1930	12	2626
1931	2988	2163
1932	1778	1363
1933	739	1287

Notes:
a) *The employment figures for 1922-1926 refer to the average employment level over the year; those for 1927-1933 refer to the employment level recorded at the end of June in each year.*
b) *1922 figure only.*
Sources: *Hans Seper, 100 Jahre Steyr-Daimler-Puch. Der Werdegang eines österreichischen Industrieunternehmens, Mally & Co., Vienna (1964), 79-80; Bericht des Vorstandes des Österreichischen Metall- und Bergarbeiterverbandes über seine Tätigkeit in den Jahren 1930, 1931, 1932, Verlag des Österreichischen Metallarbeiterverbandes, Vienna (1933), 14; Verzeichnis jener Betriebe, welche über fünf Kammerumlagepflichtige beschäftigen, 1927-1933 editions (1927-1933).*

dispute at the works)[41], to the local boom which followed the significant rise in production and employment at the works in 1928 and 1929, and to the dramatic contraction of the local economy which accompanied the severe cutbacks in production and employment made in 1929-1930 and the prolonged stagnation at the works which set in thereafter.

Of particular importance in the politics of the Social Democratic *Hochburg* in Steyr is the period of rising production and employment at the car works at the end of the 1920s. Despite an appearance to the contrary, this display of economic 'success' concealed serious flaws in the economic structure of the works, which were exacerbated by a number of curious, if not downright incompetent, management decisions. On the basis of sales which had been higher than forecast in 1927 and 1928 the management embarked on an overoptimistic expansion of output. The result was rising over-production, with stocks mounting throughout the latter half of 1928 and during 1929. In this period a high turnover was maintained only by selling vehicles at less than cost price on the export market. At the same time, however, dividends were maintained at a recklessly high level - consuming some 80-90% of net profits - in an attempt to court the good favour of the financial markets with view to a new share issue which could be used to cut an escalating debt burden. Inevitably, as Table 3.4 shows, the balloon burst, and in 1929 a dramatic loss was revealed in the company's accounts.[42]

Despite the series of adverse economic indicators shown in Table 3.4, the company took no remedial action until August 1929, when the works was temporarily shut down and plans for a rationalisation of production announced. The management of the Steyr-Werke - condemned as 'monstrously dilettantish'[43] by Austria's most respected economic journal - had sustained the favourable conditions of 1927 and early 1928 without economic justification into 1929. This 'bogus' boom is of crucial importance in understanding the development of Social Democracy in Steyr. In the medium term it decimated the economic

Table 3.4 The Financial Performance of the Steyr-Werke, 1924-1929

Year	Net Profits (1,000 Sh.)	Dividends (1,000 Sh.)	Dividends as % of Net Profits	Debts (1,000 Sh.)
1924	1,217	1,008	82.8	11,027
1925	1,685	1,512	89.7	16,771
1926	1,850	1,512	81.7	29,338
1927	1,914	1,512	79.0	35,228
1928	824	756	91.7	57,720
1929	-24,160	0	---	93,306

Sources: *ÖVW Bilanzen, 4-8-1928, 523-524; 27-7-1929; 489-490; 3-8-1930; 7.*

basis of the firm, plunging Steyr into a deeper economic trough than experienced, on average, elsewhere in Austria. More immediately, though, it thrust the town into a two-year upswing between 1927 and 1929 which equally was not experienced, on average, elsewhere. In this period, the national unemployment rate remained fairly constant at around 10%, reflecting the sluggish recovery of Austrian industry from the post-inflationary recession of 1922-1924. In Steyr, however, the unemployment rate dropped, abnormally, from around 10% in 1927 to just 5-6% in 1928-1929.[44] This bogus boom, as becomes clear below, was of pivotal importance to the Social Democratic *Hochburg* in Steyr.

Social Democratic Hegemony

Hochburg politics in Steyr by and large conformed to the patterns followed in other industrial centres in the provinces. They consisted of a quest to deflect the antipathies expressed by the movement's opponents by closing ranks and cementing the solidarity of the movement's supporters, and by marking out and guarding the *Hochburg's* 'territory' against external incursion. This quest, again as in other industrial centres, had ready-made foundations to build upon in the form of densely populated and socially homogenous manual worker communities in certain parts of the town: in the Wehrgraben, an area criss-crossed by the streams and water channels which had provided power for the early factories and which still formed a locus for working class housing; and in the Ennsleite, an estate built next to the Steyr-Werke during the First World War. These were areas in which the SDAP could command from 75-90% of the vote in First Republic elections.[45]

What distinguished Steyr from other industrial centres was the local economic upswing of 1927-1929. This generated the resources for the Social Democratic movement to mobilise its inherent electoral and organisational strength in the local community to a degree which established a localised political hegemony without doubt unparalleled elsewhere in provincial Austria.

Looking first at the attempt to 'close ranks', four factors in particular - all dealt with at length in subsequent chapters of this book - are worth pointing to. First, the paradoxical combination at the Steyr-Werke of a superficial appearance of economic success and extreme underlying economic weakness simultaneously strengthened the power of the MAV and weakened the bargaining hand of the works management in industrial relations. Local trade unionism in Steyr consequently remained strong, evading the anti-unionist employer offensives being conducted elsewhere in Austria by this time, and was thus able to defend the wage levels and working conditions of its supporters effectively until 1930 (see Chapter Four). Second, an important result of this ongoing strength in industrial relations was that a closed shop arrangement won by the MAV after the First World War remained intact. With the expansion of employment at the Steyr-Werke after 1927 this closed shop gave the MAV unusually extensive powers of patronage - covering ultimately over 5,000 jobs - in the local labour market. These powers were consciously used, as far as possible, to tie the workforce to the Social Democratic movement. At the same time, the SDAP-run municipal council, fed by the local tax revenues generated by the booming Steyr-Werke, was also able to extend and manipulate its own powers of patronage in the town. Municipal and MAV patronage were together used to reward, and thus cement allegiances to the movement and in this way to broaden significantly the scale of Social Democratic influence over local politics and society (Chapter Five). Third, expanding tax revenues also allowed the SDAP council to 'do something' for its electorate through the expansion of its manual worker-oriented social policy programme in the period 1927-1929 (Chapter Seven). And fourth, the same period also saw the peak of the scale and influence of the local network of Social Democratic auxiliary organisations - over *fifty* in all - which offered myriad opportunities for the organisation of social and leisure activities in a socially demarcated Social Democratic environment (Chapter Six).

Taken together, the various activities of MAV, local council and auxiliary organisations in Steyr deeply penetrated and helped to structure the everyday lives of well over a quarter of the town's inhabitants. The net result was the establishment by the various Social Democratic organisations of an extraordinary degree of control over their collective 'realm', a degree of control underlined by the periodic mass parades and rallies held by the Social Democratic movement, when up to 5,000 participants took to the streets in a calculated display of local Social Democratic hegemony.[46] This was, very clearly, exclusive Social Democratic territory, a safe haven of the Left on which the local opposition could play only the most subordinate of roles.

The territorial senstitivities of the Social Democrats were illustrated in dramatic fashion in July 1928, when Steyr's German Nationalist 'Gymnastics' Club - a field of activity dominated since the first half of the nineteenth century by the extreme wing of German nationalism - hosted a gymnastics festival in the town. The festival attracted participants from the whole range of German nationalist organisations, including the National Socialists. The Social Democratic response was a typical illustration of the *Abgrenzung nach außen* discussed above, the marking out of the streets of the local *Hochburg* as a 'no-go' area for the movement's opponents. Parading Nazis were attacked, mainly by younger Social Democrats, and stripped of their swastika banners in what the local CSP-oriented newspaper, the

Steyrer Zeitung, called a 'scarcely believable witchhunt of non-Social Democrats'.[47] The quest to 'punish' 'transgressors' of the local political rules then continued in the days after the festival in calls for the boycott of the businessmen and shopkeepers who supported the festival and in the demand by the MAV that the 25 or so white-collar workers from the Steyr-Werke who marched in the festival parade be summarily dismissed.[48]

As the events surrounding the Gymnastics Festival showed, the opportunities for the free expression within Steyr of allegiance to forces opposed to Social Democracy were limited. The scale of the suppression of non-Social Democratic views had even led the *Steyrer Zeitung* to declare a year earlier, in August 1927, that the 'only hope' for the 'bourgeois element' in the town was, in view of the 'peculiar conditions' which existed locally, to seek external help and reinforcement, drawing presumably on the anti-Social Democratic majority in the surrounding area, 'at the soonest opportunity'.[49] The 'help' and 'reinforcement' desired by the *Steyrer Zeitung* was that of the *Heimwehr,* whose potential as a anti-Social Democratic force had been amply illustrated elsewhere in Austria in its breaking of the communications strike called in response to the events of 15 July 1927 in Vienna. The help of the *Heimwehr* eventually came in late 1929/early 1930, and ultimately succeeded in breaking local Social Democratic hegemony, but not without initially being rebuffed by further, belligerent defence of the *Hochburg's* territory. This confrontation between Social Democracy and *Heimwehr* is examined in Chapter Five. The remainder of this chapter, though, points to some of the wider implications, and above all the weaknesses, of *Hochburg* politics in Steyr and elsewhere in provincial Austria.

The Weaknesses of *Hochburg* Politics: Insularity, Fragmentation, Vulnerability

A first point to reiterate in examining these weaknesses is that local-level Social Democracy was a highly insular movement, absorbed in marking out and defending the local Social Democratic territory against its enemies and in maximising the power and cohesion of its organisations and supporters within that territory. And, it has to be said, this insular orientation was in many cases extremely successful in establishing a sphere of autonomy and freedom of expression which was otherwise denied Social Democrats in the provinces. But it also has to be said that the successful establishment and maintenance of the sphere of autonomy and territorial integrity of the *Hochburg* always stood on unfirm, fragile foundations. The insular mentality which underpinned each individual *Hochburg* also, simultaneously, undermined the cohesion of the provincial movement as a whole.

Hochburg politics were ultimately a politics of fragmentation. Each *Hochburg* was, by definition, consumed in its particular, immediate local concerns. Each was thus separated from its counterparts not just by force of geography, but also by its very insularity. There is no indication in the literature - or in my own fieldwork research - that views were shared or information exchanged between the various provincial *Hochburgen* on the similar problems they faced. The politics of local-level Social Democracy was the politics of each to one's own. The Social Democratic movement was, in other words, an organisation which was not just fragmented *vertically*, in terms of national-local and provincial-local relations, but also *horizontally* at the local level itself.

This multiple fragmentation was not a promising recipe for sustaining industrial centres in the long run as Social Democratic *Hochburgen* in the political environment outlined in Chapter One. In the militaristic terminology which so often aptly describes First Republic politics, each *Hochburg* could, in its isolation, be 'picked off' one after the other by its opponents. And this is, indeed, broadly what happened. *Hochburg* politics were dependent on the maintenance of the cohesion and solidarity of the Social Democratic community. This cohesion and solidarity was, however, subject to erosion by the effects of economic dislocation - endemic in inter-war Austria - and right-wing (employer, provincial government, *Heimwehr*, church or other) intimidation. Once cohesion was lost, the local Social Democratic territory invariably 'fell' to the political organisations of the Right.

The best researched example of this process concerns the *Hochburgen* of Upper Styria[50] where persistent economic uncertainty and high unemployment weakened the fabric of the Social Democratic movement sufficiently for a steadfastly anti-unionist employer to step in in the mid-1920s and - with the help of a militant *Heimwehr* organisation - begin an anti-Social Democratic drive which had 'virtually emasculated'[51] the movement by early 1929. A similar pattern prevailed in the Upper Austrian coalfield,[52] while the key event in Wiener Neustadt was the *Heimwehr* parade, mentioned above, of October 1928. This broke the local Social Democratic monopoly of the streets, and with it the morale - already tested by the high local unemployment levels which had prevailed since the war - which had previously underpinned the *Hochburg*.[53]

Steyr's experience was similar to that of Wiener Neustadt, yet - considering the conditions which had reigned towards the end of the 1920s - far more abrupt. The key lay in the economic performance of the Steyr-Werke and in particular in the legacies of the mismanagement of the works in the second half of the 1920s. In August 1929, the works finally acted on the huge losses associated with the over-production of the bogus boom of 1928-1929. Production was run down from August, and by mid-September over 1,000 workers had been dismissed, originally on a temporary basis while the production line was rationalised to cut costs and restore competitiveness. The intention was to complete the reorganisation of production by the end of November. However, an event which had extensive ramifications for the Steyr-Werke (and ultimately the local Social Democratic movement) intervened. On 6 October 1929 the collapse of the Boden-Credit-Anstalt (BCA), one of Austria's biggest banks, and financial patron of the Steyr-Werke, was announced. The BCA's collapse was due in large measure to its patronage of the Steyr-Werke, to which it had injudiciously lent around 90% of its total assets. Having staked it assets and reputation on the Steyr-Werke, the BCA pressed the car works to do everything to preserve a healthy appearance, including the payment of over-high dividends and the sale of cars at less than cost price. The result was the massive loss recorded by the Steyr-Werke in 1929 (see Table 3.4), which could no longer be covered by the BCA and which led to the bank's collapse.[54]

The immediate result of the BCA's collapse was the complete shutdown of car production in Steyr, pending the announcement of any financial rescue package for the bank. Baron Rothschild was 'persuaded', allegedly at machine-gunpoint,[55] to step in, and his Credit-Anstalt assumed all the industrial holdings, assets and liabilities of the BCA. The future of the Steyr-Werke was only assured in January 1930, when a return to normal working was promised as soon as the excess stocks from 1929 had been sold.[56] In the meantime, the car production line remained idle, leaving over 3,000 car workers unemployed. Even when the production line was eventually reopened in July 1930, employment and production levels never recovered to anything near the pre-1929 levels (see Table 3.3).

The abrupt transition from boom to crisis destroyed the bases of the Social Democratic *Hochburg* in Steyr. Mass local unemployment undermined the MAV's position of strength in industrial relations in the Steyr-Werke, a problem compounded by the installation of a new and aggressive management at the works by Rothschild's Credit-Anstalt. The result was a deterioration of wage levels and working conditions. Moreover, although the MAV's closed shop remained intact, its significance in terms of patronage was reduced in direct proportion to the sharp decline in employment levels at the works. The same decline in employment also slashed the local tax revenues collected by the Municipal Council, effectively throwing it into bankruptcy and striking out both its powers of patronage and its social policy programme. In other words, the key elements on which the cohesion of the Social Democratic community had been based - the movement's powers in industrial relations, patronage and municipal politics - were eliminated. As a result, the organisational strength of the movement began to ebb, with the SDAP, the MAV and the network of Social Democratic auxiliary organisations all suffering serious drops in membership .

The decline in the organisational strength of the movement inevitably opened up opportunities for its opponents to emerge from their previous position of subordination. There followed an at times violent struggle to break the local Social Democratic monopoly of the streets (discussed fully in Chapter Five) in which the *Heimwehr*, encouraged and supported by the local parties of the Right, eventually emerged triumphant, capping off its victoiy, as in Wiener Neustadt, with a mass rally on the town's previously 'red' streets in August 1930.

The experience in Steyr was symptomatic of the underlying weakness of the Social Democratic movement at the local level in the provinces. Social Democracy in Steyr and the other *Hochburgen* this chapter has discussed was rooted in the sense of identity which emerged in dense and closed manual worker milieux located on one side of the 'front lines' of a deeply segmented society. The form of politics which arose from this environmental background was territorially focused and inward-looking, largely bound up in organisational penetration and self-assertion within the confines of the stronghold. Conditioned by this insular, *Hochburg* mentality, the local-level movement was inevitably separated out into a series of isolated enclaves. Lacking, as the previous chapter made clear, in effective support from the higher levels of the SDAP, it could in this situation only confront the challenge of the Right on the basis of the resources available to it locally. Those resources were in many cases effectively marshalled, albeit often briefly, to establish a 'safe haven', a *Schutzgemeinschaft* for the expression of Social Democratic identity. In the face of economic uncertainty and the growing confidence and inherent superiority in power and numbers of right-wing forces, those resources, however, were never sufficient - even in the peculiar conditions of Steyr - for the movement to hold its own in the long run. As a result, all of the Social Democratic *Hochburgen* had, by the end of 1930, fallen, no longer able to reproduce themselves as 'safe havens' for the unhindered expression of Social Democratic identity and values.

The distinctive features of this process of rise and fall in the Social Democratic *Hochburgen* of the provinces - along with the wider implications it threw up both for the Social Democratic movement and for Austrian politics in general - are the subject material of Part Two of this book. The next three chapters examine the core features of *Hochburg* politics: the attempt to mobilise - respectively - trade union power, political patronage, and Social Democratic auxiliary organisations in the service of the *Hochburg Schutzgemeinschaft* . The final two chapters then examine the wider impact of *Hochburg* politics on the provincial Social Democratic movement: first the tendency to an ultra-cautious reformism, borne of insularity, which had emerged by the later 1920s; and second the militant rejection of reformist politics by a leftist faction which became conscious of the weaknesses of an insular and fragmented movement after 1930 and which sparked Social Democratic resistance in the Austrian Civil War of 1934.

Notes

1   See, among many examples, Grabner, Hangler, Hawle, Kammerstätter (1984), 11; Karl Flanner, *Wiener Neustadt im Ständestaat. Arbeiteropposition 1933-1938*, Europaverlag, Vienna (1983), 6; Schlag (1983), 778. There are more hyperbolic variations on the same theme, most notably a phrase reminiscent of the so-called 'Socialist Republic of South Yorkshire' in Britain in the early 1980s: the 'Red Coalminers' Republic' in the Upper Austrian coalfield in the First Republic. See Hubert Hummer, 'Der Widerstand auf dem Land', in Stadler (1984), 76.

2   The figures for the percentage of the local population from an industrial occupational background need to be treated with some caution. They refer, in the absence of more detailed local-level figures and with the exception of the towns of Steyr and Wiener Neustadt, to the *Gerichtsbezirk* (Judicial District) in which the locality was situated. Since *Gerichtsbezirke* contained a number of communities, some non-industrial, the percentage figures given tend to underestimate the size of the industrial population. At the same time though, the term 'industrial occupational background' comprises all social groups - manual workers, white-collar employees, managers and owners - engaged in indutry. These different social groups unfortunately could not, with the available information, be disaggregated. Moreover, due to the absence of directly comparable data from any one year, the population figures are from the 1934 census and the election figures from the 1927 national election.

3   C.f. Bauer, (1988c), 6.

4   The phrases *'Integration nach innen'* and *'Abgrenzung nach außen'* are adapted from Bernhard Natter's discussion of Catholic attempts to shield and 'immunise' the flock from the Social Democratic arch-enemy. That they seem just as appropriate in a reverse usage perhaps underlines the depth of the divide between the political sub-cultures of provincial politics. See Natter (1989), 107.

5   See Maria Jahoda, Paul F. Lazarsfeld, Hans Zeisel, *Die Arbeitslosen von Marienthal. Ein soziographischer Versuch mit einem Anhang zur Geschichte der Soziographie*, Verlag für Demoskopie, Allensbach (1960), 11-16.

6   See Ingrid Bauer, Wilhelm Weitgruber, *Vom Dorf zur Vorstadt - Ein Spaziergang durch Itzling. Arbeiteralltag und Arbeiterkultur in Itzling: 1860-1945*, SPÖ-Sektion Itzling, Salzburg (1985), 48-54.

7   For example the Flugfeldviertel around the Daimler works in Wiener Neustadt. See Flanner (1983), 36.

8   See Hummer (1989).

9   A general introduction to the municipal activity of the SDAP in the provinces is given in Robert Schediwy, 'Die Blütezeit des kommunalen Sozialismus', in Fröschl, Mesner, Zoitl (1990). The role of the SDAP in municipal administration in the First Republic is addressed in more depth in Chapter Seven.

10   Quoted in Bauer (1987), 205.

11   *Die Wahrheit*, 13-4-1924, quoted in SPÖ Mauthausen (1989), 93.

12   See e.g. Ingrid Bauer's discussion and documentation of trade unionism in Salzburg: 'Zwischen konkreter Utopie und den Zwängen der Realität. Die 1920er Jahre', in Bauer (1988b), 113-124. See also Jill Lewis' discussion of industrial relations in Upper Styria in the early post-war years in Lewis (1991), 89-108.

13   See Bauer (1988a), 203-206.

14   Quoted in ibid., 204.

15   Surprising in the senses that there existed no legal basis for closed shop agreements and that closed shops could exist even in areas where Social Democracy and the Free Trade Unions were especially weak, like Tirol and Vorarlberg. See Wanner (1983), 21; Dreier (1984), 183-184; Oberkofler (1986), 186. Most of these agreements fell victim during the 1920s to the anti-unionist offensives of employers and were formally killed off in 1930 under the terms of the so-called 'Anti-Terror' industrial relations law. On all these points see further in Chapter Four.

16   The evidence here is more impressionistic, relying almost exclusively on the accusations of corrupt malpractice by anti-Social Democrats. See e.g. Nasko (1986), 140; Otto Hwaletz, Karl Stocker, 'Dokumente und Flugblätter zu den Gemeinderatswahlen in Eisenerz 1928 und 1932', in Hwaletz et al. (1984), 121-146; Lewis (1991), 134, 171.

17   See Chapter Six.

18   This is a function which is frequently misunderstood. There exists a tendency to see in these networks of auxiliary organisations parallels - however modest - to Social Democratic organisational life in Red Vienna. As Chapter Six argues, such parallels tend both to misportray the purpose of auxiliary activiy in the provinces and to perpetuate a rather simplistic, romanticised view of auxiliary activity in Red Vienna.

19   Erika Thurner, 'Vom proletarischen Insel-Dasein zum Leben im "Roten Salzburg". Salzburger Impressionen nach dem Zweiten Weltkrieg', in Greußing (1989), 174.

20   Quoted in Bauer, (1988e), 126.

21   This theme is addressed in greater depth in Chapter Six.

22   See Wolfgang Quatember, 'Generalstreik im Dorf. Der Aufstand des Republikanische Schutzbundes im Februar 1934 in Ebensee', in Greußing (1989), 146.

23   See Gutkas (1983), 861 and Chapter Five of this book.

24   Flanner (1983), 6. Much the same applied in the case of Steyr. See below.

25   See, for a general survey of 'violence in politics' in the First Republic, Gerhard Botz, *Gewalt in der Politik. Attentate, Zusammenstöße, Unruhen in Österreich*, 1918-1934, Oldenbourg, Munich (1976).

26   Schlag (1983), 778.

27   See e.g. Gulick (1948), 725-728.

28   See e.g. Hinteregger, Schmidlechner, Staudinger (1984), 201-207 and Lewis (1991), 133-137. See also Chapter One of this book.

29   Quoted in Gulick (1948), 793

30   See ibid., 790-806.

31   See e.g. Rabinbach (1983), 211; Gulick (1948), 1279; Ilona Duczynska, *Der demokratische Bolschevik. Zur Theorie und Praxis der Gewalt*, List, Munich (1975), 235.

32   Bundesamt für Statistik (Ed.), *Gewerbliche Betriebszählung in der Republik Österreich vom 14. Juni 1930. Ergebnisse für Oberösterreich*, Verlag der Österreichischen Staatsdruckerei, Vienna (1932), 15.

33   In 1930 66% of manual workers in Steyr were skilled or semi-skiled, while another 15% were in training as apprentices. Only 19% were unskilled. See ibid.

34   See e.g. Lewis (1991), 24ff.

35   STB 14-8-1927, 1.

36   Calculated from *Verzeichnis jener Betriebe in Oberösterreich, welche über fünf Kammerumlagepflichtige beschäftigen*, 1927-1933 editions, Kammer für Arbeiter und Angestellte in Linz a. Donau, Linz (1927-1933). The statistics on which these figures are based include only those employees whose firms employed five or more employees subject to subscriptions to the Chamber of Labour. They refer to the number employed at the end of June in each year.

37   In 1928, the membership of the Steyr District Organisation of the SDAP, which included the villages in the surrounding area, stood at 9,938. Around half of these are likely to have originated in Steyr. In addition, the manual workforce of the Steyr-Werke - a closed shop of the MAV - peaked at 5669 in 1929. Allowing for unionised metalworkers in other local firms the overall membership figure would have been pushed up towards, or over 6,000: See Sozialdemokratische Partei Oberösterreichs. Tätigkeitsbericht 1928, Gutenberg, Linz (1929), 9, and *Verzeichnis jener Betriebe in Oberösterreich, welche über fünf Kammerumlagepflichtige beschäftigen*, (1929).

38   See Table 6.1 in Chapter Six.

39   See Bundesamt für Statistik (1935a), 156, 159; idem (1927), 10-12.

40   Among the many and varied examples, see SZ 14-6-1927, 4; 4-9-1927, 14; 18-8-1929, 4; 16-9-1928, 1; 17-12-1929, 21-6-1932, 6-8; 16-1-1934, 4; LTP 25-8-1929, 6; 17-12-1929, 1-2; LVSt 2-7-1932, 3; 19-2-1933, 4; SJ 1-8-1930, 7; OÖAZ 29-10-1927, 4; 16-1-1932, 5.

41   This is discussed in detail in the next chapter.

42   See ÖVW Bilanzen, 27-6-1929, 489.

43   Quoted in ÖVW, 11-1-1930, 393.

44   For the derivation of the Steyr figures, see note 28 in Chapter Eight.

45   See the election results for wards 3, 4, 5, 11, 12 and 13 in the 1927 municipal and federal elections as reprinted in STB 26-4-1927, 9.

46   For example at the Mayday parade of 1929. See STB 4-5-1929, 7-8.

47   See STB 12-7-1928, 10; 3-8-1928, 8; SZ 12-7-1928, 3-4; 17-7-1928, 5; OÖAZ 21-7-1928, 4; Magistrat der Stadt Steyr, Registratur: Faszikel J/d 25-45 Vereine.

48   STB 17-7-1928, 10; LTP 11-7-1928, 1.

49   Quoted in STB, 12-8-1927, 8.

50   See Hinteregger, Müller, Staudinger (1984); Hwaletz et al (1984); Lewis (1991); Staudinger (1985)

51   Lewis (1991), 160.

52   See Hummer (1989), 96-97; idem (1984), 76; AVA Sozialdemokratische Parteistellen, Karton 54.
53   See McLoughlin, (1983-1984), 135, 142-143; Flanner (1983), 6-10.
54   See Karl Ausch, *Als die Banken fielen. Zur Soziologie der politischen Korruption*, Europaverlag, Vienna (1968), 314-317, 359-361; ÖVW Bilanzen 27-7-1929, 489; 3-8-1930, 7; ÖVW 11-1-1930, 393.
55   Gulick (1948), 858.
56   ÖVW 11-1-1930, 393.

Part Two

Social Democratic 'Stronghold' Politics
in the Provinces

4 Controlling the Workplace: Power and Conflict in Industrial Relations

The Social Democratic Free Trade Unions (FTUs) played an especially significant role in the politics of Social Democratic provincial *Hochburgen*. More than any other Social Democratic organisations in the provinces they had access to levers of political power which could be mobilised to strengthen and deepen the cohesion of the Social Democratic community at the local level. As the last chapter indicated, they were able to offer benefits to their members both in their function as an interest group in industrial relations and through the powers of patronage which at least some of them possessed at the workplace. The benefits offered by the FTUs helped to generate and deepen popular commitment to the Social Democratic movement, and in this way to consolidate the community solidarity and identity upon which the *Hochburgen* were based. In these respects the FTUs might aptly be described as the 'backbone' of *Hochburg* politics. An examination of this trade union 'backbone' is therefore an appropriate starting point for Part Two of this book.

The first section of this chapter presents a survey of FTU politics across the industrial centres of the Austrian provinces. Although the available sources in the secondary literature are rather uneven in coverage and quality, it is possible to identify a broad pattern of development: the strengthening and flexing of the union 'backbone' in the years immediately after the First World War, followed, normally from the mid-1920s at the latest, by a process of contraction and erosion which was everywhere complete by 1930, leaving the FTUs as a broken force in provincial politics.

The remaining sections of the chapter focus on the 'backbone' of the Social Democratic *Hochburg* in Steyr, the Metalworkers' Union (MAV) in the Steyr-Werke. The experience of the MAV passed through the same phases of strengthening and contraction seen elsewhere, but in a rather different rhythm and on a much more extreme scale. Section two shows that the MAV emerged from the First World War in an unusually strong position in industrial relations in the Steyr-Werke. By exploiting this position of strength it was able to win for itself a number of extraordinary powers, supplementary to those granted by post-war legislation. The significance of these powers extended far beyond the bounds of the works and served to buttress the broader influence and strength of the Social Democratic movement in the town as a whole.

Section three then examines the course and implications of a major industrial dispute at the works in 1925. This was engineered by the Steyr-Werke management in the attempt to remove from the MAV the extraordinary powers it had won after the war. That attempt failed, leaving the MAV in possession of its those powers - and guaranteeing the broader strength the movement as a whole gained from them - until 1930.

The framework for industrial relations at the works was, however, as section four shows, abruptly redefined in favour of the Steyr-Werke management by changing economic and political conditions after 1929. Following a short industrial dispute in the summer of 1930, the management succeeded in stripping the MAV of its extraordinary powers and the union as a result limped through to its dissolution in 1934 in a state of near-impotence. This reversal of fortunes was, as this final section argues, the catalyst for the collapse of the local *Hochburg*: deprived of its 'backbone', any structure will tend inevitably to crumble and fall.

The Rise and Fall of Union Power in the Provinces

The period immediately after the end of the First World War was one of unprecedented upswing for the FTUs. This upswing owed much to the strengthening of the statutory position of the unions in industrial relations by the social and employment legislation passed after the war by the SDAP-led coalition government. This lifted most remaining restrictions on the right of association, created a new framework for the regulation of collective bargaining and working conditions, and introduced a limited form of worker/union codetermination in the management of the firm.[1] Moreover, the unions' position at the workplace was further strengthened indirectly by the atmosphere of militancy which had reigned in industrial relations in the last months of the war and which extended, if only temporarily, into the post-war era. The new legal position and the legacy of industrial militancy together pushed employers and employers' associations onto the defensive.

These were conditions in which many union organisations at the local level were able not only to make effective use of their powers under the new employment legislation, but also to force, in some firms, the addition of extra, non-statutory powers to their armoury on the shopfloor. These included the deduction of union dues direct from the pay-packet and the establishment of closed shop arrangements. Direct dues deduction is a far more efficient means of generating income than member-to-member collections. It helped secure the resource base of the union organisation and thereby enhanced its wider effectiveness. In some cases, moreover, an additional 'political levy' of subscriptions to the SDAP or to other Social Democratic organisations was also deducted direct from the pay packet.[2] In other words, union strength at the workplace could in some cases be mobilised to feed into to the resource base of the wider Social Democratic movement.

The most important among the non-statutory powers won by the FTUs in the early post-war years was, however, the establishment of closed shops.[3] Closed shops have a central significance in the conduct of industrial relations in that they establish a united, cohesive, and therefore more powerful, union front in workplace negotiations with management, a factor of particular importance in a country which had rival Christian and German Nationalist (and, in later years, *Heimwehr*) trade unions.

All the above factors - closed shops, dues deduction arrangements, industrial militancy and postwar employment legislation - point to an especially favourable framework for the conduct of union activity. This is not to say that the FTUs had an open field in industrial relations, since employers almost everywhere remained trenchantly opposed to greater union rights and committed to reasserting their traditional supremacy on the shopfloor.[4] However, the unions were able, at least temporarily, to play a more effective role in defending and asserting labour interests than ever before. This is confirmed in various regional studies which point to local FTU success in defending working conditions and in particular in securing an index-linking of wages in the period of Austrian hyperinflation in 1921-1922.[5] A broader picture is given in Gerhard Botz' quantitative analysis of strikes during the First Republic. Botz splits the First Republic into four periods, the first two of which - 1919-1921 and 1922-1924 - saw an especially high level of industrial conflict as measured in working days lost to strikes and lockouts. This reflected in part the high level of distributional conflict caused by the economic upheavals of the early post-war years. It also reflected the antipathy of many employers to the labour and employment rights of the new republic. Botz shows, however, that the outcome of 90.7% of strikes called in the period 1919-1921 and 95.3% of those called in the period 1922-1924 was 'successful' from the perspective of the FTUs.[6] In other words the Austrian FTUs were, at the very least, holding their own in distributional conflicts and had some success in defending their new rights in the early post-war years.

Botz' figures are unfortunately not disaggregated province by province. As a result they are to an extent skewed by the outcome of industrial conflicts in Vienna, where the FTUs were at their strongest. Nevertheless, the high 'success' rate averaged across Austria as a whole suggests a broadly effective period for the FTUs in the provinces as well. This success was reflected, as Table 4.1 shows, in an extremely rapid expansion of FTU membership in the provinces between the end of the war and the postwar peak of union membership in 1921-1922, over which period at least a threefold, and in some cases a fivefold increase was registered. The FTUs were acting as a popular magnet, attracting new support to the Social Democratic movement and deepening the penetration of the movement into local society. This

Table 4.1 Free Trade Union Membership in the Provinces, 1918-1931[a]

Province	1918	1922	1927	1931
Burgenland				
Membership	n/a[b]	15,304	13,366	10,817
Index	n/a[b]	100	87.3	70.7
Carinthia				
Membership	6,361	31,039	17,530	14,253
Index	20.5	100	56.5	45.9
Lower Austria				
Membership	67,992	21,2088	143,357	99,934
Index	32.1	100	67.6	47.1
Salzburg				
Membership	5,620	19,547	16,920	13,081
Index	28.8	100	86.6	66.9
Styria				
Membership	31,363	128,222	67,074	48,104
Index	24.6	100	52.3	37.5
Tirol				
Membership	6,851[c]	22,981	15,929	12,527
Index	20.7[c]	100	69.3	54.5
Upper Austria				
Membership	14,656	98,912	62,253	49,151
Index	14.8	100	62.9	49.7
Vorarlberg				
Membership	n/a[c]	10,158	4,860	2,839
Index	n/a[c]	100	47.8	27.9

Notes:
a All index figures are calculated on the basis of 1922 membership figures.
b Burgenland was still part of Hungary in 1918. Hence, no figures are available.
c Tirol and Vorarlberg constituted a single unit within the Free Trade Union movement until after the First World War. The 1918 figures for Tirol are thus compared to (and in the case of the index, calculated from) the composite figure of Tirol plus Vorarlberg after the First World War.
Sources: Fritz Klenner, Die Österreichischen Gewerkschaften. Band I, Verlag des Österreichischen Gewerkschaftsbunds, Vienna (1951), 464-465; Protokoll der Verhandlungen des Parteitages der Sozialdemokratischen Arbeiterpartei Deutschösterreichs1923, 72; Jahrbuch der österreichischen Arbeiterbewegung 1928, 55; Wirtschaftsstatistisches Jahrbuch 1931-1932, 164.

penetrative function was enhanced wherever closed shops existed. Although the current state of research does not allow any detailed analysis of the scope and frequency of closed shop arrangements, it is clear that they existed across provincial Austria, not just in the more highly unionised provinces of Lower Austria and Styria, but also (of course less frequently) in areas of union weakness, like Tirol and Vorarlberg.[7] Closed shops, by implication, gave the FTUs control over employment opportunities in the locality concerned and were openly used to reward card-carrying Social Democrats with jobs (and, equally, to discriminate against non-Social Democrats). In other words, closed shops did not just strengthen the unions' bargaining position in industrial relations, but also secured for them powers of patronage whose significance extended well beyond the workplace. This was an extra incentive to seek membership in Social Democratic organisations and thus deepened the 'magnet' effect of the FTUs.

The effectiveness of union powers both within and outside the workplace proved however to be unsustainable. The first flush of assertiveness and success after the First World War was soon replaced by a generally losing rearguard action whose tempo was conditioned by a combination of the following factors:

• *Industrial structure*. The size and geographical distribution of firms played an important role, with smaller firms and firms or sites isolated from other centres of union strength typically experiencing an early erosion of union powers.
• *Labour force structure*. FTUs generally proved less able to retain organisational strength in firms and industries in which unskilled labour was predominant.
• *Economic situation*. Trade unions are normally weaker in sectors or periods experiencing economic downturn. Economic problems were faced from the early years of the First Republic in sectors which had difficulties adapting from war-time to peace-time production and/or which were most severely affected by the break-up of the formerly coherent economic unit of the Habsburg Empire. More generally, the Austrian economy as a whole experienced a sharp downturn in the 'stabilisation crisis' of 1922-1925 which followed the end of the post-war hyperinflation. This, as Table 4.1 shows, was clearly reflected in a substantial decline in provincial FTU membership.
• *Union competition*. The position of the FTUs *vis-à-vis* employers was weakened to the extent that rival union organisations were able to maintain and extend their organisations at the workplace.
• *Employer opposition*. While employers generally opposed the rights won by unions at the workplace after the war, some developed especially consistent and hostile anti-union policies. The intensity of employer opposition is therefore an important factor in explaining the weakening of the FTUs.

• *Wider opposition.* In some areas, as Chapter One showed, provincial authorities (and the police and army units they controlled) and the *Heimwehr* could also be mobilised in the quest to break FTU organisations.

With this range of adverse factors stacked against them, the FTUs gradually lost the advantages they held in industrial relations in the early postwar years. Employers took advantage of weaknesses arising from industrial and labour force structure, economic situation and the presence of rival trade unions to strip the FTUs of any non-statutory rights they may have won, to ignore the statutory rights they were entitled to, and ultimately to marginalise them at the workplace, at times with the assistance of the *Heimwehr* and the provincial authorities. The scale of marginalisation is illustrated baldly in the figures in Table 4.1, which show a dramatic decline in FTU membership in the years 1922-1931.

The process of marginalisation and decline occurred most rapidly in western Austria,[8] where an extremely sparse distribution of industrial centres combined with small-scale production, low skill levels, a strong Christian trade union movement and a reactionary political environment to undermine the FTUs by the early 1920s.[9] The most devastating decline in the FTUs was, though, undoubtedly that in the heavy industrial centres of Upper Styria, where two-thirds of the FTU membership - some 80,000 members - were lost in the years 1922-1931.

This 'failure of Styrian labour'[10] was attributable to a particularly unfavourable combination of all the factors mentioned above. The emphasis in the region was on the production of raw materials and basic metal products which did not require a highly skilled workforce. Unskilled workers generally have a lower propensity for union organisation. This had led the emergent metalworkers' FTU to concentrate its efforts in the late nineteenth century on organising the less numerous, but more amenable skilled workers of the region. As a result there was no engrained union tradition among the unskilled to draw on in the First Republic, so that despite a rapid initial expansion of membership, union loyalties remained weak and open to erosion. The nature of Upper Styrian industry also proved disadvantageous in two other respects. Firstly, the production of raw materials and basic products is generally more vulnerable to economic fluctuation than the manufacture of finished products. Indeed, following the currency stabilisation of 1922, Upper Styrian industry faced constant crisis conditions. The consequent unemployment, aggravated by progressive rationalisation measures, compounded FTU weakness. Secondly, the geographical dispersal of industrial centres in upper Styria in the valleys descending from the Alps made united action by the FTUs difficult. These structural problems left a clear opening for the dominant employer, the AMG, to pursue a consistently aggressive and sophisticated anti-union strategy in which it found a willing helper in the form of the *Heimwehr* and its 'Independent' Trade Union. The result of this combination of unfavourable conditions was that the FTUs were a spent force as a labour interest group in Upper Styria by the late 1920s.

Some industrial centres, for example the Upper Austrian coalfield, Lower Austrian St. Pölten and, as will be discussed below, Steyr, were able to hold their own as focal points of FTU strength until the onset of the Great Depression.[11] The more typical experience was, though, closer to that of western Austria and Styria: the marginalisation of the FTUs well before the mass unemployment of the depression years could take its effect. It is against this background that the experience in Steyr stands out as an unusual case.

Controlling the Workplace I: Union Dominance in the Steyr-Werke

The dominant FTU in Steyr in the First Republic - in a town with a long metalworking tradition - was the Metalworkers' Union (MAV), whose organisational focal point lay in the Steyr-Werke. This section focuses on the nature of industrial relations in the Steyr-Werke from the end of the First World War to 1930, a period in which the MAV established and was able to maintain an unusually strong position in the works *vis-à-vis* a generally weak management. The MAV's strength resulted from a number of complementary factors.

Of fundamental importance was the successful transition of the works from war-time armaments production (although a small-scale sports gun operation was continued) to the peace-time production of cars. As a result there was no major economic dislocation after the war, unlike that experienced by another major war-time arms-producing town, Wiener Neustadt, where the arms industry failed to diversify effectively.[12] Transitional unemployment did not therefore debilitate MAV strength in the early post-war years. On the contrary, directly after the war the works recorded some of its highest employment levels during the whole First Republic (see Table 3.3 in Chapter Three). These high employment levels allowed the MAV to draw on and mobilise a long tradition of metalworkers' unionisation (extending back to 1890)[13] to establish very quickly a strong organisation in the works. On that basis MAV membership in Steyr rose by over 1,000% from around 600 in 1915-1916 to 6,822 by 1922.[14]

A further point to note is that this tradition of unionisation was a tradition of *skilled worker* unionisation, reflecting Steyr's centuries-long pedigree as a centre of skilled metal manufacturing (as opposed, for example, to the basic production and lower skill levels of Upper Styria). As elsewhere, these skilled workers were especially amenable to union organisation. Just as important, the skills base in the labour force enhanced the bargaining power of the MAV and weakened that of management in the car works. The skilled workers the MAV organised were essential to maintain production; management could not do without them. This factor took on particular importance given the nature of the commercial market in which the Steyr-Werke was operating. This was highly competitive and increasingly dominated by mass-produced, low-cost imports from the USA. It was imperative that management avoid industrial conflict which might interrupt production and thus endanger the works' toehold in the market. In these circumstances, the balance of power in industrial relations was firmly tilted towards the MAV. This power advantage allowed the MAV to negotiate for itself - through the Works Council it dominated throughout the First Republic[15] - a series of non-statutory rights at the works. These supplementary rights served in the following years to perpetuate that advantage.

The Non-Statutory Rights of the MAV

The non-statutory rights won by the MAV-controlled Works Council after the First World War were quite exceptional.[16] Alongside a Works Council veto power over manual worker recruitments and dismissals, the workforce had a specific right to hawk the SDAP press, display Social Democratic political notices and hold collections for political purposes on the shopfloor (for example for the paramilitary *Schutzbund* and the SDAP election fund). In addition, MAV dues, including a special supplementary political levy for the *Kinderfreunde* (the SDAP Children's Organisation), were centrally deducted from wages by the firm's finance office. Finally, twice the amount prescribed by law was deducted from wages to fund Works Council activities, one third of Works Council costs were paid by the firm, and Works Councillors were paid as normal for Works Council activities undertaken in the firm's time.

These rights had the effect of establishing the shopfloor of the works as a vehicle for Social Democratic agitation and fund-raising, as well as providing for the free administration of both union and non-union (*Kinderfreunde*) dues-collection. They also gave the Works Council the final say in manual worker personnel issues, establishing a closed shop among the manual workforce. The latter point ensured that the MAV was able to perpetuate its domination of the shopfloor. Through the right to veto new recruits, the Works Council was able to exclude 'unfriendly' elements from the works - above all members of the Christian Metalworkers, who had a minor presence in the town[17] - and to give preferential treatment to card-carrying Social Democrats (allegedly in collusion with the SDAP-run municipal Unemployment Office)[18].

However, the supply of employable card-carrying Social Democrats began to dry up in the late 1920s. These were years of high and expanding employment at the Steyr-Werke and unusually low unemployment in the town. An inevitable corollary of the MAV's closed shop policy in these circumstances was that non-Social Democrats came to join the MAV merely to get work.[19] Such workers had purely *instrumental* reasons for joining the MAV, directed at one particular outcome: to secure employment. Beyond that they had no interest in the MAV or any commitment to the wider aims of Social Democracy or free trade unionism. This is a point which becomes significant in the reversal of the balance of power in industrial relations at the works, and is examined further below.

The Works Council was also able to make political use of the subscriptions it levied from the manual workforce. These were set at one per cent of wages (twice the half per cent required by law) and raised, in relative terms, enormous sums. In 1929, for example, the levy on wages raised 166,866 shillings, boosting total Works Council income to 221,139 shillings. For purposes of comparison, this was just under a tenth of total municipal income for the town of Steyr in that year.[20] The Works Council had, in effect, a lucrative private tax at its disposal, which was used to subsidise a series of Social Democratic causes and activities.

Table 4.2 reproduces, in modified form, the expenditure column of the Steyr-Werke balance sheet for the first six months of 1929. As the table shows, over a quarter of Works Council funds were set aside to reimburse some 200 Works Councillors and other MAV functionaries who, according to the local SDAP newspaper, lost wages for carrying out MAV work in the firm's time. These payments bore little relation to the possible work a functionary might have carried out. Averaged out, over six shillings, or around four hours' pay, were allocated per functionary per week to look after the interests of thirty or so workers.[21] It is hardly conceivable that each functionary could have had so much work to do on behalf of so few workers. The implication is that these payments were straightforward perks which came with the status of functionary.[22] This in turn raises the questions of whether functionaries were motivated by genuine trade unionist commitment, or merely by the perks on offer, and if so to what extent the instrumentalist tendencies noted above also extended into the MAV's functionary network. Again, the implications of instrumentalism are discussed below.

Table 4.2 Expenditure of the Steyr-Werke Works Council, first half-year, 1929 (in Austrian shillings)

Item	Amount
Income	120,813.05
Expenditure:	
Reimbursement of wages of Works Councillors and MAV functionaries	35,454.03
Subsidy to the Social Democratic Housing Cooperative	15,271.00
Subsidy to the *Kinderfreunde*	18,993.00
Subsidy to the *Verein Arbeiterheim*	18,993.00
Educational expenditure	3,172.00
Welfare expenditure	5,544.80
Delegation costs	4,157.63
Reimbursement of wages for magistrate's and jury duty, rent tribunal attendance etc.	1,590.23
Stationery, telephone etc.	2,087.50
Other	394.74
Balance	15,155.12
Total	120,813.05

Source: *SZ 18-3-1930, 1.*

The proceeds of the Works Council's 'private tax' also served, as Table 4.2 shows, to subsidise other organisations in the wider Social Democratic movement. For example, Works Council money had purchased, under the auspices of subsidies to the *Verein Arbeiterheim* (analogous to a British Labour Club), both the building which housed the local SDAP headquarters and expensive cinematic projection equipment for the party meeting hall.[23] In addition, sizeable subsidies were paid to the local Social Democratic housing cooperative and to the *Kinderfreunde*. The latter complemented the *'Kindergroschen'* ('children's penny'), the special supplement to basic MAV subscriptions deducted at source by the Steyr-Werke finance office and passed directly to the children's organisation. With this twofold support from the workforce at the Steyr-Werke, the *Kinderfreunde* organisation for the Steyr district easily had the greatest income per head in Austria.[24]

The subsidisation of other Social Democratic organisations had a dual significance. It was first and foremost a potent expression of the MAV's control of the shopfloor of the Steyr-Werke. But it also helped indirectly to reinforce that control both by placing the wider Social

Democratic movement on a sturdier financial footing and by ensuring a sense of indebtedness of the wider movement to the MAV. As the next section shows, if the Steyr-Werke chose to challenge the dominant position of the MAV in the works, it would be faced by the opposition not just of the union, but also of the organisations which had benefitted from the union's munificence.

The 1925 Lockout: Course and Consequences

On 29 September 1925, the manual workforce at the Steyr-Werke was locked out. The proclamation of the lockout was the culmination of a confrontational and aggressive anti-union attitude taken by management during the summer of 1925, which had the ultimate aim of stripping the MAV of its non-statutory rights at the works. Throughout the summer, the works had been preparing for the transition to assembly line production methods. To facilitate a smooth transition, the MAV Works Council had agreed to an 'economic peace', a temporary suspension of industrial conflict at the works. By September, however, it was felt by the MAV that management was exploiting the 'economic peace' to hold down wages below average levels in the industry. A new wage claim, which even normally anti-MAV sources considered justified,[25] was tabled by the MAV but flatly rejected by management. The developing wages conflict between management and MAV was then flanked by a more serious conflict between the Social Democratic white-collar workers' union at the Steyr-Werke, the *Bund der Industrieangestellten*. Management had refused to recognise and implement nationally negotiated supplements to the existing collective agreement and had begun to negotiate pay on an individual basis, ignoring the statutory collective bargaining rights of the white-collar union.

These management-initiated conflicts pointed to the adoption of an anti-union policy at the works, similar to those pursued elsewhere in the provinces. This was confirmed on 28 September, when 28 manual workers, 25 of them MAV functionaries, were arbitrarily 'picked out' (*'herausgegriffen'*) and sacked. This was presented as a punitive measure taken because of attempts by manual workers to intervene in the management-*Angestellte* dispute and because the MAV's wage claim represented an 'unjustified' disturbance of the 'economic peace' which had been agreed at the works.[26] More realistically it has to be seen as a deliberate escalation of a wages dispute into a more fundamental conflict about the position and rights of unions in the firm, especially since it openly flouted the MAV's personnel policy veto. The union (MAV and white collar) response was to down tools and (also somewhat arbitrarily) to 'fetch out' various officials of the firm to explain management's actions. At least one official was physically assaulted; upon hearing this, management proclaimed the lockout of the manual workforce.[27]

The sudden transition of wages conflict into lockout - without intervening negotiation - suggests that management had been planning a major confrontation with the MAV. The timing of the lockout backs up this view. Between 1923 and 1925 the recovery of the car works from the post-inflationary recession in Austria had been sluggish, and, excepting the post-1929 period, 1925 was the year of the lowest employment at the Steyr-Werke during the First Republic (see Table 3.2). This may have suggested a temporary decrease in MAV bargaining power, especially since the union had agreed to a temporary 'economic peace'. The willingness to enter this agreement, which in effect amounted to a restriction on normal union activities, may have been interpreted by management as a sign of further weakness. In addition, three other major disputes in the Austrian metal industry - at the AMG works in Donawitz and Eisenerz, at Siemens und Halske in Vienna, and at the St. Egydyer steelworks in Hainfeld - were simultaneously coming to a head. Each of these had resulted, by early October in lockouts of the workforce, suggesting a concerted employers' anti-unionist offensive in the metal industry.[28] In view of the need to coordinate several conflicts simultaneously, the MAV's overall effectiveness in national terms was significantly diminished at this time.[29] In all, the various factors pointed to a short-term lowpoint in MAV strength and a window of opportunity for management to attempt to assert its authority in the works.

The publication on 8 October of management's 'guidelines' for resolving the dispute confirmed that this was its reasoning. According to these 'guidelines', the directors were prepared to reopen the works only under the existing manual worker pay structure, and remained unprepared to implement the supplements to the collective agreements of the white-collar workers. Upon reopening the works, the manual workers who were to be reemployed would be specified by name, presumably to the exclusion of further MAV functionaries. Finally, and most significantly, 'the manual workers shall not lay claim to rights which exceed the rights granted them by law': MAV dues would no longer be deducted centrally, the Works Council would lose its influence on staffing matters, the works would no longer subsidise the running costs of the Works Council, and newspapers would no longer be hawked on the shopfloor.[30] Unsurprisingly, the MAV refused to negotiate on these terms - which would have destroyed its powers and privileges in the works - and for the next seven weeks the dispute entered a stand-off, during which time the real distribution of power in industrial relations at the works became evident.

As the length of the dispute increased, it became clear that management had seriously miscalculated its ability to impose its will on the MAV. Its own position was weakened by the timing of the conflict, which, although geared to an assumed temporary lowpoint in MAV strength, wholly failed to take into account the pressures on the firm created by the nature of the Austrian car market. The lockout was started at a time when important preparations for the launch of a new, mass-produced, assembly line *Steyr* model were in progress. The demand for cars in Austria was highly seasonal in view of the hard, Alpine winters. Preparations therefore had to be completed in time for sufficient stocks to be ready for the increase in demand for cars in the spring season. The longer the dispute continued, the more pressure management was under to resume launch preparations for the new model. This was an extra bargaining counter for the MAV, especially since the market in cars was so competitive. In the mid-1920s, cheap mass-production Model T Fords began to conquer an increasing proportion of the European market. If the Steyr-Werke missed the start of the season, cheap foreign competition could easily swallow its market share.[31]

A further problem for management was that the company could in no way *afford* a lengthy dispute. As the last chapter showed, reckless and profligate financial management had left the firm walking a financial tightrope during most of the 1920s; a lengthy industrial conflict could have signalled collapse and liquidation.

In view of these weaknesses in the management's bargaining hand, it can be assumed that it did not expect the lockout to last more than two or three weeks. It had, in effect, staked its all on an early collapse in the MAV's resolve. This was a disastrous miscalculation which vastly underestimated the inherent strength of the union and the support it could expect to receive from other Social Democratic organisations which had previously benefitted from its generosity. One example of this was the cooperation of the local *Schutzbund* - past beneficiary of shopfloor collections at the works - with the municipal police (themselves taking orders from the SDAP Mayor) in 'policing' the picket lines of the locked-out workers.[32] If the plan had been - as was the practice elsewhere in the provinces - to bus in blackleg labour, effective security for any attempt to cross the picket lines could not be guaranteed.

Of greater significance was the input of the *Kinderfreunde* - the major beneficiary of MAV funding - into the dispute. In cooperation with its National Executive, the local *Kinderfreunde* organised a national Social Democratic fostering scheme to look after the children of the locked-out workforce for the duration of the lockout. Within fourteen days, 802 children were living with temporary foster parents.[33]

This impressive mobilisation was supplemented by a further *Kinderfreunde* campaign aimed at providing meals for another 3,500 children in Steyr.[34] Moreover a *Kinderfreunde* appeal for donations to support the dispute raised some 113,352 shillings.[35] This amounted, as a simple average, to around four shillings per worker per week during the lockout. In addition the locked-out workers received full union strike pay - eighteen shillings per week according to one source[36] - and a special 13% discount at the Social Democratic consumer cooperative.[37] If donations, strike pay, coop discount and the savings made by parents as a result of the *Kinderfreunde* campaigns are taken together, it is clear that the locked-out workforce had a standard of living, which though poor in comparison with normal times, was entirely tolerable in the short term. As a result, the MAV was able to endure, without any loss of solidarity among its members, a longer dispute than management had reckoned with. This unexpected endurance in turn had severe implications for the weaknesses of management's own position.

The result was that when the MAV Works Councillors suggested the resumption of negotiations on 21 November, management was forced to accept. Two days later agreement had been reached. The management was forced to retract the demands it had made on 8 October. Moreover, it agreed to recognise the supplements to the collective agreements of the white-collar workers and to a one-off, lump-sum payment to manual workers, equivalent to a 6% pay bonus over the year, pending the negotiation of a new collective agreement. The MAV made one concession, whereby it was agreed to phase out the deduction of MAV dues at source by the end of the year. No mention at all was made of the other statutory rights called into question during the dispute.[38] There is even evidence to suggest that dues deduction at source continued after 1925 and that the practice was only ended by the 'Anti-Terror Law' of 1930. Certainly the Christian Social *Steyrer Zeitung* was still complaining about it in 1930,[39] and the *Kinderfreunde* were still receiving the benefits of the MAV *'Kindergroschen'* in the late 1920s.[40]

The outcome of the dispute was thus an unequivocal victory for the MAV. Management had challenged the bases of MAV dominance in the works, but had clearly failed in the attempt to assert its own authority (while simultaneously exposing its own tactical ineptitude and financial weakness). The immediate material outcome of the dispute, concerning wages and collective agreements, is not the issue of significance. Far more important is the fact that the MAV's non-statutory rights remained intact.[41] This reconfirmed the control over the workplace the union had established immediately after the war, a control which management was unable to challenge again until 1930, when mass unemployment had established a wholly different framework for industrial relations at the works. The reconfirmation of MAV dominance allowed the union and its Works Council to continue to raise and distribute funds for other Social Democratic organisations in the town, underpinning the wealth and organisational effectiveness of the movement as a whole. Most significantly it left the Works Council in control of recruitments and dismissals among the manual workforce. This power of patronage was, as the next chapter shows, central to the entrenchment of the Social Democratic *Hochburg* in Steyr in the late 1920s.

Controlling the Workplace II: Management Dominance in the Steyr-Werke

As noted in the previous chapter, car production at the Steyr-Werke was completely shut down in August 1929, recommencing only eleven months later in July 1930. The consequence was mass local unemployment. This vastly changed local economic background radically altered the framework for industrial relations which had previously sustained MAV dominance on the shopfloor and which had marked out Steyr as an unusual case in industrial relations. As a result, the balance of power on the shopfloor of the Steyr-Werke was sharply and swiftly shifted in favour of management. Two further factors also emerged at the same time to bolster management's position. Firstly, the takeover of the Steyr-Werke by Rothschild's Credit-Anstalt in October 1929 had led to the dismissal of the existing management and its replacement by a new, and more determinedly anti-unionist Rothschild management team. Secondly, new federal legislation - the so-called 'Anti-Terror Law' of 1930 - restricted FTU activities to the advantage of employers. This section examines the ways in which economic collapse, a more assertive management and a new legal framework combined to marginalise the MAV and establish management dominance in industrial relations at the Steyr-Werke.

The Credit-Anstalt had been forced to overreach itself financially in taking over the BCA, and consequently placed stringent financial restrictions on its industrial holdings, in particular the previously profligate Steyr-Werke. Credit-Anstalt firms also had a reputation for aggressive anti-union policies.[42] These factors had a deep impact on the conduct of industrial relations at the works. When negotiations opened in June 1930 on the pay and conditions which would apply on the planned resumption of production, the new management immediately sought to weaken the MAV's position at the works. It served notice to terminate the existing collective agreement and announced its intention to cut costs by reducing top wages by 10% and, most significantly, to abolish all non-statutory rights enjoyed by the Works Council. Unsurprisingly, these terms were, as in 1925, immediately rejected. In contrast to 1925, however, the MAV's ability to resist management had been severely weakened in the preceding ten months of zero car production at the works.

Most importantly, well over 3,000 MAV members had been unemployed for those ten months and had no obvious alternative sources of employment in view of the dominance of the Steyr-Werke over the local economy. In these circumstances, the overriding concern of the average car worker was no longer to defend the powers of the Works Council, but to get back to work. Mass unemployment sapped the commitment of the membership to preserve the MAV's position on the shopfloor. This problem was underlined by the fact that the MAV's powers of patronage in manual worker staffing were redundant as long as there was zero employment in car production. The union thus no longer had a 'hold' over the non-Social Democratic instrumentalists who had joined the MAV just to get work. With the MAV unable to provide work, instrumentalists' commitment logically disappeared. The same would apply to any functionaries whose motivation lay in the perks the Works Council had previously been able to dispense to them. By mid-1930, it was evident that the financial restrictions placed on the works and the general reduction in demand during the depression would mean that the works could not operate at full capacity for the foreseeable future. With lower employment levels the Works Council would generate less income and thus have little to offer in the way of perks. Without perks, the commitment of instrumentally motivated functionaries too began to fall away, further buckling the closed front necessary for effective union action.

The MAV was further handicapped in that the supply of funds generated by Works Council subsidies and MAV subscriptions had dried up during the period of shutdown. Consequently the MAV could not rely on a support operation being launched, as in 1925, by its previous beneficiaries in the *Kinderfreunde* and elsewhere. The union's position was made worse still by the extensive rationalisation of the production line which had taken place after August 1929. This had reduced the dependence of the works on skilled labour, increasing the significance of unskilled workers, with their generally weaker attachment to trade unionism. The new management at the works recognised this and sought to exploit the implications of rationalisation by driving a wedge between unskilled workers and the skilled worker-oriented MAV, displaying a tactical acumen which contrasted strongly with its predecessor's ineptitude in 1925. Accordingly it added the promise of a substantial increase in lower-end wages - i.e. those of the unskilled - to its original terms in the attempt to 'divide and rule' by undermining the cohesion of MAV organisation.[43]

The 'divide and rule' tactic was repeated in a different form a few days later in an act of coercion designed to circumvent the right to the Works Council to negotiate on behalf of the workforce. Management appealed to those workers (also members of the MAV works organisation) still at work in the small bicycle and ball-bearing factories annexed to the car works to accept its conditions for the resumption of *car* production. If an overwhelming majority of the bicycle and ball-bearing workers accepted the stated conditions on behalf of the car workers, they would be 'permitted' to keep their jobs, otherwise ... [44]

The pursuit of such aggressive tactics, more reminiscent of the Styrian than the Steyr tradition, underlines the new bargaining power management enjoyed after the long shutdown of car production. Although the next stages of the conflict are unclear, it seems that this new aggression was serious enough for it to merit the intervention of the National Executive of the MAV. Against the opposition of the local MAV, the National Executive apparently stepped in and accepted management's conditions. This action provoked intense criticism from the Steyr MAV at the MAV National Congress of September 1930. Both the president of the Steyr-Werke Works Council, August Moser, and his fellow Works Councillor, Franz Schrangl, attacked the National Executive's intervention and capitulation to the Steyr-Werke management.[45] Moser complained that wage cuts and the elimination of union rights should not be accepted without resistance, even in the face of high unemployment levels. On the contrary, it was, he asserted, still possible for unions in certain firms - like his - to assert themselves and hold out against employers.[46] But, he continued:

> ... it often happens that the Works Councillors are shut out of negotiations and that only the more senior functionaries are involved. We Works Councillors wish to protest against such tactics and therefore appeal to the Executive that such things do not happen again in the future ... Day-in day-out we do the spadework, but when it comes to the moment when the cause should decisively be defended, someone brings up the catchword 'crisis', and the battle is given up without a determined fight.[47]

It is, however, unlikely that the defiant attitude of Moser and Schrangl and their calls for a more activist and offensive approach to industrial relations would have stood any chance of defending the MAV's position if the National Executive had not intervened. Ten months' unemployment had undermined the rank and file will to resist, had exposed the eroding commitment of instrumentalists, and had broken off the supply of funds to potential support organisations within the wider Social Democratic movement. In addition, rationalisation had further weakened the MAV's bargaining hand by reducing the dependence of the works on skilled workers. In these circumstances, the intervention of the National Executive was the product of an entirely realistic assessment of power relations in the Steyr-Werke, and can best be seen as an exercise in damage limitation designed to maintain an organisational presence of the MAV at the works. This interpretation is given added weight when the implications of the 'Anti-Terror Law' of 5 April 1930 are taken into account.

The 'Anti-Terror Law' reflected the conservative perceptions of Social Democratic 'terrorism' at the workplace which were discussed in Chapter One: 'Terrorism' consisted of discriminatory closed shop arrangements and the associated compulsory payment of subscriptions and political levies to Social Democratic organisations. To counter such 'terrorism', the law was designed to ensure a 'negative right of association' at the workplace: the right of the individual *not to have to* join a particular (i.e. Social Democratic) labour organisation, and the right *not to have to* pay any kind of (Social Democratic) trade union subscription or political levy.[48] The 'Anti-Terror Law' was thus aimed explicitly at undermining the organisational cohesion of the FTUs and at reducing their financial strength. Its implementation had serious implications for the June 1930 conflict at the Steyr-Werke. Some of the rights the local MAV was committed to defend were now *illegal*. A full-blown union mobilisation in their defence could have given management the pretext to deny an 'illegal' MAV recognition in industrial relations and to draft in a more management-friendly bargaining partner from the range of non-Social Democratic trade unions in Austria. In this respect it is interesting to note that a *Heimwehr* list won 5% of the vote in the 1930 Works Council election at the Steyr-Werke (before disappearing again).[49] The MAV National Executive's intervention can be seen from this perspective as a successful attempt to prevent the MAV in Steyr from following its counterpart in Upper Styria and being replaced on the shopfloor by the *Heimwehr's* 'Independent' Union. This is especially so since there is evidence that the MAV at the Steyr-Werke somehow managed, despite the 'Anti-Terror Law', to retain a near-closed organisation on the shopfloor through to 1934.[50]

The realistic assessment by the MAV National Executive of power relations in the Steyr-Werke was confirmed when a mass meeting of car workers was held early in July 1930 to vote on management's terms for resuming production. Only *ten* of those present rejected the terms,[51] reflecting the new-found impotence of the union. As a result top pay rates were cut, lower-end wages increased and the MAV's catalogue of extra-statutory rights formally abolished: the MAV's closed shop and central dues deduction were scrapped, confirming the provisions of the 'Anti-Terror Law'; political activity on the shopfloor was proscribed; newspapers and other publications could no longer be hawked; and no political notices could be posted in the works. In addition, the Works Council levy on wages was reduced to the statutory level, and Works Councillors now had to carry out their tasks in their own time with no financial support from the firm.[52]

It is against the background of this humiliating expulsion of the MAV from its previous positions of power at the Steyr-Werke that the protests of Moser and Schrangl at the 1930 MAV National Congress need to be seen. Put simply, their local 'world' was falling in as the positions of power they had built up and exploited since the First World War were swept away. Moreover, this 'world' was not just falling in in the Steyr-Werke, but also, more broadly, in Steyr as a whole. Just as MAV powers had been central to the entrenchment of the local Social Democratic *Hochburg* in the 1920s, so the removal of those powers in the face of economic crisis, assertive management and national legislation fatally undermined the bases of the Social Democratic *Hochburg* after 1930. Moser and Schrangl were expressing their frustration and anger at the loss of the stronghold. They were also venting that anger at a national union leadership which had not only proved unable to help out but which also seemed to have accelerated the process of decline by fatalistically 'selling out' to the Steyr-Werke management. Their protest in this sense looked beyond the narrow realm of industrial relations and reflected a wider disaffection with the inability of the national-level Social Democratic movement to defend its outposts in the provinces. As such it was one of the first indications of the emergence of an opposition grouping within the local Social Democratic movement in the early 1930s, which began to oppose and reject with progressively increasing vehemence the priorities and politics of its national leaders.

The sense of frustration which fed this emerging intra-movement opposition was compounded by the experience of the MAV in the Steyr-Werke in the years 1930-1934. These were years in which the management dominance established in 1929-1930 was consolidated. This was largely due to the continuing economic problems which afflicted the works and maintained local unemployment at a high level. Having overcommitted itself in taking over the BCA in 1929, Rothschild's Credit-Anstalt itself collapsed in May 1931. After the Austrian National Bank had assured its future, the Credit-Anstalt's financial assistance to industry, which had not been especially bountiful before May 1931, was further curtailed. A result was that the level of car production in Steyr had to be reduced in July 1931 to six per day, when seventeen per day had been made a few weeks beforehand, and when fifty per day could have been produced if the works was operating at full capacity.[53] In view of the continuingly high unemployment which resulted from undercapacity at the car works, there was always a reservoir of unemployed workers willing and able to replace current employees. This 'reserve army' of the unemployed compounded the MAV's weakness and allowed the Steyr-Werke management to abandon any form of consultation or negotiation and rule, in effect, by decree in the works.

In March 1931, for example, a number of manual workers were sacked for refusing to accept management's decrees on working hours and conditions.[54] In December 1931, both manual and white-collar workers were given an ultimatum on wages to the effect that 'the works will be completely shut down if the white collar and manual workers do not unconditionally accept the proposed wage and salary cuts by 4pm'. After the MAV called management's bluff, 80 manual workers were immediately sacked and another 170 promised the same fate if the union did not comply. Unsurprisingly, the MAV then backed down.[55] By February 1934, management even felt able to ignore the MAV completely and to take up negotiations on a new collective agreement with the *Viennese* (!) Christian Metalworkers' Union. It was confidently announced that the MAV would be 'decisively finished off' and rumoured that there would be a forced enrolment of manual workers into the Christian union.[56]

The negotiations between management and the Christian union provoked an unexpectedly passionate response from a previously supine MAV and its members. Meetings held by the MAV to protest against management's actions and the terms offered to the Christian union were the best attended for years and produced passionate opposition to management's intentions. As a result of this apparently determined mood among the workforce, management abruptly dropped negotiations with the Christian union.[57]

The success of the MAV in forcing a management backdown in February 1934 does not, of course, reflect any change in the balance of power in industrial relations at the Steyr-Werke. The MAV was probably at its weakest point in conventional terms of union strength, with only around a thousand workers employed at the works, ranged against a 'reserve army' of 3,600 registered unemployed in Steyr itself and another 4,000 in the surrounding area.[58] The explanation for the MAV's successful defiance of management lies rather in the broader political situation of 1933-1934.

By early February 1934, the dictatorship of the Christian Social Chancellor, Engelbert Dollfuss, had been established for over ten months. These months had seen a gradual, systematic, 'salami-tactic' suppression of the remaining bases of Social Democratic power and influence in Austrian politics (parliament, the *Schutzbund*, the Social Democratic press, the Chambers of Labour, Red Vienna). An increasingly fatalistic national leadership of the Social Democratic movement had acquiesced passively in the establishment of dictatorship and the erosion of Social Democratic power. This acquiescence had provoked increasing dissatisfaction in the movement, particularly at the local level. The local level, isolated and neglected in the internal politics of the movement, had already experienced the progressive erosion of its provincial strongholds and was now forced to stand by as the same process repeated itself at the national level. Its dissatisfaction was manifested in increasing opposition to the passivity and fatalism of the national leadership and in growing calls for an active defence of what remained of the movement. This dissatisfaction was reflected in Steyr in the consolidation of an opposition faction during 1933 which unconditionally rejected the passivity of the national leadership (and of a similarly minded local counterpart). It was led by Moser and Schrangl, who had first displayed their opposition to the passivity and acquiescence of the national level in the MAV-management conflict of 1930. It had its support in the workforce at the Steyr-Werke, the Steyr *Schutzbund* and the local Social Democratic youth movement. By early 1934, this opposition was willing, even determined - given sufficient provocation - to put up violent resistance to dictatorship.

These themes are developed at length in the final chapter of this book, but provide in this chapter the necessary background for assessing the conflict in early 1934 over the right of the MAV to represent the Steyr-Werke workforce. For Moser, Schrangl and their supporters on the shopfloor, this was not an issue limited to the confines of the works, but rather reflected wider political developments in Austria. At the turn of the year, Dollfuss had issued a further series of anti-Social Democratic decrees, one of which sought to eliminate Social Democratic influence in Works Councils. Management's actions at the start of February 1934 were presumably an attempt to put the new decree into practice. This was very much the last straw for Moser, Schrangl and colleagues. The MAV's control over the Works Council of the Steyr-Werke was effectively the last bastion of Social Democratic power in Steyr. The attempt to remove it compounded the sense of frustration felt at the progressive erosion of local Social Democratic power since 1930 and was seen as sufficient provocation to take to the streets in active resistance to dictatorship. In Moser's words:

> As long as the workforce is behind us, the unreasonable course taken by management will be rejected. It will come to a strike, and we will, of course, set up a picket line. This could cause clashes with the police, the gendarmerie and other reactionary elements. We have a certain police official in Steyr ... who is a suspected National

Socialist. If there is any trouble, he will certainly join in with his people. And then there is the *Heimwehr*, which would, of course, intervene immediately, and that will trigger hostilities. And we expect the support of the whole Austrian working class.[59]

It was for this reason - the commitment of the MAV to resist violently any further attacks on the Social Democratic movement - that management backed down in early February 1934. It was unwilling to spark a conflict which, given the mood of the workforce, could easily escalate into violence. It could, in any case, reasonably expect that the Dollfuss government would remove the remnants of FTU power in the near future. That expectation was fulfilled just days later in the aftermath of the Civil War of mid-February 1934 when Dollfuss decreed the abolition of the FTUs and thus ended the presence of the MAV in the Steyr-Werke.[60]

This chapter has set up some of the central themes which run through the rest of the case study of Social Democracy in Steyr which forms the core of Part Two of this book. These are, in conclusion, worth reviewing. An issue of fundamental importance is that the MAV, unlike most other provincial FTUs, was able not just to establish, but also to maintain a decisive advantage in industrial relations, against employer opposition, throughout the 1920s. As the following chapter shows, that advantage, as manifested in particular in the MAV's powers of patronage in the local labour force, was utterly crucial in the establishment of a local Social Democratic *Hochburg* whose scale and scope was unparalleled in provincial Austria.

The MAV's powers were not, however, sustainable in the economic and political conditions which prevailed after 1929. In these conditions its advantage in industrial relations was lost and it became exposed to the forms of employer dominance which had already been in most cases the experience of provincial FTUs for some years. The loss of the MAV's powers was, as the following chapter again shows, equally crucial in the collapse of the local Social Democratic *Hochburg*. More broadly, though, and as a result, the loss of power, and with it the 'backbone' of the local Social Democratic movement, provoked a deep resentment and frustration among some of those who had previously wielded that power. This frustration was, in the 1930s, increasingly directed at a national party leadership which proved signally unable to prevent the erosion of Social Democratic power either in the context of local-level politics, or more broadly and in later years, in the national political arena in Austria. This growing frustration, as the discussion in a number of the following chapters shows, led to the emergence of a militant activism in various organisations in the local Social Democratic movement which coalesced in 1933-1934 into an opposition faction which sought release from the perceived inadequacies of the movement's leadership in violent resistance to dictatorship.

Notes

1   See Gulick (1948), 175-255; Klenner (1951), passim; and on codetermination, Wilhelm Filla, *Zwischen Integration und Klassenkampf. Sozialgeschichte der betrieblichen Mitbestimmung in Österreich*, Europaverlag, Vienna (1981), 60-118.
2   See Staudinger (1985), 72-73.
3   Either through formal agreements with employers or through the more informal means of threatening industrial action in cases where management planned to take on non-FTU labour. See ibid., 73; Filla, 82.
4   See e.g. Filla (1981), 82-95; Staudinger, 72-78.
5   See e.g. Dreier (1984), 244; Lewis (1991), 89; Nasko (1986), 241-243.
6   Gerhard Botz, 'Streik in Österreich 1918-1975. Probleme und Ergebnisse einer quantitativen Analyse', in: Botz, Hautmann, Konrad, Weidenholzer (1978), 815-816.
7   See e.g. Nasko (1986), 145, 235, 241; Staudinger (1985), 72-73; Dreier (1984), 183; Oberkofler (1979), 186.
8   Although Table 4.1 shows that Tirol and Salzburg retained a relatively high proportion of union members over the period 1922-1931, it should be remembered that they started from a low base. They never managed to attract sufficient numbers in absolute terms to carve out an important role in industrial relations.
9   See e.g. Bauer (1988e), 113-124; Dreier (1984), 158-186; Oberkofler (1979), 182-202.
10   The term is that of Lewis (1991), on whose work the following account is based.
11   On St. Pölten, see Nasko (1986), 258-260, and on the Upper Austrian coalfield, see Hummer (1989).
12   See e.g. Flanner (1983), 3-15.
13   In which year the forerunner of the MAV, the 'Association of Iron and Metalworkers and their Labourers' was founded. This in turn had drawn on an organisational tradition extending back to the foundation of the Steyr Workers' Educational Association in 1869. For a description of these early organisational developments see Radmoser (n.d.), 12-39.
14   Josef Stockinger, *Zeit, die prägt. Arbeiterbewegung in Steyr*, Gutenberg, Linz (1988), 101.
15   The MAV typically won between 80-90% of the vote in Works Council elections. The remainder was won by a Communist list which remained, however, organisationally within the MAV. Only in the 1930 election did a third list - that of the *Heimwehr* - stand for election, winning 5.1% of the vote. This election followed mass dismissals at the works in 1930 which affected Social Democrats disproportionately, and coincided with management attempts to undermine the MAV by encouraging the *Heimwehr's* 'Independent' Union. The *Heimwehr* did not, however, establish a lasting presence and failed to put forward a list in subsequent years. See below and in Stockinger (1988), 102.
16   The following list draws from *Bericht des Vorstandes des Österreichischen Metallarbeiterverbandes über seine Tätigkeit in den Jahren 1924, 1925, 1926,*

Verlag des Österreichischen Metallarbeiterverbandes, Vienna (1927), 24-26, 161; AVA BKA Inneres 22/Oberösterreich Karton 5100: 168.481-30; OÖAZ 15-9-1928, 5; SZ 22-6-1930, 6.

17   Stockinger (1988), 113-114.

18   See OÖAZ 12-12-1925, 2-3.

19   This point is developed further in the next chapter.

20   STB 30-3-1930, 8.

21   Given that around 6,000 manual workers were employed at the time. See STB 6`4-1930, 11.

22   This implication is supported by one of the points in the catalogue of non-statutory rights won by the MAV at the works - that Works Councillors in any case were paid as normal for Works Council activities undertaken in the firm's time. For them at least, these payments were naked, 100% perks.

23   SZ 23-3-1930, 4.

24   See the national *Kinderfreunde* annual reports, *Rote Saat*, 1926-1929.

25   See e.g. SZ 1-10-1925, 2; LVS 3-10-1925, 2.

26   STB 30-9-1925, 1 reproduces the dismissal notice for the 28 manual workers. See also STB 1-10-1925, 1; AZ 30-9-1925, 8; 7-11-1925, 7; SZ 1-10-1925, 2.

27   STB 30-9-1925, 1.

28   See e.g. STB 2-10-1925, 3.

29   *Bericht des Vorstandes des Österreichischen Metallarbeiterverbandes* (1927), 156; STB 2-10-1925, 3; 28-11-1925, 1. All four conflicts are reported in AZ and ÖMA throughout September and October 1925.

30   These terms are reprinted in *Bericht des Vorstandes des Österreichischen Metallarbeiterverbandes* (1927), 156.

31   See *Bericht über die wirtschaftlichen Verhältnisse in Oberösterreich im Jahre 1926*, Verlag der Kammer für Handel, Gewerbe und Industrie in Linz, Linz (1927).

32   STB 1-10-1925, 1-2.

33   See *Sechzig Briefe der Solidarität*, Jungbrunnen, Vienna (1926).

34   AZ 13-11-1925, 7.

35   STB 24-11-1925, 1; AZ 1-12-1925, 7; *Sechzig Briefe der Solidarität* (1926), 7.

36   OÖAZ 5-12-1925, 2.

37   STB 9-10-1925, 2; 13-10-1925, 1, 7; 15-10-1925, 3; 3-11-1925, 4.

38   The full terms of the settlement are reprinted in *Bericht des Vorstandes des Österreichischen Metallarbeiterverbandes* (1927), 163, and are discussed in STB 28-11-1925, 1-3.

39   SZ 6-2-1930, 1.

40   See *Rote Saat* 1926, 42-43; 1927, 61-62; 1928, 59-60; 1929, 22, 58.

41   This point is completely missed by Josef Stockinger in the only other existing account of the lockout. See Stockinger (1988), 107-108.

42   SZ 3-1-1932, 4.

43   SZ 24-6-1930, 6; ÖVW Bilanzen 28-6-1930, 453-454.

44   AVA BKA Inneres 22/Oberösterreich Karton 5100: 168.481-30.

45   *Verhandlungen des 15. Verbandstages der Österreichischen Metallarbeiter*, Verlag des Österreichischen Metallarbeiterverbandes, Vienna (1931), 146, 157-158.

46   Ibid., 146-147.

47   Ibid. C.f. Interview with Josef Mayrhofer, 4-7-1986.

48   See Klenner (1953), 850-858; Karl Stubenvoll, 'Zur Genesis und Funktion des Anti-Terror-Gesetzes', in Helmut Konrad, Wolfgang Maderthaner (Eds.), *Neuere Studien zur Arbeitergeschichte. Zum 25jährigen Bestehen des Vereins für Geschichte der Arbeiterbewegung*, Europaverlag, Vienna (1984).

49   Stockinger (1988), 102, and footnote 14 above.

50   See Peter Kammerstätter (Ed.), *Der Aufstand des Republikanischen Schutzbundes am 12. Februar in Oberösterreich. Eine Sammlung von Materialien, Dokumenten und Aussagen von Beteiligten*. Band II, unpublished manuscript, Linz (n.d.), 1123-1124.

51   OÖAZ 12-7-1930, 3.

52   AVA BKA Inneres 22/Oberösterreich Karton 5100: 168.481-30.

53   AVA BKA Inneres 13/6 Karton 2382: 180.781-31; 164.285-31; ÖVW Bilanzen 4-8-1928, 523.

54   OÖAZ 28-3-1931, 6.

55   Dokumentation der Kammer für Arbeiter und Angestellte in Wien, Kommunalpolitik 1928-1932/33: *Neues Wiener Tagblatt* 30-12-1931; AVA BKA Inneres 13/6 Karton 2382: 104.738-32.

56   See STB 6-2-1934, 5; Magistrat der Stadt Steyr, Sitzungsniederschriften des Gemeinderates der Stadt Steyr, 15. Sitzung, 28-12-1933, 131; Kammerstätter (n.d.), 1125-1127.

57   Ibid., 1127; STB 6-2-1934, 5.

58   STB 8-2-1934, 5.

59   Quoted in Kammerstätter (n.d.), 1127.

60   One ironic feature of the Civil War in Steyr, given the reluctance of the Steyr-Werke management to risk provoking violence, was the fact that the first local fatality was the extremely unpopular *Werksdirektor* Herbst. See Stockinger (1988), 161.

5 Patronage, Power and Impotence in the Social Democratic *Hochburg*[1]

The following two chapters discuss further the implications of the insular and defensive mentality which pervaded Social Democracy in Steyr, and which was typical of a movement pinned down at the local level behind the 'front-lines' of provincial politics. Chapter Six presents a detailed examination of the network of Social Democratic auxiliary organisations in Steyr which helped to demarcate and shield the local supporters of Social Democracy from the hostile 'outside' world of provincial conservatism. This chapter focuses first, though, on the significance of political patronage as a feature of *Hochburg* politics in Steyr. The discussion in Chapter Three has already noted the potential for patronage to be used as a means of deepening the organisational penetration and control of the Social Democratic movement within its provincial *Hochburgen*. This chapter builds on and confirms that discussion, arguing that patronage was consciously employed in Steyr and elsewhere as a means of drawing a local 'clientele' into a relationship of indebtedness to the movement and that this sense of indebtedness was used to consolidate the movement's influence at the local level.

The chapter's first section establishes a framework for the examination of political patronage in the context of the First Republic by drawing on the insights provided by the study of party patronage in Second Republic Austria. The subsequent sections then give a detailed analysis of the use and implications of Social Democratic patronage in Steyr. Section two examines the patronage 'resources' available to the Social Democratic movement in Steyr and the ways in which these were employed to deepen Social Democratic organisational influence over local politics and society. Particular emphasis is placed on the MAV's powers of patronage in the local labour market, which, as the last chapter indicated, formed the 'backbone' of the local *Hochburg*, although attention is also given of the patronage resources controlled by the SDAP-run Town Council. Section three examines the finely balanced and fragile relationship which existed in the town between Social Democratic patrons and their local clients. The implications of this fragile relationship are then drawn out in section four, which deals with the erosion of the movement's wider social and political influence after it lost of control over local patronage resources following the economic collapse of 1929. The central theme is that patronage politics, along with the *Hochburgen* they helped to sustain, proved to be an unstable and transient means of securing political power.

The Politics of Party Patronage in the First Republic

The use and abuse of party patronage[2] are important characteristics of the political system of the Austrian Second Republic.[3] A large public sector and an interventionist regulatory tradition together created an enormous potential for the distribution of political patronage after the Second World War. This potential was recognised and tapped after 1945 in the practice of *'Proporz'*, the distribution of posts in state ministries according to party strengths. It was subsequently developed further and institutionalised in the service of the parties of the Grand Coalition of 1947-1966, the ÖVP and the SPÖ. In this way patronage became a central means of political mobilisation in the Austrian party system - both in terms of voter-generation and membership recruitment - which outlived the break-up of the Grand Coalition in 1966. Party patronage has therefore remained, even in the 1990s, and despite growing public disillusionment with patronage politics, a more or less entrenched feature of the Austrian political system.[4]

In view of this extensive influence of party patronage in the Second Republic, it is remarkable that there has so far been no systematic and detailed investigation of the scale and significance of the phenomenon in the First Republic. The parties which have shaped the politics of the Second Republic are, after all, in most respects direct successors of the major parties of the inter-war years. It is certainly not inconceivable that the patronage strategies of Second Republic parties had their roots in the activities of their predecessors in the First Republic (or, indeed, in other eras of modern Austrian history). This supposition is supported by a brief theoretical discussion of the bases of patronage politics.[5]

The basis of party patronage is the possession by parties and their related organisations of control over access to certain scarce and desirable patronage 'resources'. Such resources include, just to name some of the more common examples, tax concessions, subsidies and other financial benefits from the public purse as well as housing, jobs and other material benefits available either in the public or the private sectors. Party patronage consists of the distribution of such patronage resources in a discriminatory way which is designed to build up a privileged, and therefore grateful and indebted party 'clientele'. This clientele, by accepting party patronage, obliges itself to some kind of political 'repayment', normally votes, party membership or some other form of commitment to the party cause. These political 'repayments' help to consolidate the power of the party concerned. The mutual relationship of party and clientele is normally asymmetrically tilted in favour of the party. The financial and material resources which lie in the party's gift are often of crucial, existential importance to the individual client, whereas the 'repayment' of any one client - *one* vote or *one* membership card - is only of marginal importance to the party. The party is therefore the stronger partner in the relationship - but only if it can maintain its control over access to the desired patronage resources. If it loses that control, it will, in the course of time, also lose its clients, and the relationship will dissolve.

With the above in mind, it is clear that there was at the very least a considerable potential for party patronage in the First Republic. Parties did, at the national, provincial and local levels, have a power of disposal over public finances and public goods. They also had links to private sector interests which brought patronage resources within their grasp. These points have periodically been acknowledged in the literature in discussions of the parties of the Right in the First Republic. Instances of right-wing party patronage in the public sector would, for example, include the discriminatory (i.e. anti-Social Democratic) army recruitment (and dismissal) policies of the CSP Army Minister Carl Vaugoin, the discriminatory allocation of positions in the administrative apparatus of the province of Salzburg by the CSP-led provincial government, the discriminatory allocation of public housing by the CSP in Innsbruck, and the financial malpractice conducted by the German Nationalist Party in the Salzburg Town Council for its members' own benefit.[6] As regards the private sector, a number of banking scandals unfolded during the First Republic which uncovered extensive corruption by CSP and German Nationalist politicians,[7] and - as was made clear in Chapter One - any number of discriminatory, anti-Social Democratic, staffing policies were conducted in the private sector, in some of which cases the CSP[8] and most notoriously the *Heimwehr*[9] controlled access to jobs.

None of these examples has, unfortunately, been discussed in detail from the analytical perspective of party patronage (although they raise obvious and often striking parallels to Second Republic patronage strategies, especially those of the CSP's successor, the ÖVP). Rather, they have tended to feed into the partisanship of writing on contemporary history in Austria. They have generally featured in works sympathetic to the SDAP as thinly disguised condemnations of the 'moral standards' of right-wing parties, and/or as examples of the overwhelming odds stacked against the Social Democrats during the First Republic. On one level, such depictions are entirely valid. The parties of the Right in the First Republic did not have especially high 'moral standards' and did manage to assemble a formidable battery of anti-Social Democratic discriminatory powers. That is not to say, though, that SDAP 'standards' were necessarily always and everywhere higher or that the SDAP itself did not use powers available to it, where it could, in a discriminatory way.

Unfortunately, such questions about the self-serving manipulation of political power by Social Democrats have not been raised in the often partisan literature on the Social Democratic movement. As the Introduction to this book pointed out, this is a glaringly obvious failing in work on Red Vienna, where the SDAP city administration controlled access to the immense patronage resources which derived from Vienna's status as city-cum-province: the massive financial resources of the city budget, the numerous jobs available in the municipal workforce, and above all the much-sought fruits of the city housing programme. During the First Republic some 60,000 flats were built by the Vienna City Council. It does not seem conceivable that these flats - and the other potential patronage resources in Vienna - were not distributed, in the confrontational atmosphere of First Republic politics, to build up and to favour an indebted Social Democratic clientele. This point was indeed acknowledged by a contemporary observation on the city housing programme: 'Outside Utopia one cannot anticipate that the public administration of extensive properties occupied by voters can be kept free from partisanship'.[10] Unfortunately this observation has not been picked up by a post-war historiographical tradition which has elevated Red Vienna and its policies to icons of the Austrian Left.[11]

This gaping lacuna in the study of the public administration of Red Vienna is matched in the literature on Social Democracy in the provinces. No effort has been made to examine the scope and significance of Social Democratic patronage in the provinces, despite the fact that there was a clear (albeit limited) potential for the development of patronage strategies. Although the SDAP was kept away from the exercise of significant power in provincial government,[12] it was nevertheless either the majority party or the leading coalition partner in hundreds of local councils throughout Austria.[13] These councils did not, of course, have a wide range of autonomous powers at their disposal. The powers they did possess still brought with them, though, modest patronage resources, in particular the opportunity to dispose 'creatively' of the council budget,[14] of jobs in the council workforce[15] and of flats built in (small-scale) local public housing schemes.[16] The extent to which these resources were distributed in a discriminatory way remains, without further research, uncertain, although occasional clear hints have been dropped to suggest they were: in local scandals about the distribution of council monies in Eisenerz and Bruck an der Mur in Upper Styria,[17] in suggestions that posts in municipally-run local police forces were reserved for Social

Democrats in St. Pölten and possibly Bruck again,[18] and in complaints about the distribution of public housing in SDAP-run St. Pölten.[19]

Moreover, as the last chapter showed, Social Democratic FTUs also controlled the distribution of local jobs wherever they were able to establish closed shops. In other words, there existed a clear potential for the development of patronage strategies by councils and FTUs in the strongholds of Social Democracy across the provinces. That potential was tapped with great effectiveness by the Social Democratic movement in Steyr.

Patronage and Power in Steyr

In no other area was the quest of Social Democrats in Steyr to seal their town off from the 'outside' world and build it up yet further as a *Hochburg* of the movement pursued so systematically as in the use of patronage. The Social Democrats consciously used the levers of political power available to them to generate highly desirable patronage resources. Anyone wanting to secure access to those resources had, of course to rely on their benevolence and good favour. In this way the local movement was able to build up a large, indebted clientele which was bound to the organisations whose favours it had received. This patronage strategy thus acted as an instrument to deepen the organisational penetration of the Social Democratic movement into Steyr society. It was based on the manipulation of the powers of the MAV, as discussed in the last chapter, and the Town Council, which was controlled by the SDAP throughout the First Republic, and was conducted in three main arenas: the local labour market, the municipal police force, and the Social Democratic functionary network.

The most significant arm of the Social Democratic patronage strategy in Steyr was the control exerted by the MAV over the local labour market by virtue of its manual worker closed shop at the Steyr-Werke. In the years of highest employment at the works in the late

Table 5.1 The MAV and the Steyr Labour Market 1927-1933

Year	1927	1928	1929	1930	1932	1932	1933
MAV jobs	3,757	5,316	5,891	2,198	1,734	1,057	1,056

Note: *as represented in the level of manual worker employment at the Steyr-Werke on 1 July in each year.*
Source: *Kammer für Arbeiter und Angestellte in Linz a. d. Donau, Verzeichnis jener Betriebe, welche über fünf Kammerumlagepflichtige beschäftigen, 1927-1933 editions, Linz (1927-1933).*

1920s, up to 6,000 local jobs at the car works were dependent on MAV patronage (see Table 5.1). In a town of some 20,000 inhabitants, this degree of control over local job allocation represented an enormous patronage resource.[20]

The second major arena of Social Democratic patronage in Steyr was the local police force. The local police were a municipal force directed by the Town Hall. This local policing power was unusual in that the federal police force was normally responsible for law and order in Austria's towns, while the provincial gendarmeries normally policed rural areas. Steyr's local autonomy in policing matters (like that of St. Pölten and Bruck an der Mur mentioned above) was the remnant of an imperial privilege granted to Steyr in the nineteenth century. It was jealously guarded by the Town Council after the First World War[21] and was used to purge the police force of non-Social Democrats during the 1920s and to replace them with party members and activists. By 1930, according to reports of the federal police in Linz, only one of eight officers in Steyr could be assessed as a 'solid bourgeois type' (*'gutbürgerlich'*). The remaining seven officers and most of the 50-plus constables were card-carrying Social Democrats.[22]

The force fell under the direction of the SDAP mayor, Franz Sichlrader, and his deputy Julius Rußmann, both of whom used their powers to ensure that the practice of law and order in the town was conducted in the interests of the party. This political manipulation became most evident (and, as will be seen below, especially controversial) when the *Heimwehr* was attempting to gain a foothold in the town in 1929-1930. The police openly discriminated against *Heimwehr* members but managed to be 'looking the other way' when *Heimwehr* members fell victim to sometimes violent intimidation by Social Democrats.[23] The ability to manipulate the police was tremendously significant in Austrian politics. The events of 15 July 1927 had shown how the police - even in the Viennese 'citadel' - could be used as a weapon against the Social Democratic movement. This, as the local Christian Socials immediately recognised and bewailed in 1927 under the impression of the events in Vienna,[24] was simply not possible in Steyr. On the contrary, the police could be, and indeed were, used in the following years to defend the local *Hochburg* against the resurgent forces of the Right in Austrian politics.

The final major element of Social Democratic patronage in Steyr concerned the manipulation of the powers of MAV and Town Council to grant material perks to union and party functionaries. As was shown in the last chapter, the MAV was able to reward its functionaries in the Steyr-Werke with a Works Council bonus payment equivalent to around half a day's normal pay per week. Moreover, 'plum' jobs in a strictly party-book municipal administration were reserved for key party activists. The Director of the Steyr *Magistrat* (the local 'civil service') and primary adviser to the mayor, Ferdinand Häuslmayr, was for example a leading member of the SDAP District Executive Committee. Similarly, the post of manager of the Municipal Enterprises, the local public sector, was reserved for the military leader of the Steyr *Schutzbund* (above because of the logistical support the transport and storage facilities of the Municipal Enterprises could offer the Social Democratic paramilitaries)[25]. In terms of pay, hours of work, pension arrangements and tax concessions, these activists - and the other card-carrying Social Democrats in municipal employment - enjoyed conditions of employment markedly superior to those of equivalent jobs in the private sector and elsewhere in the Austrian public sector.[26] The implication is clear: union functionaries and municipal employees were in substantial material debt to the Social Democratic movement.

It emerges clearly from the above that patronage was a central feature of Social Democratic politics in Steyr. The patronage resources available to the Social Democratic movement were purposefully exploited, above all in the labour market, to recruit an indebted clientele. In addition, the activities of the municipal police force were politicised and manipulated on the basis of a party-book staffing policy to underline the local preeminence of the movement and to discriminate against its opponents. And finally, the whole patronage system was glued together by the provision of perks to union and party functionaries whose commitment was essential to the management of Social Democratic patronage resources of the MAV and the municipal administration.

This patronage system served to deepen the organisational penetration of the Steyr Social Democratic movement into the political and social fabric of the town. Through it the movement was able to establish an extensive control over areas of daily life which were not normally open to political manipulation (at least not by Social Democrats). The local political dominance of Social Democracy could in consequence extend far beyond the formal local political arenas of elections, town hall politics and industrial relations to become an integral component of the broader political culture of the town. This not only helped to enhance the perception that the Social Democrats in Steyr were willing and able to 'do something' for their supporters (and thus strengthened the grip of the movement over its adherents). It also, and perhaps more importantly, neutralised the local opponents of Social Democracy, who, enfeebled by the 'cocoon' of patronage in the town, were forced indignantly to accept and acknowledge Steyr's status as a *'rote Hochburg'*, a 'bastion' and 'bulwark' of Social Democratic power.[27]

The Fickle Relationship between Patrons and Clients

Social Democratic patronage in Steyr evidently had an unusually broad scope and a deep significance in consolidating the local *Hochburg*. With this in mind, the discussion now moves on to examine in more depth the character of the relationship between the givers and takers of patronage, between patrons and clients, in Steyr.

'Love at first job offer'

The essence of the relationship between patrons and clients in Steyr is easily distilled. The patrons in party and union needed a compliant clientele in order to secure and extend their political power in the town. And the clients accepted Social Democratic favours - and the obligations which went with them - in order to make their lives materially more comfortable. The bases of this relationship raise important questions about the quality of the commitment given by the clientele to the Social Democratic movement. In many cases it was undoubtedly a matter of rewarding long-term loyalty and commitment, of 'doing something' for the membership. Others, though, who lacked long-term ties and conviction and were recruited as passive or active members wholly or mainly because of the perks on offer did so for *instrumental* reasons. Their commitment was at least in part opportunistic and expedient, conditional on the ability of party or trade union to continue to supply the fruits of membership. Such instrumentalists were not 'conviction' Social Democrats and would in all probability not have joined party or union if perks were not on offer. Rather, they were inevitably, in many cases, political indifferents or - given the scale of patronage in Steyr, particularly in the labour market in the late 1920s - even outright opponents of the Social Democratic movement.[28] A significant part of the organisational strength of the movement in Steyr thus rested on the instrumentally motivated membership of non- and anti-Social Democrats.

This relationship between patronage and instrumentalism can be illustrated most clearly in the case of labour market patronage. In 1928-1929, 5,000-6,000 local jobs in the Steyr-Werke stood at the disposal of the MAV (see Table 5.1). In a town whose economy was dominated by this single works, many non-Social Democrats simply had to join Social Democratic organisations to stand a chance of finding a job. This applied in particular to the numerous new recruits of 1928-1929. An example has survived of a Catholic worker, a member of the Christian Metalworkers' Union, who was taken on at the works in September 1928. Asked about his union background, he declared his membership of the Christian union but stated his readiness nevertheless to *pay subscriptions* to the MAV (*einzuzahlen*).[29] In other words, his proposed commitment to the MAV was expressed purely in formal, financial terms, almost as an arrangement fee for being granted work. Also instructive in this context is the information supplied by a First Republic MAV Works Councillor at the car works, Alois Zehetner, who described the recruitment process as follows:

> When manual worker were taken on, the person concerned also had to get a signature from the Works Council. This decided 'Yes' or 'No'. *In the process, the recruitment into the trade union was completed if the person was not yet organised'.*[30]

In other words, MAV membership for many was simply a formality, a means to the end of finding work, and not an expression of commitment to free trade unionism. This was indeed a case of 'love at first job offer'!

In a similar vein, the bonuses received by MAV functionaries and the exemplary working conditions enjoyed by municipal employees indicate - although the evidence is less conclusive - that instrumental motivations also played a part in the Social Democratic functionary network. Even active members of the Social Democratic movement could be - as Robert Michels recognised in his analysis of the pre-First World War German labour movement - open to a commitment based not on conviction but material expediency:

> It is ... indisputable that to the average man the close association of his own economic existence with his dependence on the Socialist Party seems a sufficient excuse for the sacrifice of his own conviction in order to remain within a party with which he is in truth no longer in full sympathy.[31]

The End of the 'Affair'

The longer-term stability of such a patron-client relationship will normally depend on the ability of the political patron to maintain a high degree of control over access to the resources desired by their clients.[32] If the patron loses this control, the relationship is likely to break down. This point is particularly important in the context of patron-client relations in Steyr since Social Democratic control over local patronage resources, although extensive in the 1920s, was never secure in the longer term. The powers of patronage of both MAV and Town Hall in Steyr were always dependent on, indeed proportionate to, the level of employment at the Steyr-Werke. The major source of municipal income was a form of local income tax, to which the manual workforce of the Steyr-Werke, by far the largest employer in the local economy was easily the greatest aggregate contributor. The municipal budget, and thus implicitly the scale of municipal powers of patronage, was therefore dependent on the economic performance of the Steyr-Werke. Similarly, the MAV's powers of patronage in the local labour market and its ability to levy enough funds from the workforce to reward its functionary network, were even more directly dependent on employment levels at the works.

This dependence of Social Democratic patronage on the Steyr-Werke was by no means a problem during the 1920s, and particularly in 1928-1929, when employment levels were especially high. However, as Table 5.1 shows, the size of the manual workforce was slashed under the impact of the Great Depression and continued to decline into the 1930s. The economic problems of the Steyr-Werke inevitably had a devastating impact on the powers of patronage of the Social Democrats and their ability to maintain the patron-client relationship established during the 1920s.

An immediate effect was the decimation of the municipal budget. As employment levels fell at the car works, so did local income tax receipts, forcing the SDAP majority on the Town Council to introduce drastic economy measures. One of the first sacrifices was municipal control over the local police, an item which accounted in 1929 for fully one sixth of total municipal expenditure.[33] Negotiations between the Town Hall and the Federal Government in late 1929 led to agreement to 'federalise' the local police with effect from 1 July 1930. As it turned out (see below), the Social Democrats effectively lost their police powers rather earlier than July 1930. But even so, their willingness to bow to financial necessity and lose that rarity in Austria - a friendly and manipulable police force[34] - symbolises their inability to sustain their patronage network into the 1930s.

The most important aspect of Social Democratic patronage - the MAV's influence over the local labour market - was also decimated by the collapse in employment at the Steyr-Werke. Although the MAV was able to retain a more or less closed organisation in the works into the 1930s, the size of the workforce was a fraction of the pre-1930 level: in 1929 almost 6,000 had a 'Social Democratic' job in the car works; a year later it was just 2,198, and in 1933 barely more than 1,000 (see Table 5.1).

For the instrumentalists among the thousands of former car workers who had joined the MAV just to get a job, there was no logical reason to remain a member of the union. Organisational commitment to Social Democracy was no longer a passport to employment. As a result, instrumentally motivated members began to retract their support, as it were to cancel their part in the patron-client relationship, and thereby to loosen the 'hold' of Social Democracy over local politics and society. This tendency was enhanced as the material incentives associated with active membership in the movement began to disappear. The generous employment conditions of the municipal workforce were downgraded as council expenditure was cut back, and the MAV was forced to end the practice of paying its functionaries in the Steyr-Werke as its income too dried up. The Social Democratic patrons became ever less able to maintain the ties of instrumentally motivated clients to the movement.

The extent of instrumentalism in the Social Democratic movement - and therefore the extent of retracted instrumentalist support after 1929 - cannot easily be precisely quantified. If full membership lists were available (which they unfortunately are not) there would still be no way to distinguish between 'instrumentalists', 'conviction Social Democrats' or those with other forms of motivation. Studies of the motivation structures of party members in later, and better documented, eras have shown that a wide range of different motives can - often simultaneously - contribute to the decision to join a party.[35] Even in the analysis of party patronage in the Austrian Second Republic, where patronage has long been recognised as an important feature of the political system, attempts to distinguish instrumental from other types of motivation have been notoriously unreliable and in part contradictory.[36] It is therefore only possible to present a crude and impressionistic quantification of instrumentalism in the Social Democratic movement in Steyr, based on the scale of retracted support after 1929.[37]

It is interesting to note, for example, the reduced participation at SDAP events in 1930 as compared to their equivalents a year beforehand. In 1930 3,500 attended the Mayday celebrations in Steyr; in 1929 the figure had been around 5,000.[38] And when Otto Bauer, the most prominent SDAP leader, spoke at a mass meeting in the town in July 1930, 900 turned up to listen; in September 1929, a lesser-known member of the SDAP National Executive, Wilhelm Ellenbogen, had attracted 2,000.[39] More generally, the membership level of the Steyr SDAP fell by around 25% between 1929 and 1932.[40] Furthermore, as discussed in the previous chapter, only a handful of those present at a mass meeting of car workers in July 1930 voted to reject the draconian terms of the Steyr-Werke management for a resumption of car production. By this time it had become clear that the size of the workforce would remain for the foreseeable future much smaller than in the 1920s, undermining the MAV's ability to allocate jobs and distribute perks to its functionaries.

The sinking membership of the SDAP, the reduced levels of participation at party events and the acquiescence of the Steyr-Werke workforce symbolise the 'end of the affair' between Social Democratic patrons and instrumentalist clients in Steyr. After 1929 the Social

Democrats found themselves unable to maintain their control over access to patronage resources. As a result their previous clients no longer felt obliged to wave the party flag when required or to demonstrate a spurious trade union solidarity based on compulsion. This inevitably had wider implications for the maintenance of the local Social Democratic *Hochburg*. Up to the autumn of 1929, the political preeminence of the Social Democrats in Steyr was underpinned by their ability to neutralise opposition by making key aspects of daily life in the town dependent on their patronage. After the autumn of 1929, however, the patronage network began to disintegrate. The next section discusses how the declining ability to dispense patronage freed the town from its 'cocoon' of obligation to the Social Democratic movement and paved the way for the revival of local opposition.

Patronage and Impotence in Steyr

The first sign of challenge to the Social Democratic *Hochburg* was the foundation of a *Heimwehr* unit in Steyr on 10 August 1929. The aims of the *Heimwehr* unit were made clear at the inaugural meeting: the 'red foremen' were to be thrown out of the Steyr-Werke and Social Democracy in Steyr was to be 'overthrown' as in Vienna (i.e. on 15 July 1927) and Donawitz, the Upper Styrian town where the *Heimwehr's* 'Independent' Trade Union had all but eliminated Social Democratic influence in the works of the AMG.[41] A more immediate aim was to win the right to walk (or, more precisely, march upon) the streets of Steyr openly and unmolested, and thus to breach symbolically the fortifications of the Social Democratic *Hochburg*. To this end a series of parades and meetings were held in the second half of 1929 in the villages around Steyr both to drum up support and symbolically to 'approach' and 'encircle' the town.[42] Buoyed by this self-styled 'march on Steyr',[43] the *Heimwehr* felt confident enough by December 1929 to hold regular, informal, but fully-uniformed Sunday afternoon musters on Steyr's main square (deemed with some understatement and unusual irony to be 'Sunday strolls', as a means of avoiding potential municipal - i.e. SDAP - police restrictions on formal meetings).

The Social Democratic response to the symbolic provocation of the 'march on Steyr' and the subsequent *Heimwehr* musters in Steyr reflected an undiminished confidence in the power of patronage to secure political compliance. With tactics reminiscent to those which greeted the German Gymnastics Festival of July 1928,[44] the Social Democrats attempted to call in the 'debts' of their clients and convert their sense of obligation to the movement into a rebuff to the challenge of the *Heimwehr*. They were confident that they could either mobilise their clients directly - even physically - against the *Heimwehr*, or, at the very least, that they could neutralise any potential sympathies for the *Heimwehr* from within their clientele. This they attempted by generating a 'witchhunt' atmosphere in the town, designed to intimidate and deter both *Heimwehr* members and potential supporters. They organised, for example, a boycott of the businesses of *Heimwehr* sympathisers which was brashly proclaimed from advertising hoardings owned by the Town Council and which was supervised closely by detachments of the *Schutzbund*.[45] They also issued, with some success, a series of incitements to violence against *Heimwehr* members. For example, Vice-Mayor Russmann pregnantly stated that 'we simply do not let the *Heimwehr* into Steyr',[46] a sentiment the local party leader, Franz Schrangl expressed more explicitly in a party meeting:

> Prudence and reason will continue to be the mottoes of our party. But if we should be attacked ..., then we shall have reached our limit - get in there and thrash their skulls in![47]

Subsequently local farmers present in Steyr for the weekly market who wore the characteristic cock's feather or other livery of the *Heimwehr* were subject to vilification and intimidation.[48] More dramatically, the passage of *Heimwehr* vehicles through Steyr *en route* for a rally in a nearby village in October 1929 produced such uproar that the local police, despite its political allegiance, had to arrest 25 Social Democrats. Two Social Democrats even fired live shots at *Heimwehr* members returning from the festival.[49] This campaign of confrontation reached its highpoint, though, between December 1929 and February 1930 when the *Heimwehr* held its regular Sunday musters. Several hundred, mainly younger Social Democrats sought to defend the sanctity of Steyr's streets in open assaults on *Heimwehr* 'strollers'.[50]

The anti-*Heimwehr* 'witchhunt' was underpinned by the complicity of the municipal police. Constables were instructed by Mayor Sichlrader to close their eyes where possible to Social Democratic intimidation and faced reprimands if they tried to take action against Social Democratic offenders. If police action did become absolutely necessary, miscreants were dealt with with the utmost leniency: fines and periods of detention were kept to minimum, token levels and the files of those named in private prosecutions were conveniently 'lost' in the Town Hall.[51]

The Social Democrats were able in these ways to repulse the *Heimwehr* challenge in the short-term. The atmosphere of intimidation in the town was a clear deterrent to the expression of support for the *Heimwehr* in a situation where the Social Democrats controlled access to key patronage resources. This strategy could not, however, be maintained indefinitely. As was noted above, the Social Democrats began, from late 1929 onwards, to lose their powers of patronage in the Town Hall and Steyr-Werke. At the same time as they were attempting to secure the compliance of their clients in countering the *Heimwehr* challenge, they had less and less at their disposal to offer in return for this compliance. They were steadily losing their ability to 'do something' for their clients, to tie them to the movement, and thus ensure that they supported, or acquiesced in, their campaign of intimidation.

The corollary of this breakdown of the local patron-client relationship was not, however, a sudden expansion of the *Heimwehr*, an 'outside' force which was at its strongest in Upper Austrian rural areas and thus had no real tradition or social basis to draw on in the town. It lay rather in a revival of the established local parties of the 'bourgeois' Right. Since the end of the monarchy the local Christian Social and German Nationalist Parties had had to submit themselves to the dominance of the Social Democrats. Muzzled by the pervasiveness of Social Democratic patronage, they had been forced to accept Social Democratic hegemony in the town. But as the 'hold' of the Social Democrats over their clients crumbled and, by implication, as former Social Democratic instrumentalists returned their allegiance to their 'natural' party-political homes, the parties of the Right enjoyed an increasing room for manoeuvre. Suddenly released from the shackles of Social Democratic patronage, they used the issues raised by the *Heimwehr* challenge as a catalyst to break Social Democratic hegemony in Steyr.

A crucial factor here was a growing public outrage in Steyr (and throughout 'bourgeois' circles in Upper Austria as a whole) about the open persecution of the *Heimwehr* and of local *Heimwehr* sympathisers and about the role of the local police in allowing that persecution to take place. This outrage produced an anti-Social Democratic momentum at the popular level which allowed the parties of the Right in Steyr to emerge from their previous torpor. For example, they ostentatiously quitted a Town Council meeting in December 1929 in protest against Social Democratic intimidation of local *Heimwehr* sympathisers.[52] They also called upon provincial and federal governments to ban the local *Schutzbund* for its role in overseeing the boycott of *Heimwehr*-friendly shopkeepers in the town.[53] Most importantly, though, the local Christian Socials and German Nationalists gave expression to the growing local anti-Social Democratic feeling by sending a series of protest delegations to provincial and federal authorities during December 1929 and January 1930. These demanded either the immediate 'federalisation' of the local police force or, failing that, the dispatch of outside police reinforcements to the town to guarantee a more congenial form of law and order.[54] This unprecedented display of political independence bore its fruit when the political atmosphere in Steyr became especially fraught towards the start of February 1930. The *Heimwehr* had announced its intention of holding a 'stroll' on 2 February, which was to be attended for the first time by supporters from outside, from some 26 nearby villages.[55] Against the wishes of a party leadership increasingly worried about the policing issue, rank and file militants in the Social Democratic youth organisation and the *Schutzbund* styled the 2 February as a 'showdown' over the 'right to the streets' in the town. The week preceding 2 February saw the announcement of a rival 'stroll' by the *Schutzbund*[56] and 'unusually strong' gatherings of young Social Democrats, supported by local Communists, who were in 'fighting mood' and prepared to defend their view that Steyr was 'a pure workers' town, where the *Heimwehr* had no business to be'.[57]

The prospect of such a 'showdown' led the provincial government to respond to the demands of the local parties of the Right and to dispatch its own police units to Steyr on 2 February. This led Mayor Sichlrader to intervene at the last minute to prevent a 300-strong *Schutzbund* formation from confronting the *Heimwehr*, presumably to prevent the possibility of violent confrontation with the police. The *Heimwehr* was thus able to walk the streets if not exactly undisturbed, then certainly with adequate protection against Social Democratic protestors.[58] More importantly, the dispatch of outside police units set a precedent. Future militant protest against the *Heimwehr* could easily result in the intervention of a politically unfriendly police force under the orders of the CSP-led provincial government. The confident and unrestrained actions of the local right-wing parties which led to this *de facto* abrogation of Steyr's autonomous policing powers - months before the local police were formally federalised - signalled the caving in of the Social Democratic *Hochburg* in Steyr. After 2 February 1930, the Social Democratic leadership was forced (to the evident disgust of 130 *Schutzbündler* who had been in the vanguard of the anti-*Heimwehr* campaign, and who immediately defected to the local Communists)[59] to call for restraint and abandon their tactics of confrontation and intimidation.[60] By mid-March 1930, *Heimwehr* members were able to go about their business in Steyr openly and without interference. The new political balance in the town was then confirmed when the federal police took over responsibility for law and order. In approving a mass rally of the *Heimwehr* on 31 August and in banning a planned counter-rally of the *Schutzbund* on the same day, the federal police formally consigned the Social Democratic *Hochburg* to history.[61]

The conclusion is quite clear: the use of patronage by a political party (and in this case an associated trade union) can certainly contribute to the consolidation of the power and influence of that party as long as it can continue to control access to things its clients want. If it loses that control, though, it inevitably loses power and influence. The two sides of this coin emerged especially clearly in Steyr. Social Democratic hegemony in the 1920s rested on a patron-client relationship in which the political support of instrumentalist clients was exchanged for the material benefits the Social Democratic patrons could provide. After the autumn of 1929 the Social Democrats could no longer uphold their part of this relationship, with the result that the instrumentalists ended the 'affair'. From the autumn of 1929, the negative implications of a patronage system which could underpin the *rote Hochburg* of the 1920s, but which could now equally shatter the bases of that *Hochburg*, became increasingly evident. These negative implications of patronage formed the starting point of a period of constant decline which, spurred on by the unfavourable economic and political climate of the early 1930s, was to culminate in the events of February 1934. A once hegemonic and super-confident movement was thus transformed into an impotent, demoralised and ultimately crushed political force.

This flawed patronage strategy in Steyr also casts rather broader light on some of the wider characteristics of local-level Social Democratic politics in the provinces. The driving force behind the use of patronage was the desire to extend the organisational tentacles of the Social Democratic movement as far as possible into as many areas as possible of local politics and society. Patronage was in this respect a potent expression of an insular *Hochburg* mentality, of the territorial politics of organisational integration and demarcation which pervaded the isolated outposts of Social Democracy in the provinces. A further reflection of this insular mentality - and of the emphasis on organisation that it promoted - can be seen in the extensive network of auxiliary organisations which every provincial *Hochburg* strove to establish. These organisations are the subject of the next chapter.

Notes

1   An earlier and abbreviated version of this chapter was published as Jeffery (1992a).

2   'Patronage' is a notoriously imprecise concept which is used in different ways in different academic disciplines ranging from political science to social anthropology. The usage of the concept in this chapter is based on 'modern' party patronage, as discussed for example in: Christopher Clapham (Ed.), *Private patronage and public power*, Pinter, London (1982); S.N. Eisenstadt, René Lemarchand (Eds.), *Political clientelism, patronage and development*, Sage, Beverly Hills (1981); Ernest Gellner, John Waterbury (Eds.), *Patrons and clients in Mediterranean societies*, Duckworth, London (1977); Müller (1988).

3   A useful empirical overview of party patronage in the Second Republic, placed in the framework of a broader discussion of theoretical approaches to the study of party patronage, is given in Müller (1988).

4   Müller (1988), 475-482.

5   The following account draws in particular from Müller (1988).

6   See respectively: Martin Kitchen, *The coming of Austrian fascism*, Croom Helm, London (1980), 87ff; Bauer (1988d), 88; Gulick (1948), 454; Hanisch (1983), 915.

7   See Ausch (1968), passim; Gulick (1948), 245-246, 327-328, 702-709.

8   Access to some jobs in Mauthausen in Upper Austria was, for example, allegedly dependent on regular church attendance, which would clearly have been designed to favour CSP members. Equally, anti-Social Democratic staffing policies in the Upper Austrian coalfield are likely to have borne the imprint of the CSP, since the CSP-led provincial government was a major stakeholder in the provincial coal industry. See respectively SPÖ Mauthausen (1989), 114-115; Hummer (1984), 76.

9   The most obvious example here is the *de facto* closed shop established by the *Heimwehr* Independent Union in collusion with the AMG management in various AMG plants in Upper Styria. See in particular Staudinger (1985), 64-77.

10   C.O. Hardy, *The Housing Programme of Vienna*, Washington D.C. (1934), 95-96, as quoted in Gulick (1948), 454.

11   See the Introduction to this book.

12   See Chapter Two.

13   The SDAP had, for example, 387 mayors in Austria in 1931. See *Jahrbuch der österreichischen Arbeiterbewegung 1931*, 268-271.

14   The evidence here is rather impressionistic, relying primarily on allegations of corrupt financial malpractice made by non-Social Democrats. See e.g. Nasko (1986), 140; Hwaletz, Stocker (1984), 121-146; Lewis (1991), 134, 171.

15   There were, for example, 436 municipal employees in Wiener Neustadt in 1929 (Flanner, (1983), 5) and presumably similar if not greater numbers in the other larger SDAP cities like Linz and Graz.

16   For example in Linz, in Hallein and Gnigl-Itzling in Salzburg, in Lower Austrian St. Pölten and in Upper Styrian Bruck an der Mur. See respectively Brigitte Kepplinger (Ed.), *Wohnen in Linz. Zur Geschichte des Linzer Arbeiterwohnbaues von den Anfängen bis 1945*, Böhlau, Vienna (1989); Bauer (1988e), 101, 110-111; Nasko (1986), 140; Lewis (1991), 171.

17   Hwaletz (1984), 121-123; Lewis (1991), 133-134.

18   Nasko (1986), 167; Hinteregger, Schmidlechner, Staudinger (1984), 201.

19   Nasko (1986), 140.

20   Also worth mentioning, but of far less significance in respect of job allocation, are jobs in the municipal workforce and in Social Democratic organisations, both of which were on party-book lines. The former peaked at 212 in 1929 and the latter at 103 in 1928.

21   See e.g. LTP 21-12-1929, 2.

22   AVA BKA Inneres 22/Oberösterreich Karton 5100: 103.821-30.

23   See AVA BKA Inneres 22/Oberösterreich Karton 5100: 103.821-30, 115.035-30; SZ 17-12-1929, 3; LTP 25-12-1929, 2. See further below.

24   This was reflected in the CSP fraction's call to transfer local police jurisdiction to the federal level in the Town Council sitting of 25 July 1927. See SZ 31-7-1927, 6; STB 29-7-1927, 7-8.

25   See e.g. AVA BKA Inneres 22/Oberösterreich Karton 5101: 218.507-31, 232.007-31; Karton 5102: 120.680-32, 134.958-32.

26   OÖLA Bezirkshauptmannschaft Steyr Präsidialakten Faszikel 8: 'Die Finanzlage der Stadt Steyr', von Dr Josef Walk.

27   See STB 12-8-1927, 8; SZ 18-3-1930, 1-2; LVB 2-9-1930, 8-9; SJ 5-9-1930, 7-9; see also below.

28   In much the same way that many Social Democrats joined the *Heimwehr* in Upper Styria to get access to jobs controlled by the *Heimwehr's* 'Independent' Trade Union. See Staudinger (1985), 77.

29   OÖAZ 15-9-1928, 5. My italics.

30   See Letter to the Author from Alois Zehetner, 19-11-1987. My italics.

31   Robert Michels, *Political parties. A sociological study of the oligarchical tendencies of modern democracy*, Dover, New York (1959), 116.

32   On this point see John Waterbury, 'An attempt to put patrons and clients in their place', in Gellner, Waterbury (1977), 330-331.

33   STB 30-3-1930, 8.

34   After federalisation in July 1930 the police - with a force three times the size of the old municipal one - 'veered off into the bourgeois *Lager*' and became 'particularly dangerous' for Social Democracy, according to a leading local functionary. Quoted in AVA BKA Inneres 22/Oberösterreich Karton 5100: 227.225-30.

35   See e.g. the discussion in Müller (1988), 470ff.

36   Ibid.

37   The followng statistics need to be read with caution. The declining commitment of previous supporters and members of the movement could also be explained in part by reasons other than revoked instrumental support. The classic study by Jahoda, Lazarsfeld and Zeisel of long-term unemployment in the Lower Austrian village of Marienthal showed for example that long-term local unemployment led to a progressive withdrawal from political life (See Jahoda, Lazarsfeld, Zeisel (1960)). A similar process can be seen in an increasingly 'tired' working class in Steyr (see e.g. AZ 1-1-1932; STB 29-3-1931, 9 and Chapter Eight). Also important was the deterrent effect on continued commitment of state repression, to which the Social Democrats throughout Austria were exposed sporadically from 1930 and constantly from the end of 1932. In these circumstances it can be assumed that many long-serving Social Democrats turned their back on the movement unwillingly but for the urgent, pragmatic reason of securing their livelihoods in a new - and for Social Democrats unfriendly - political climate.

38   STB 4-5-1929, 7-8; AVA BKA Inneres 22/Oberösterreich Karton 5100: 144.375-30.

39   STB 11-91-1929, 8-9; SZ 15-7-1930, 5.

40   VGA. Parteiarchiv Mappe 67/2.

41   STB 14-8-1929, 8.

42   See e.g STB 29-8-1929, 9, 30-8-1929, 8, 27-9-1929, 8, 1-10-1929, 7, 4`10-1929, 8, 26-10-1929, 7-8, 17-11-1929, 14, 22-12-1929, 14.

43   So the Upper Austrian *Heimwehr* leader, Starhemberg, in July 1929. See STB 29-6-1929, 8.

44   See Chapter Three.

45   LVB 25-12-1929, 6-7.

46   Quoted in AVA BKA Inneres 22/Oberösterreich Karton 5100: 111.425-30.

47   Quoted in STB 11-9-1929, 9.

48   See for example Magistrat der Stadt Steyr, Registratur Faszikel B/a 12509-1929.

49   STB 26-10-1929, 7-8; SZ 22-10-1929, 1, 27-10-1929, 11; AVA BKA Inneres 22/Oberösterreich Karton 5100: 115.035-30.

50   See the many federal police reports on the situation in Steyr in AVA BKA Inneres 22/Oberösterreich Karton 5100.

51   SZ 10-12-1929, 4; OÖTZ 17-12-1929, 3; AVA BKA Inneres 22/Oberösterreich Karton 5100: 103.821-30, 114.424-30, 115.035-30.

52   STB 24-12-1929, 1-2.

53   See ibid. and SZ 24-12-1929, 3.

54   See e.g. STB 20-12-1929, 1-2; SZ 17-12-1929, 3.

55   SJ, 7-2-1930, 3.

56   AVA BKA Inneres 22/Oberösterreich Karton 5100: 111.430-30.

57   AVA BKA Inneres 22/Oberösterreich Karton 5100: 110.113-30, 111.424-30, 111.430-30; STB4-2-1930, 6-7; SJ 7-2-1930, 3.

58   AVA BKA Inneres 22/Oberösterreich Karton 5100: 111.430-30.

59   AVA BKA Inneres 22/Oberösterreich Karton 5100: 121.881-30. See further in Chapter Eight.

60   AVA BKA Inneres 22/Oberösterreich Karton 5100: 117.933-30, 118.776-30.

61   AVA BKA Inneres 22/Oberösterreich Karton 5100: 190.414-30.

6 On the Way to the 'New Human Being'?: The Social Democratic 'Cultural' Organisations

Social Democracy in inter-war Austria was a movement of tremendous organisational diversity. In addition to the SDAP and the FTUs, there were over forty other nationally organised Social Democratic organisations in Austria. The aggregate national membership of these auxiliary organisations was, in 1931, 652,761 (compared with a national party membership of 653,605 and a national union membership of 582,687 in the same year).[1] Their activities and membership were, unsurprisingly, concentrated in Vienna.[2] Nevertheless, auxiliary organisations also played an important role in the movement in the provinces. Even the smallest Social Democratic provincial *Hochburgen* could boast, in relative terms, an impressive spectrum of auxiliary activities. These ranged, to take the example of the Upper Austrian quarrying village of Mauthausen, from straightforward leisure clubs in the fields of sport and music, to a tenants' pressure group and a consumer cooperative, and through to children's and youth groups.[3] Larger centres of Social Democratic strength displayed a real zest for auxiliary activity, with Gnigl-Itzling in Salzburg claiming at least sixteen auxiliary organisations and Fohnsdorf in Styria a similar amount.[4] In Steyr there were over *fifty*, with an aggregate membership of around 20,000.[5]

These figures show quite clearly that an immense amount of Social Democratic energy was expended throughout Austria on activities outside the immediate realms of party politics and free trade unionism. The aim of this chapter is to examine why, and with what implications for the Social Democratic movement, such energies were expended in the Austrian provinces.

The vast range of non-party and non-union organisations in the Social Democratic movement have often been referred to, following the terminology of Karl Renner, a leading figure of the inter-war SDAP, as 'cultural' organisations: they represented a third, auxiliary dimension of the 'class struggle' which existed alongside the more orthodox 'political' (i.e. party) and 'economic' (trade union) dimensions.[6] 'Culture' in Renner's sense was not taken merely to mean artistic and intellectual enlightenment and achievement, but referred much more broadly to the 'ways of life', the social attitudes, behaviour and relationships of the members of the Social Democratic movement.[7] The 'cultural' activities of the movement, viewed in this light, collectively represented an attempt to shape and organise the ways of life of the members of the movement in accordance with, and in support of, its wider political and economic aims in the Austrian 'class struggle'. As neatly summed up in the title of Joe Weidenholzer's 1981 book, *Auf dem Weg zum 'Neuen Menschen'* ('on the way to the "new human being"'), 'cultural' activity was seen - and has generally been seen in the literature - as a means of educating and moulding the supporters of Social Democracy into the 'new', model socialist citizens who would be needed to run the socialist society which would be created following the SDAP's 'inevitable' electoral victory.

As its title suggests, this chapter, using the example of the Social Democratic 'cultural'/auxiliary[8] organisations in Steyr, seeks to question the image of auxiliary activity as some kind of preparatory step towards creating the model citizens of the socialist future. The first section develops a critique of the broader historiographical trends in this field of study. This critique casts doubt on the extent to which the attempt to shape 'new human beings' had any practical significance when viewed from the perspective of the movement's rank and file. A discussion of the situation in the provinces then throws up an alternative view of the meaning of auxiliary activity: that it should be understood not as some kind of preparation for the future, but as a defensive organisational response to the immediate, present-day problems of 'front-line' politics.

This hypothesis forms the basis for a detailed investigation both of the purposes of auxiliary activity in Steyr, and of the significance of auxiliary activity for understanding the wider character of the local Social Democratic movement. Section two demonstrates the limited resonance of the 'new human being' message in Steyr, while section three builds on the arguments presented earlier in Chapter Three to examine the auxiliary organisations in the town as a central component of the insular *'Schutzgemeinschaft'*, the 'protective community' of the provincial *Hochburg*, which afforded Social Democrats a realm of freedom of expression organisationally shielded from the everyday hostilities of provincial conservatism. The final section of the chapter then discusses the wider relevance of auxiliary activity for the politics of Social Democracy in Steyr. It suggests that auxiliary activity and the shielding function it performed tended to become a *Selbstzweck*, an end in itself, for many local Social Democrats. As such it helped to consolidate the insular outlook of the local movement and - as some of the auxiliary organisations began to recognise by the early 1930s - to diminish its capacity to respond to wider political problems.

Auxiliary Activity and the 'New Human Being'

The view that Social Democratic auxiliary activities represented a
strategic quest to shape the 'new human beings' of the socialist future
has long been part of the received wisdom of the historiography of
Social Democracy in the First Republic. This section argues that this
view needs to be qualified. It is beyond doubt that the small elite of
Social Democratic educationalists in Vienna which attempted to direct
the Social Democratic auxiliary organisations - both within Vienna and
beyond - viewed the shaping of some kind of 'new human being' as the
theoretical goal of their work. More careful consideration needs to be
given, though, to the question of how much the Social Democratic rank
and file ever came *in practice* - either in the provinces or, for that
matter, in Vienna - to be 'shaped' in accordance with that goal. This
need becomes clear in a brief examination of trends in writing about the
Social Democratic auxiliary organisations.

The Historiography of the 'New Human Being'

During the First Republic, Vienna was the site of an ongoing debate
among a small group of Social Democratic educationalists and
theorists about the character of the 'new human being'.[9] Although this
debate did not produce any uniform and uncontested definition of this
'new human being', some combination of the following, broad
characteristics was certainly envisaged: s/he was to be emphatically
secular, fired by a liberal humanism, dismissive of modern *Kitsch*
culture, imbued with a spirit of social and class solidarity and (last and
probably least) guided by the classics of socialist thought. The aim of
auxiliary activity was to provide a comprehensive organisational
framework, held separate from 'decadent', 'bourgeois' society, in which
these characteristics could be instilled and developed in the everyday
activities of the Social Democratic membership. No area of daily life
beyond the workplace (which unavoidably remained under 'bourgeois'
control) was to be left open to the influence of the cultural 'enemy'. The
auxiliary organisations were to act collectively as a hermetically sealed
'state within the state'[10] in which ordinary Social Democrats could
make a clean break with 'bourgeois' cultural forms and begin to develop
a new socialist lifestyle and morality.

The ambitious commitment to a comprehensive organisational
demarcation inspired, mainly in the late 1970s and early 1980s, a great
burst of research and publication on Austrian Social Democracy. This
veritable *'Kulturwelle'*,[11] which was focused almost exclusively on
auxiliary activity in Vienna, sought to demonstrate the particular steps
taken in shaping 'new human beings' in the Social Democratic

movement by one or other of the Social Democratic auxiliary organisations. There were works on the contributions made by leading individual educationalists,[12] the programmes of the Central Educational Office,[13] the Social Democratic library network,[14] the youth organisation,[15] the *Kinderfreunde*,[16] the Social Democrats' sports clubs,[17] their choral and musical societies[18] and political cabarettists,[19] the Religious Socialists[20] and the Socialist Students.[21] This seemingly irrepressible urge, mainly among Austrian historians, to map out the myriad strides on the way to the 'new human being' reached its zenith in the mounting of an exhibition on 'Workers' Culture'[22] in Vienna in 1981 and in the catalogue which accompanied it.[23] Exhibition and catalogue were both extraordinarily popular and probably did more than anything else to entrench the image of the 'new human being' firmly in the historiographical canon surrounding inter-war Social Democracy in Austria.[24]

This entrenchment of the 'new human being' in Austrian historiography is unfortunate since the 1981 exhibition/catalogue and, indeed, many of the works cited above have serious flaws. Many of them combine the dual failing of Austrian historiography which was identified in the Introduction to this study. They display on the one hand a methodological traditionalism which is restrictively focused on formal organisational structures, key personalities, and their ideas and policy programmes. They tend on the other towards 'in-house history', history written by authors close to the SPÖ who, writing in the era of SPÖ single party government (1970-1983), sought, in Gruber's words, to shape 'a heroic past to serve as a tradition usable by' the SPÖ in the present.[25] The visionary 'new human being' stood out proudly for many on the Left - alongside the municipal socialism of Red Vienna and the SDAP's doomed resistance in the Civil War of 1934 - as a point of orientation, identity and mobilisation in an era of remote and bureaucratised party politics.[26]

Emerging from this background, the works of the *'Kulturwelle'* had inevitable limitations. They tended to take the 'new human being' aims of the various organisations at a rather uncritical face value and to present the activities undertaken and the organisational advances made as systematic steps on the way to achieving those aims. Few took the time to address consistently and rigorously the question of how the addressees of auxiliary work, the Social Democratic rank and file, perceived, were influenced by, or contributed to, the activities and organisations of their putative socialist reeducation.[27] Fewer still attempted, aside from the odd, isolated and cursory sub-section, to broaden the scope out from Vienna and examine auxiliary activities in any detail in the provinces. The result was a series of narrow 'histories from above', which, taken together, produced a vast, Vienna-centred chronicle of largely unsubstantiated assumptions of 'success' in the quest to create the 'new human being'.

In more recent years, these assumptions have, as far as the situation in Vienna is concerned, come under the sustained and convincing attack of Helmut Gruber. Gruber punctuated the 1980s with a series of incisive and world-wearily critical articles on the organisational life of the Social Democratic movement in First Republic Vienna.[28] These collectively laid the groundwork for his magisterially iconoclastic *Red Vienna. Experiment in Working Class Culture, 1919-1934*, published in 1991. In *Red Vienna* Gruber raises important and far-reaching qualifications about the quest to create the raw, human material of the future socialist society in Vienna. He highlights in particular a gaping gulf of mentality and interest which existed between educationalist elite and mass membership in the Social Democratic auxiliary organisations, a gulf which prevented the 'new human being' message from ever developing a genuinely popular resonance. The vision of the 'new human being' propagated by the Social Democratic educationalists had, in consequence, to be 'satisfied with reaching only an "aristocracy" of workers' in Vienna.[29] This conclusion begs not only further studies on what kind of motivation - if not to contribute to the making of the new society - lay behind rank and file membership and activity in the proliferation of auxiliary organisations in Vienna.[30] It also raises, by implication, questions about the function of auxiliary activity in the provinces.

The 'New Human Being': the View from the Provinces

There has unfortunately been little attempt to pick up the iconoclastic baton from Gruber in the provincial context. There exist only isolated and rather fragmentary discussions of the auxiliary organisations in the provinces, and most of these tend in some way to reproduce rather uncritically the imagery of a quest to shape 'new human beings' through auxiliary activity. One extreme example is that of Werner Dreier's account of Vorarlberg Social Democracy, where a discussion of the auxiliary organisations in the province is prefaced in ritualistic manner by references to leading Viennese educationalists and their vision of educating the 'new human being'.[31] The implication is that the influence of the educationalists stretched from Vienna to even the furthest flung province, and that the quest for the 'new human being' was, *ipso facto*, the driving force behind auxiliary activity in Vorarlberg.

This would be an extremely unsound conclusion to draw. Gruber's work has shown that the influence of the educationalists was limited even within Vienna. As might be expected in a movement whose national organisations were inherently neglectful of their provincial components, the level of that influence was weaker still outside Vienna. Moreover it diminished the further away any particular province was situated. A clear indication of this is given in Table 6.1, which shows the number of lectures organised by the Viennese Central Educational Office (*Bildungszentrale*) in each province over the period 1921-1932, and which sets out a pattern broadly replicated in the other educational programmes organised centrally by the *Bildungszentrale*.[32] Beyond Lower Austria the level of activity, and by implication the influence, of the *Bildungszentrale* was at best limited, and at worst - as in Carinthia and Dreier's Vorarlberg - utterly negligible.

Table 6.1 *Bildungszentrale* Lectures in the Provinces, 1921-1932

Province	Lectures
Lower Austria	2150
Styria	306
Upper Austria	94
Salzburg	89
Burgenland	24
Tirol	24
Carinthia	9
Vorarlberg	8

Source: *Josef Weidenholzer, Auf dem Weg zum 'Neuen Menschen'. Bildungs- und Kulturarbeit der österreichischen Sozialdemokratie in der Ersten Republik, Europaverlag, Vienna (1981), 243.*

The evident inability of Vienna's educationalists to spread their word into the provinces does not, of course, necessarily mean that there was no conception of the 'new human being' in the provincial auxiliary organisations. Indeed, *Bildungs- und Kulturarbeit* in some areas was very much directed by individuals with a clear sense of the future society in their work. Especially noteworthy were the activities of Otto Stammer in Styria and the triumvirate of Ernst Koref, Edi Macku and Otto Stöber in Upper Austria.[33] Macku and Stöber in particular were renowned for the innovative and avant-garde methods with which they shaped some of the major Social Democratic festivals in Linz,[34] leading to Denkmaier and Janko's confident assertion that 'in Linz too - above all in the 1920s - the programme of culture and events was characterised by the pledge to educate the "new human beings" ... '[35] The question needs to be asked, though, as in Vienna, whether such activities had any *widespread* influence and significance. The network of activities directed by Stammer in Styria was focused on a small number of urban centres, while that of the Upper Austrian triumvirate seems to have had little noticeable impact outside the Upper Austrian capital, Linz, where it was based.[36] Even within the immediate spheres of influence of these provincial educationalists, it remains unclear, moroever, whether the messages underlying their auxiliary work had any great popular resonance. Their work has tended to be assessed on its artistic and/or educational merits - which were often considerable - but not with regard to its impact on, or significance to, the local rank and file.

In other words, studies of auxiliary activity in the provinces have tended, as in Vienna, to view their subject from above, from the perspective of those who sought to shape those activities, rather than to assess its impact and meaning at the grass roots. Just as Gruber has shown in the case of Vienna, there is a clear need for new studies which shift the focus away from the leading educationalists and their ideas, and towards the 'ordinary' Social Democrats who may well have given a meaning and direction to auxiliary activity in the provinces which did not coincide neatly with the educationalists' intentions. This hypothesis is given some support (unfortunately in rather short and scattered passages) in a number of works focused on the *Hochburgen* of Social Democracy in the province of Salzburg written by or under the guidance of Ingrid Bauer.[37] Based primarily on interviews with contemporaries, these offer original and perceptive, 'grass roots' insights into the purpose of auxiliary activity in the provinces.

The 'grass roots' perspective taken in the work of Bauer and her colleagues has done much to illuminate the character of the manual worker milieu on which the Social Democratic *Hochburgen* of the provinces were based, in particular the everyday hostility, discrimination and persecution which Social Democrats were forced to confront. In particular it highlights the continual struggle of the Social Democrats in Salzburg to create, on their own terms, opportunities for personal and social development which were otherwise denied to them by the chicaneries of employers, church and state. They succeeded in doing so largely through their collective, voluntary input into the various local auxiliary organisations: by giving up their evenings and weekends to help run them and thus to provide 'untainted' social and leisure opportunities for Social Democrats; by giving donations they could ill afford to help establish a local workers' club, sports field or some other facility; by helping physically to build such facilities in their spare time, and so on. The fruits of this collective effort were substantial: 'All this helped that relationship of intimacy, that feeling of solidarity, of being a part to grow, [a relationship] which comprised so much more than merely being a member of some leisure organisation'.[38] The Salzburg auxiliary organisations collectively provided 'something like a protective community: a dense network of solidaristic relationships which prevented a wall of social isolation and a loss of perspective from forming around these [workers'] families'.[39] Membership and activity in auxiliary organisations acted as a point of reference for, and, at times, a defiant assertion of, the shared identity of an embattled minority social group:

> Being a Social Democrat, being a member of a Social Democratic club, reading a Social Democratic newspaper, having Social Democratic friends meant above all being embedded in a political home, meant a sense of belonging together, meant being cemented together: 'You're a worker just like me'. Membership of the *Kinderfreunde*, the Workers' Athletics Club, the Free Thinkers and all the other Social Democratic cultural organisations demonstrated a sense of belonging to the labour movement - and a 'Red' was by no means welcome everywhere. [40]

Seen in this light, the function of input into and identification with the auxiliary organisations in Salzburg was a reactive one. There was no conception here of anticipating the future in the present, no ideological vision of a 'new human being', no 'great political principles, utopias and grand social designs'.[41] Auxiliary activity was tied to a pragmatic, thoroughly non-utopian present.[42] It was directed against the 'outside', anti-Social Democratic world, and served to create a form of collective organisational shield against that outside world. It formed part of the provincial Social Democratic *Schutzgemeinschaft*, of the 'safe haven' within which individuals could express and develop relatively freely their sense of collective identity through the Social Democratic movement. As such it points back to a key element of the *Hochburg* politics discussed in Chapter Three: the drive for an *Integration nach innen* in the Social Democratic movement, for a closing of ranks against the broad front of anti-Social Democratic forces which dominated provincial politics and society.

The interpretation given in Bauer's work to the purpose of auxiliary activity in Salzburg presents a clear and useful contrast to the traditional vision of a quest to shape 'new human beings'. For Bauer, auxiliary activity is defensive, reactive and focused on the present; in the 'traditional' view, it has an anticipatory, pro-active orientation towards the future. This contrast provides a useful framework against which to examine auxiliary activity in Steyr.

The 'New Human Being' in Steyr

Table 6.2 lists the Social Democratic organisations which existed alongside the SDAP and the FTUs in Steyr. It is, for a relatively small town, a long and imposing list with an immense aggregate membership.[43] The remainder of this chapter examines the purpose and

Table 6.2 Social Democratic Auxiliary Organisations in Steyr [44]

Organisation	Membership (Year)
Abstinents	n/a
Alpine Costume and Folk Dance Preservation	n/a
Animal Protection	n/a
Artists and Sketchers	n/a
Arts Centre	n/a
Athletics	n/a
Brass Band	n/a
Canary Breeders (two clubs)	n/a
Chess	91 (1927)
Choral Societies (three clubs)	230 (1927)
Consumer Cooperative	n/a
Crematorial Association	4,172 (1927)
Cyclists	n/a
Educational Committee	22 (1930)
Esperantists	35 (1930)
Flying Sports	n/a
Football (three clubs)	n/a
Free-Thinkers	1,042 (1927)
Gymnasts (three clubs)	1,403 (1928)
House-Building Cooperative	1,000 (1929)
Kinderfreunde:	
- Adults	1,521 (1929)
- Children	2,046 (1929)
Library	446 (1929)
Mandolin Players	64 (1928)
Military Gymnasts (*Wehrturner*)	360 (1930)
Motorcyclists	n/a
Pensioners (accident)	n/a
Pensioners (old age)	288 (1930)
Philatelists	n/a
Political Cabarettists	n/a
Radio Hams	300 (1930)
Red Falcons	88 (1930)
Samaritans	n/a
Savers and Annuitants	n/a
Schutzbund	650 (1930)
Secondary School Students	72 (1930)
Shooting and Hunting (two clubs)	n/a
Shopkeepers and Small Businessmen	142 (1928)
Skiers	n/a
Small Animal Breeders and Allotment Gardeners	n/a
Tenants Association	1,434 (1929)
Tourists (*Naturfreunde*)	817 (1929)
Watersports	n/a
Weightlifting, Wrestling and Tug-o-War	n/a
Women's Organisation	1,582 (1931)
Youth (SAJ)	605 (1929)
Zither Players	n/a
Aggregate total membership	**17,190**

implications of such an immense organisational effort, beginning in this section with a discussion of efforts to infuse a sense of the 'new human being' into auxiliary activities in Steyr.

Socialist Education in Steyr

Like Koref, Macku and Stöber in Linz and Stammer in Styria, a small number of amateur educationalists presided over *Bildungs- und Kulturarbeit* in Steyr. Their organisational base was in the SDAP District Educational Committee and the most prominent among them were its Chair, Alois Huemer, and, in particular, Josef Kirchberger, who, as editor of the local SDAP newspaper, the *Steyrer Tagblatt*, had a high-profile platform for his ideas. A first point to note about their work serves as a reiteration of the findings of Chapter Two on central-local and provincial-local relations in the Social Democratic movement: it was normally undertaken in isolation, with minimal interaction or coordination with the higher organisational levels of the movement. During the First Republic there was, for example, only one official meeting which brought together local educationalists from across Upper Austria. This seems to have produced one solitary batch of provincially coordinated party 'schools', but nothing more.[45] Equally, there was no regular interaction with the national *Bildungszentrale* in Vienna, apart from a small (and, in the 1930s declining) number of 'flying visits' by guest speakers from the national political arena.[46]

In their isolation, Steyr's educationalists did though attempt to propagate a message similar to (if rather less sophisticated than) their counterparts in Linz and Vienna. This saw Marxian socialist theory and the liberal-humanist tenet of 'knowledge is power, education liberates' as dual and complementary foundations of the future, post-capitalist society: 'Only those of a high intellectual level will one day be able to build up a better society, the socialist society, on the ruins of the collapsed capitalist world'.[47] This simplistic version of the wider commitment in Austrian Social Democracy to educating 'new human beings' was brought to bear in the range of functions exercised by the Educational Committee in Steyr. These included the organisation of instruction in socialist theory in 'schools' and lectures, the direction of the artistic programmes of the various socialist festivals and of a broader programme of 'high' culture for local consumption (classical music, drama, and so on), the organisation of the Steyr 'Workers' Library', and more generally the 'elevation' of the content of Social Democratic organisational life in the town. Many of the organisations listed in Table 6.2, especially those involved is some way in music, but also the *Kinderfreunde*, the Social Democratic youth organisation (the SAJ), the Women's Organisation and the various sports clubs (which played a role in the major socialist festivals), regularly came into contact with, and fell at least in part under the influence and direction of, the Educational Committee.

The extensive organisational 'reach' of the Educational Committee did not necessarily mean, however, that it had much success in propagating its vision of the 'new human being'. Analagous to the situation Gruber found in Vienna, there existed a clear gulf between leaders and masses in auxiliary activity in Steyr. This was based in part on the distinctly paternalistic attitude displayed by local educators towards their potential educatees, and in part on a related emphasis on promoting 'highbrow' activities which were not attuned to the interests or tastes of their target audience.[48]

A clear example of educationalist paternalism was given in a 1927 description of the structure of local party 'schooling' in socialist theory. In the attempt to promote a serious attitude to study, the *Steyrer Tagblatt* prescribed not just a prohibition of obviously unsuitable pursuits like drinking and smoking while in 'school', but also an apparent attempt to re-create the didactic and disciplinary atmosphere of an early twentieth century classroom, complete with blackboard and chalk and attendance register for every session![49] The underlying message was that the rank and file Social Democrats who attended these sessions were to sit still, be quiet, and be instructed and 'improved'.

The quest to 'improve' carries with it an implicit assumption that the rank and file stood at some 'lower' intellectual level which had to be hauled up to the 'higher' level represented by those on the Educational Committee. This was certainly an attitude which underlay Josef Kirchberger's journalism, and was illustrated in a number of blustering tirades about the failings of his readership, which, it seemed to him, was more interested in reading about trivial local gossip than the 'serious' issues he tried to illuminate.[50] It also underlay the rather pompous fanfare which accompanied the launch of a (short-lived) local, 'high-cultural' Social Democratic Arts Centre by the Educational Committee in 1928. This brought together the usual talk of a new age approaching with a haughty condemnation of the 'rubbishy *Kitsch* and shallow or even vulgar jokes',[51] which, presumably, the addressees of the Educational Committee's work were normally interested in.

The impression was that rank and file Social Democrats had to be tutored in leaving behind their enduring interest in local trivia and their traditional working class tastes and forms of expression for the 'better' ways the Educational Committee could lead them to. This naked paternalism would not seem to be the ideal method of securing popular appreciation for these 'better' ways. It seems highly likely - though there is no direct evidence for this - that many rank and file Social

Democrats would have felt alienated from the work of the Educational Committee by virtue of repeatedly being told that their traditional, everyday customs and tastes were just not good enough.

Rather more concrete evidence of a gulf between educationalists and rank and file can, though, be found in the level of participation by the rank and file in Educational Committee programmes. The Committee attempted to present its message of intellectual elevation primarily through the media of unashamedly 'highbrow' - and, it seems, low-appeal - activities. The party 'schools' in socialist theory (not to mention the periodic guest lectures by national party notables)[52] were, for example, pitched at a high intellectual level which would seem inappropriate to the great majority of local Social Democrats who had enjoyed only limited educational opportunities. An almost inevitable result was a low level of participation. In early 1928, for example, when a coordinated educational drive was being undertaken throughout Upper Austria (for the first and only time), the following, highly ambitious themes were covered in the 'schools': 'The History of Social Movements', 'Basic Concepts of Economics', 'Economy and Society', 'The Essence of Capital', 'The Central Features of the Marxist Theory of History, Society and the State' and 'Means and Paths to the Victory of our Class'. The attendance in Steyr was a mere fifty (just five of whom, incidentally, were women).[53] A number of less ambitious and locally conceived 'schools' put on later in 1928, covering 'The Party Programme', 'Ancient and Medieval History' 'Constitutional History' and 'Macroeconomics', also had a limited attendance.[54] Thereafter - and it is tempting to suggest *in consequence* of these low levels of participation - this form of 'schooling' seemed to peter out, with only token efforts being made in subsequent years.[55]

A similar pattern can be seen in the attempts by the local Education Committee, through its Arts Centre, to establish a programme of 'high culture' in Steyr. Arts Centre and Educational Committee organised a range of events, particularly in the late 1920s, which were of clearly high artistic merit. The founding event of the Arts Centre in January 1928 for example combined dance, operatic singing and a piano recital in a concert featuring works from Bach, Brahms and Puccini.[56] Other events in the same period included a poetry reading, a lecture on the Borgias, a 'Schubert Festival' featuring the local Social Democratic brass band, and a performance by a Russian orchestra. These events all formed part of the Educational Committee's wider educational strategy: 'Genuine art', according to the founding aims of the Arts Centre, formed an integral part of the programme of 'socialist education'.[57] But just as in the case of the more explicitly 'socialist' education in the field Marxist theory, it had a limited appeal in Steyr. Events such as those listed above, no matter how worthy artistically, often played to half-empty halls.[58] The reason for this was pointed to in an unusually candid Educational Committee report on a poorly attended concert given by the local brass band and one of the choral societies: the rank and file evidently preferred what were seen and condemned as 'dubious' forms of entertainment. Ordinary Social Democrats would, the report noted indignantly, much rather go to 'kitschy' films than revolutionary ones, and would much rather listen to foxtrot and jazz music than symphony concerts or choral recitals.[59]

Put in another way, the local educationalists were fighting a losing battle against the attractions of an emerging, modern, urban entertainments industry. The appeal of modern and commercialised forms of entertainment, in a predominantly working class town hardly famed for a 'high-cultural' tradition, was far greater than the ideologically 'sound', but almost ostentatiously highbrow offerings of the Arts Centre were ever likely to be. It seems doubtful, though, that the members of Steyr's Educational Committee ever fully recognised or appreciated the relative attractiveness of popular versus highbrow culture. As a result, their programmes always had a limited audience and appeal. This problem can be seen in a slightly different respect in the case of the Social Democratic Workers' Library. The library became the centrepoint of the efforts of the Educational Committee in the early 1930s, providing educational opportunities which were cheap and 'recyclable' in a period of mass unemployment and widespread local poverty. The library loan statistics, set out in Table 6.3 for the period 1928-1933, make interesting reading. In its review of the 1928 figures, the Educational Committee set out the aim, consistent with its liberal-humanist tenets, of increasing loans in the field of the social and natural sciences since 'a workers' library is only fulfilling its purpose if it is able to boost the demand for scientific learning and knowledge among its readers'.[60] As Table 6.3 shows, this aim was achieved in the following years in terms of absolute numbers of loans, but certainly not in relative terms: drama and fiction persistently accounted for around nine out of every ten loans made. As a result, the same complaint about the limited readership of scientific works, and the need to expand that readership, came to be aired repeatedly right through to 1934.[61] The borrowers continued, though, to prefer the 'lighter' fiction section, remaining impervious to their Educational Committee's priorities. This finding needs to be qualified to the extent that the quality of the holdings of the fiction section was relatively high, and certainly excluded pulp fiction genres like crime, westerns and 'bluestocking and teen stories'.[62] The library may well, therefore, have promoted the reading of a different, higher literary quality of fiction. Nevertheless, in its drive to change the overall pattern of reading habits to incorporate serious works in the natural and social sciences, the Educational Committee's quest to 'create new human beings and build up a new world'[63] once again met its limits.

Table 6.3 Loans from the Social Democratic Workers' Library in Steyr, 1928-1933

Year	Drama/fiction		Social Sciences		Natural Sciences		Total Loans
	Loans	%Total	Loans	%Total	Loans	%Total	
1928	3124	94.9	120	3.6	48	1.4	3292
1929	11371	92.6	391	3.2	516	4.2	12278
1930	22749	89.3	762	3.0	1964	7.7	25475
1931	23272	89.9	722	2.8	1899	7.3	25893
1932	25211	89.4	1142	4.1	1838	6.5	28191
1933	n/a	90	n/a	10	n/a	n/a	26941

Note: *The 1933 figure of 10% for social science loans is a composite figure for both the social and natural sciences.*
Sources: *STB 3-2-1929, 3; 9-2-1930, 13; 17-2-1931, 12; 24-1-1932, 12; 31-1-1933, 4; 27-1-1934, 5.*

It would seem doubtful, in summary, that the Educational Committee encountered much success in its various activities in promoting the 'high intellectual level' it felt was needed to 'build up a better society, the socialist society'. Both its paternalistic approach and its highbrow programmes inevitably placed limits on the impact and uptake of its message in the wider auxiliary activities of the Social Democratic movement. Indirect support can be given for this in the following discussion of the functions of some of the major local auxiliary organisations.

Auxiliary Organisations in Steyr: Towards the 'Better Society'?

Probably the only auxiliary organisation in Steyr in which the quest to create 'new human beings' played an identifiable and consistent, guiding role was the youth movement, the SAJ. As examples from elsewhere in Upper Austria seem to confirm, the SAJ provided a forum in which a combination of youthful idealism and energy could be tapped to develop a new, vigorous, almost puritanical lifestyle.[64] During the 1920s, the members of the Steyr SAJ perfected a highly idealistic self-image as the auxiliary avant-garde of the Social Democratic movement, the 'builders of the coming world'[65] of socialism. They ran a full programme of events and meetings for weekday evenings and weekends, which were notable for the collectivist spirit of community solidarity in which they were undertaken. Sports, for example, were played in a way which rejected the competitive individualism and sensationalism of 'record-chasing', 'bourgeois' sport. Openly competitive sports like football were frowned upon. Instead, a collective approach at an average level of competence was preferred, as epitomised in eurhythmic displays of dance and gymnastics periodically presented during Social Democratic festivals.[66] A purposeful attempt to shape a new, socialist lifestyle was also attempted. A dogged and puritanical abstinence from alcohol and nicotine was encouraged which was often upheld for life. This was accompanied by an outright indulgence in challenging physical exercise, in particular mountain hiking. The avowed aim of these 'lifestyle' activities was to produce the mental strength of character and the physical stamina needed in the perceived future role of the youth: Alcohol and nicotine were condemned as both physically and mentally harmful, while outdoor activities were seen not only to cultivate physical health, but also to provide the mental challenges necessary for the development of strong, socialist characters.[67]

Beyond this idealistic, future-oriented zeal apparent in the SAJ, though, (which was, in any case partly abandoned for a more practical political role in the 1930s)[68] it is hard to find evidence of any consistent or purposeful steps taken on the way to the 'new human being' in the various auxiliary organisations in Steyr. This applies most obviously to the various clubs which had no other pretensions than to cater for the collective pursuit of popular hobbies. It is difficult to imagine how, for example, canary breeding (an activity which could boast two separate clubs in Steyr!), chess playing or stamp collecting could have made any notable contributions to shaping the 'better society'. Such clubs simply catered for a formal demarcation from similar, non-Social Democratic hobby clubs. More importantly, though, even auxiliary organisations which might have seemed in principle to be in a far better position to play an anticipatory, future-oriented role largely limited themselves in practice to a straightforward demarcation function. This point can be illustrated by reference to the *Kinderfreunde* and the Social Democratic Women's Organisation.

The *Kinderfreunde* in Steyr were a rich organisation. Alongside normal parental subscriptions, they received the proceeds of the MAV *'Kindergroschen'* and an annual Works Council subsidy from the Steyr-Werke (see Chapter Four). Their annual income was, at least until the collapse in employment at the Steyr-Werke in 1929-1930, far greater than that of the Steyr SDAP.[69] This generous funding supported a comprehensive network of facilities and activities. These included a kindergarten for younger children, a network of *'Kinderhorte'* for the supervision of schoolchildren after school hours, numerous organised recreational activities, mountain cabins for use during overnight hikes, sports grounds, a lunchtime soup kitchen and a Christmas-time campaign for children from needy families, holiday 'colonies' (again largely for needy children) in the foothills of the Alps during school summer holidays, and so on.[70]

This comprehensive children's programme was not geared, however, to political education in the sense of the 'new human beings' these children might some day have become. It was, rather, based on two alternative, and rather more immediate considerations.[71] These, as evidenced in the grudging flattery of envious and even admiring comments by local clericalist sources about the *Kinderfreunde* organisation, undoubtedly had considerable success.[72] The first and primary consideration was to shield children from supposedly detrimental 'bourgeois' and clerical influence:

> Our concern remains the same: to hold the child as far as is possible away from all bourgeois events and influences, to bind it to our ceremonies, festivals and meetings, to our work and institutions so strongly that they become an indispensable need.[73]

The second, supplementary function of *Kinderfreunde* activity was, as indicated above in the emphasis on support for needy children, to provide a welfare service for Social Democratic families. This supplementary function may, of course, have helped to buttress the primary 'shielding' function by generating additional instrumentalist attachments to the *Kinderfreunde* cause; the *Kinderfreunde* in Steyr were certainly able to offer greater material welfare incentives than rival Catholic Church-based children's groups.[74] The broader point is that neither of the two functions exemplified in *Kinderfreunde* activities were directed towards the inculcation and entrenchment of socialist ideological values. They were focused far more on providing a clearly and comprehensively delimited framework for everyday activities which would help entrench identification with, and loyalties to, the Social Democratic movement.

A similar pattern emerges, for rather different reasons, in the case of the Social Democratic Women's Organisation. Despite its regularly rehearsed rhetoric about gender equality and the emancipation of women,[75] the activities of the Women's Organisation remained imperviously restricted to traditional, stereotypical 'women's' activities. Even though some Social Democratic women in Steyr had assumed active public roles and functions in the First Republic - as town councillors, party or union functionaries, school or welfare officials, lay magistrates, and so on[76] - no attempt was made in the Women's Organisation either to build on the emancipatory trend or more broadly to discuss or challenge existing gender roles. The organisation adhered, on the contrary, to traditional, household-based concerns. It ran courses in sewing, crochet, knitting and home economics, and sought to mobilise women around stereotype issues. Particularly important here were welfare issues (especially after the onset of the depression), and, above all, shopping and the cost of living.[77] Indeed, women were specially singled out on the basis of their traditional role as housekeepers/shoppers as being highly suited to active service in the co-operative movement![78]

The apparent lack of ambition of Social Democratic women's activities in Steyr had a number of sources. One was tactical: women in Steyr tended to be reluctant Social Democrats, more attached to conservative, especially religious beliefs than men.[79] In these circumstances, a minimalist and traditionalist women's programme was perhaps a sensible mobilisational tactic: it was less likely to 'frighten off' socially conservative women. A more important reason for the limited scope of women's policies in the Social Democratic movement was, however, almost certainly the attitude of men. Dieter Langewiesche notes in a wider discussion of the movement in Austria as a whole that traditional social prejudices still exercised a strong restraint on any women's activities which transcended the boundaries of the home. Even in supposedly 'progressive' Social Democratic families, a traditionalist view of a woman's role in society (*Kinder* and *Küche*, but without the *Kirche*!) still prevailed.[80] Such social stereotypes became especially potent in Steyr after the collapse of the Steyr-Werke and the onset of mass unemployment and poverty in the town. Women's political activity was immediately a superfluous expense in the eyes of many men, who frequently obstructed further political involvement even though reduced subscriptions for the unemployed were available.[81]

Women's activities in Steyr, for all these reasons, failed even to attempt to break down the patriarchal-authoritarian gender roles in family relationships which were inherent in the wider Austrian (and indeed, Christian-European) tradition. The Women's Organisation, as a result, conveyed no sense whatsoever of a new society in the making. Like the *Kinderfreunde* and the vast majority - the SAJ excepted - of the auxiliary organisations in Steyr, the function of the Women's Organisation appeared to be first and foremost one of demarcation: to provide a separate organisational framework, firmly embedded in the 'old' society, which was reserved for Social Democratic women to carry out their unremarkable, traditional 'women's' activities in isolation from the similarly traditional 'women's' activities carried out elsewhere by non-Social Democratic women.

Auxiliary Activity in the Steyr *Schutzgemeinschaft*

This conclusion, viewed alongside the evidently highly limited resonance of the Educational Committee's ideas and programmes, suggests that auxiliary activities in Steyr were not driven in any widespread or consistent sense by an anticipatory, future-oriented, utopian vision of the 'better society' and the 'new human being'. The discussion of the functions of *Kinderfreunde* and Women's Organisation has, on the contrary, thrown up obvious parallels to Ingrid Bauer's findings about auxiliary activity in Salzburg province. *Kinderfreunde* and Women's Organisation had a much more reactive focus on the present, providing fora in which essentially mundane, everyday activities could be conducted in an organisational context closed off from the non-Social Democratic 'outside world'. This section builds on these parallels to the work of Bauer. It argues that the energies devoted to auxiliary activity in Steyr can best be understood as one of the characteristically defensive reactions of the local Social Democratic movement to the 'outside world' which confronted it in its embattled and isolated position on the front lines of provincial politics.

Frau Meier

An intriguing insight into the defensive function of auxiliary activity was given over forty years ago in the semi-autobiographical recollections of the former SDAP functionary Josef Buttinger.[82] While focused on Vienna - and strangely ignored since as a point of departure for research on Social Democracy in Vienna - Buttinger's recollections have clear implications for an understanding of auxiliary activity in Steyr (and, of course, elsewhere in the provinces). They evoke a vivid picture of an intense rank and file commitment to the myriad auxiliary organisations and activities of Viennese Social Democracy whose purpose was to compensate for the practical problems faced in everyday life. The following excerpt, which refers to the rank and file stalwarts of the movement, is highly instructive:

> They felt important selling badges, performing gymnastic displays, reciting poetry, embroidering flags, pasting posters in display cabinets. In choral rehearsals, in decorating their windows for Mayday, wearing party and club insignia, stewarding the *Kinderfreunde* open-air party, and even in applauding the 'appearance of the M.P., Dr Ellenbogen', they had for years felt a worthiness and importance which even the poorest are not denied when they place themselves in the service of the community.[83]

Buttinger points here to auxiliary activity in Vienna as a form of *Schutzgemeinschaft* in which the sense of *collective* strength and *community* solidarity developed through auxiliary activity helped alleviate *individual* problems. The rank and file Social Democrats, primarily from a disadvantaged and underprivileged manual working class background, were, individually, typically 'the poorest' in Viennese society, but were able to compensate for individual disadvantage through positive, collective experiences in Social Democratic organisations. On the basis of this compensatory function, a collectivist Social Democratic consciousness emerged, focused on and absorbed in organised, communal activities. Buttinger illustrates the nature of this consciousness in a pregnant parody of the archetypal active Social Democrat, '*Frau* Meier from [the Viennese District of] Alsergrund':

> In her work for the party *Frau* Meier had found a greater happiness in life. What was her life without the party? An eternal struggle to secure a meagre existence, always threatened by new economic hazards. Having to work for others, having to crawl to them, having to go without everything she wanted - every day she escaped the dreariness and degradation of this fate through her participation in the life of the socialist movement. Within the party her ravenous drive to be doing something, her need for communication, her urge to stand up for those less well off than her, her desire for social interaction were all happily satisfied ...[84]

Buttinger's evocation of *Frau* Meier is potent and persuasive, and raises a host of hitherto neglected questions about the function of Social Democratic auxiliary activity in Vienna. In particular, it would be interesting to see how Gruber's deconstruction of traditional interpretations of auxiliary activity could be complemented and extended by a grass roots approach to the study of auxiliary activity focused on the preoccupations of the numerous *Frau* (and *Herr*) Meiers of Vienna. Buttinger's work also has, moreover, clear implications for understanding auxiliary activity in the provinces. The 'Meiers' of Vienna, in Buttinger's view, thrust their considerable energies into the Social Democratic movement in reaction to, and in compensation for, the environment of economic and material disadvantage which surrounded them. The equivalents of the 'Meiers' in the provinces had, on average, at the very least, an equal experience of material disadvantage compared to that in Vienna, but, rooted in the manual worker milieux scattered around the provinces, faced in addition the extraordinary social and political disadvantages of a minority movement isolated in a hostile social and political environment. This provincial environment of multiple disadvantage would seem, in the light of Buttinger's recollections, ideally suited to promoting a reactive and defensive form of auxiliary activity whose purpose was to strengthen the cohesion and shared community identity of the Social Democrats. This was, as Bauer has shown, certainly the case in Salzburg. The following discussion examines the situation in Steyr.

A preliminary indication that auxiliary activity acted as part of a Social Democratic *Schutzgemeinschaft* in Steyr is given in the sheer scale of the network of auxiliary organisations in the town. The long list of fifty non-party and non-union organisations with, in total, around 20,000 members is, in per capita terms, almost certainly without parallel in Austria. At most there were, at peak levels, around 5,000 SDAP members and 8,000 SDAP voters in Steyr in the First Republic. Each individual Social Democrat would therefore - to take a hypothetical, average SDAP voter - have been a member of at least two and a half different auxiliary organisations. These bald statistics, however flawed and superficial,[85] clearly show an unusual level of organisational penetration by the Social Democratic movement in Steyr. They point to a defensive closing of ranks among Social Democrats, an *Integration nach innen* which bound a vast number of individuals into the Social Democratic movement in a multi-faceted web of organisational links criss-crossing local society. The comprehensiveness of this organisational web - see Table 6.2 - created, to borrow Buttinger's description, 'home, fatherland and religion'[86] rolled into one for the local *'Frau* Meiers'; it established an impenetrable organisational 'space' within which the members of a territorially concentrated and embattled minority movement could develop and express a form of social identity starkly at odds with the values of the majority in the society which surrounded it.

This defensive function of auxiliary activity in Steyr can be seen clearly in probably the two most enduring themes which pervaded the activities of the various auxiliary organisations, and which defined and sharpened Social Democratic social identity in opposition to the values of provincial conservatism: anti-clericalism and pro-republicanism.

Anti-clericalism in Auxiliary Activity

The Catholic Church was a perpetual *Feindbild* for Social Democrats in Steyr. Through its deep hostility to the Social Democratic movement and its entrenched influence in Upper Austrian society, it acted in a number of ways as a persistent, negative point of reference around which Social Democratic identity could solidify, and against which the movement could mobilise itself. Especially significant in solidifying this *Feindbild* in the First Republic were the periodic condemnations of Social Democracy (both in Steyr and in general) by Bishop Gföllner of Linz,[87] the more low-key sniping of local church figures, the friendly relationship of some local clergy with the *Heimwehr*,[88] the perpetually hostile journalism of the local clericalist newspaper, the *Steyrer Zeitung*,[89] the strong influence of the Church in the educational system, and so on.

In the face of what was seen as a veritable barrage of clericalist criticism and hostility, a steadfast anti-clericalist drive was a common feature in the activities of a number of the Social Democratic auxiliary organisations in Steyr. As was indicated above, for example, one of the most important functions of the *Kinderfreunde* was to shield younger children as far as possible from clericalist influence by developing an all-embracing programme of activities. Anti-clericalism was also important for the parents' arm of the *Kinderfreunde*, which was highly active in campaigning on the 'schools question' (*'Schulfrage'*), i.e. the Church's continued role in the education system. Easily the most outspoken organisation in its anti-clericalism was the Free Thinkers' Movement, which saw its primary task in actively reducing Church influence in Austrian society. It sought to do so in particular by promoting defections from the Church with a language and vigour which have been condemned by sources both friendly and hostile to the Social Democratic movement as 'regrettably low' and 'primitive'.[90] Probably of a more enduring significance, however, was the Crematorial Association in Steyr - unsubtly entitled 'The Flame' - which attracted a mass local membership (and, as a result, massive Catholic opposition) to the principle of cremation as opposed to the traditional Catholic funeral and burial. The mass membership of 'The Flame' equipped it with the resources both to publish its own feistily anti-clericalist journal,[91] and, most importantly, to build and open in Steyr in 1927 the first ever crematorium in Upper Austria. The crematorium provided a living and potent symbol of anti-clericalism in Steyr, a fact not lost on the *Steyrer Tagblatt*, which proudly published a monthly reminder and update of the number of cremations being carried out.[92]

Clericalist influence could not, of course, be completely expunged from the Social Democratic movement. Through its calendar of festivals (Christmas, Easter, Corpus Christi and so on), the Church provided points of social orientation which were irremovably imprinted on the minds of the whole population. Like their counterparts throughout Austria, the Steyr Social Democrats still attempted, though, to provide counterpoints to Church influence over the social calendar by developing alternative points of orientation in their own annual cycle of festivals. These were often one of the main - and one of the most assiduously prepared and eagerly awaited - focal points of activity in the auxiliary organisations. The festivals were normally scheduled at roughly the same time as, and were to an extent modelled on, their major Catholic 'competitors'.[93] There were, for example, regular

Kinderfreunde 'Sunday ceremonies' (*'Sonntagsfeiern'*), which acted as a counterpoint to Church services and Sunday schools for younger children. In similar vein, the Catholic confirmation was 'shadowed' by the Social Democratic *'Jugendweihe'*, the 'Inauguration of Youth' into the SAJ at fourteen years of age. Some of the more widely celebrated festivals had a more explicitly provocative, anti-clericalist character, designed to inflame Catholic sensitivities. Whitsun was, for example, shadowed by a festival organised by the Free Thinkers in the memory of a local 'farmer-philosopher', Konrad Deubler, who was persecuted and imprisoned for his anti-clericalist views in the late nineteenth century. All Saints Day was matched by a pseudo-pagan 'Celebration of the Dead' (*'Totengedenkfeier'*) orchestrated by 'The Flame'. Most controversially, a celebration of the summer solstice, dedicated to 'free thought', and supplemented by a 'Spring Festival' of the *Kinderfreunde*, was timed to coincide with Corpus Christi. Amid accusations that the Summer Solstice Festival was explicitly designed to undermine the Corpus Christi celebration (and that Social Democratic 'spies' were monitoring - and punishing - any participation by Social Democrats in the Corpus Christi ceremony), early June became a regular flashpoint for political confrontation in the Steyr area.[94]

Republicanism and Wehrhaftigkeit

The function of the Social Democratic festivals was not restricted simply to underscoring the movement's anti-clericalism. Festivals were also vehicles which were used to highlight the broader social and political divisions which existed in and around Steyr. To use the terminology introduced in Chapter Three, festivals were a part of the *Abgrenzung nach außen* of Social Democratic *Hochburg* politics; they helped to mark Steyr out for political friend and foe alike as Social Democratic territory. This function of *Abgrenzung nach außen* was most evident in the traditional Social Democratic celebration of 1 May and in the new, post-war festival of 12 November, the 'Day of the [proclamation of the] Republic'. Both of these were official public holidays, celebrated by the Social Democrats in tremendous displays of pomp and pageantry. Spiced with 'high-cultural' events run by the Educational Committee, and displays and exercises by the various sports and gymnastics clubs, their centrepieces were mass parades through the town, involving all the party sections, the local FTUs and the main auxiliary organisations, and capped off by a rally on the town square. Upwards of 5,000 regularly took part, a full quarter of the population of the town and a full-scale mobilisation of the Social Democratic movement.

Neither public holiday was, however, cause for celebration among non-Social Democrats in Steyr. This is unsurprising in the case of 1 May, given its traditional and historic association with the rise of the labour movement, and given that it was only accepted grudgingly, under heavy SDAP pressure, as a public holiday after the First World War. Rather more significant is the utterly passive, unmoved non-Social Democratic attitude in Steyr to the Day of the Republic, the official celebration of the founding of the democratic, republican order in Austria.

The contrasts in Steyr in the willingness to observe the 12 November holiday illustrate the divergent attitudes to the republican political system on either side of the front-lines of Upper Austrian politics. Support for the democratic system established in 1918-1919 was a core value in the Social Democratic movement in Steyr. Formal democratisation (in the guise of universal suffrage) had been, in Steyr as in the rest of Austria,[95] the central demand of the Social Democratic movement before the First World War. The establishment of democratic structures in the post-war republic not only consummated this demand but also gave the Social Democrats a much wider range of new and unprecedented powers in Austrian politics, economy and society. It was the purposeful mobilisation of these powers which had enabled the Social Democratic movement in Steyr - to the chagrin of the previously dominant Christian Social and German Nationalist representatives of provincial conservatism - to establish its local stronghold of 'red' hegemony. In this respect 12 November not only recalled the birth of the republic, but also - for both the local Social Democrats and their opponents - of 'red' Steyr as well.

For these reasons the Day of the Republic had a pregnant significance in Steyr. It threw a vivid spotlight on the social and political divisions in and around the town. These were captured and starkly visualised in the local patterns of festive decoration. 'Bourgeois' Steyr - the commercial centre of the town in and around the town square, Catholic Church buildings, the offices of the District Commissioner (the *Bezirkshauptmann*, the executive official for the surrounding rural district of Steyr-Land), the police station (after the federalisation of the police in 1930), and the more affluent, predominantly non-Social Democratic residential areas - remained ostentatiously undecorated on 12 November. So, with limited exceptions, did the great majority of public and private buildings in the villages around the town. In contrast, the 'red' town hall, local cooperative businesses and predominantly Social Democratic residential areas like the Ennsleite and the Wehrgraben were richly festooned with party and state flags, colourful bunting and night-time illuminations. These set the scene for what was invariably the best attended Social Democratic festival in Steyr - better even than 1 May - with 12 November commanding a peak participation of around 8,000 in 1928 (foreshadowed the night before by an attendance of 6,000 at a torch-lit procession of the SAJ and the Social Democratic gymnasts).[96]

The scale and spectacle of the annual celebrations on 12 November were styled as a 'mighty and powerful' demonstration of Social Democratic commitment to the democratic republic, as a 'vehement manifestation of the republican idea'.[97] Their purpose was to express in highly visual and symbolic terms Social Democratic difference, and on this basis to act as a show of the strength of the Social Democratic *Hochburg vis-à-vis* local opponents of the republican state form. This function became ever clearer after 1930, when 12 November became a day of protest against the authoritarian form of government which anti-Social Democrats, both locally and more broadly throughout Austria, increasingly favoured. For example, the 1931 Day of the Republic took place two months after an abortive *Heimwehr* putsch (the so-called Pfrimer Putsch) which had been launched in Upper Styria, but which had also spilled over, in isolated incidents, into the valleys running down from the Alps towards Steyr.[98] The proximity of the *Heimwehr* threat produced an extraordinary 'celebration' of the Day of the Republic in Steyr, far removed from the more carnival atmosphere of the 1920s. 12 November 1932 was dominated by a silent - and thereby, one imagines, an all the more impressive - mass parade through the streets of the town, which was conceived as a demonstration of commitment to take to arms, if necessary, to defend the republic. In the words of the SDAP-run *Steyrer Tagblatt*:

> Steely determination lay on the faces of all those who declared to the world on 12 November their willingness to defend the republic with all the means at their disposal. The deep seriousness and conspicuous silence, which lasted for the whole of the procession, typified the readiness of the workers in Steyr to fight and impressed a special character on the demonstration.[99]

Even allowing for an element of hyperbole in the *Steyrer Tagblatt's* reporting, 12 November 1931 gave a clear demonstration of an important corollary of republican commitment in the Social Democratic movement which fed into the activities of a number of the auxiliary organisations: *Wehrhaftigkeit*. *Wehrhaftigkeit* does not translate literally, but implies a capability and readiness to undertake physical self-defence. This readiness has already been touched upon in this work in the discussion of the quest to protect the Social Democratic monopoly of the streets in Steyr against the *Heimwehr* in late 1929-early 1930. *Wehrhaftigkeit* also had, however, a much wider significance in the fraught political atmosphere of the early 1930s as a broader statement of Social Democratic opposition to - and defensiveness towards - anti-republican politics. It not only underlay the activities of the Social Democratic paramilitary force, the *Schutzbund*, and the military gymnasts (*Wehrturner*),[100] who were responsible for the *Wehrhaftigkeit* of the Social Democratic youth, but also a range of other auxiliary organisations. Indeed, in the early 1930s, a complicated organisational division of labour in cultivating *Wehrhaftigkeit* emerged as preparation for a hypothetical, presumably *Heimwehr*-inspired *Ernstfall*, or emergency situation: *Schutzbund* and *Wehrturner* (along with much of the SAJ) practiced military drill and occasionally conducted 'field exercises'; the two Social Democratic shooting and hunting clubs gave tuition in the use of guns; a special railwaymen's and post office workers' unit planned the maintenance of lines of communication in the event of an *Ernstfall*, supported by the cyclists', motorcyclists' and radio hams' clubs; and the Social Democratic samaritans prepared for the medical orderlies' duties they were assigned to perform in an emergency.[101]

The diverse and evidently meticulous efforts put into maintaining *Wehrhaftigkeit* evoke very clearly the sense of embattlement felt within the Social Democratic movement in Steyr and the defensive response that sense of embattlement provoked. The movement had, it seems, to be permanently alert to the possibility of external threat to the freedom of expression it had been able to carve out for itself within the confines of the *Hochburg*, and to be ready to meet and counter any threat which did emerge. The inherent defensiveness embodied in *Wehrhaftigkeit* epitomises the general thrust of auxiliary activity in Steyr. Like the pro-republicanism it complemented and buttressed, and like the anti-clericalist motif which ran through much of local auxiliary actitivy, it was directed against some external - anti-republican and/or clericalist - threat. And like the comprehensive organisational network of Social Democratic clubs and societies, it was intended to help shield and demarcate Social Democrats from a hostile 'outside' world. By keeping the 'outside' world at bay, organisational demarcation, anti-clericalism, pro-republicanism and *Wehrhaftigkeit* together consolidated the Social Democratic *Schutzgemeinschaft*. They helped establish a zone of collective security for the 'Meiers' in Steyr which compensated for the manifold problems faced by Social Democrats in provincial everyday life.

Auxiliary Activity as *Selbstzweck*

The preceding discussion unambiguously suggests that the auxiliary organisations in Steyr, despite the promptings of the local Educational

Committee, had little to do with the 'new human beings' of the future. They were, on the contrary, almost entirely conditioned by the conflictual patterns of provincial politics in the First Republic. Auxiliary activity was, above all, an inward-looking reflex to an overwhelming problem: the pervasive anti-socialism which confronted Social Democrats in the provinces. This section poses the question whether the inward-looking focus of auxiliary activity inadvertently served to distract attention from the roots of the problems the Social Democrats faced and, as a result, blunted the broader political impetus of the Social Democratic movement. Tremendous amounts of time and energy must, after all, have been expended in work for the various auxiliary organisations. This was a burden which weighed down especially heavily on the more active Social Democrats, who, in addition to existing commitments, were prevailed upon from all quarters to join the most diverse organisations. The result was - as was recognised in national-level debates on the organisational fragmentation of auxiliary activities - an accumulation of functions and responsibilities by active individuals which led to 'a shallow level of organisational life and to a superficial political commitment' on the part of those individuals.[102]

This was certainly a problem faced in Steyr. As was noted earlier, it can be assumed that a considerable number of Social Democrats in Steyr were simultaneously members of several different organisations, given that the aggregate auxiliary organisation membership was around 20,000 in a town of 8,000 SDAP voters. Multiple and overlapping memberships inevitably produced conflicts of interest and conscience. These were reflected in complaints aired in the *Steyrer Tagblatt* that there were often several meetings or events taking place at the same time, and more broadly that the movement in Steyr had become afflicted by a superfluous *'Vereinsmeierei'*, an uncontrolled 'mania' for establishing and running clubs.[103] Activity in the auxiliary organisations ran the danger of becoming a *Selbstzweck*, and thus of demoting the *politics* of Social Democracy to a peripheral role. Guttsman writes informatively in the German context of the 'centrifugal tendencies' of auxiliary organisations, and of the

> ... growing danger that these organisations might become entirely self-absorbed so that the one will seek to solve the social question with song, the second through gymnastics and the third with music and the performance of plays. And if the unions or the party do not fully support such a drive, they are regarded as ignorant bureaucrats.[104]

The tendency to organisational self-absorption which Guttsman notes was certainly true, for example, of the Social Democratic gymnastics clubs in Steyr. These treated plans made in 1928 to incorporate all the local sports clubs into an overarching federation with an undisguised lack of enthusiasm. Their organisational 'patriotism' was later publicly rebuked in an SDAP activists' meeting, when it was emphasised that a 'proletarian' cannot be a *Sportler* alone, that s/he cannot regard the sports movement as a 'universal panacea', but that s/he must be first and foremost a socialist.[105] Nevertheless, some years later the gymnasts were still involved in 'territorial' disputes, this time with the *Schutzbund,* over the question of which organisation should have responsibility for the *Wehrturner.*[106] More indirect evidence of organisational 'patriotism' is given in the mere fact that a Social Democratic movement in a smallish town sustained three separate gymnastics clubs, three football clubs, three choral societies, two shooting and hunting clubs and two canary-breeding clubs. It is hard to avoid the conclusion that auxiliary activity was used by numerous petty functionaries in the Social Democratic movement as an opportunity to establish and maintain their own, jealously guarded organisational fiefdoms.

These examples, although somewhat sketchy, back up the impression of auxiliary activity in Steyr as a *Selbstzweck.* Immersed in the quest to shield and protect social and leisure activity from unwelcome, external influence, the auxiliary organisations developed their own self-centred and inward-looking momenta, focused on organisational maintenance rather than political struggle. Auxiliary activity in this light was a 'surrogate' politics. It reinforced the tendency to insularity which pervaded the Social Democratic movement in its provincial *Hochburgen.* It is worth considering, for example, the real meaning of 'republicanism' for Social Democrats in Steyr. Local 'republicanism' had little in any concrete sense to do with the democratic process as such after 1918. It was not focused on the national parliamentary struggle of the SDAP for social reform, the achievements of Red Vienna,[107] or the work of the Chambers of Labour, and so on. It was focused squarely on 'red' Steyr, on the powers made available to the local Social Democrats in the town hall and the Steyr-Werke as a result of the transition of 1918. Equally 'anti-clericalism' in Steyr was focused not on any wider conception of the relationship between church and state, but above all on clerics and clerical influence in and around Steyr.

This high degree of insularity and introspection was not a promising formula for coordinated political action between the Steyr Social Democrats and their counterparts elsewhere. It certainly diminished the capacity of the Upper Austrian movement, fragmented in its various *Hochburgen* to make any effective, or, for that matter, any noticeable province-wide response to broader political developments. In the circumstances of the early 1930s, this was a fateful weakness. As

Chapter Three has already suggested, an introspective and fragmented movement was a vulnerable one, and this vulnerability was ruthlessly exposed in a period of economic crisis by a resurgent right wing in Austrian politics.

This failing in Social Democratic politics, both in Steyr and elsewhere, went largely unnoticed among the auxiliary organisations in Steyr - with the sole and highly significant exceptions of the SAJ and the *Schutzbund*. Both these organisations progressively saw their rationales being undermined in the early 1930s. The SAJ, the 'builders of the coming world' were the Social Democratic avant-garde; the youth had been given the task of developing today the idealistic values and lifestyle which would dominate the socialist society of tomorrow. Yet economic crisis and growing political persecution were making the socialist 'tomorrow' ever more remote by the early 1930s. The SAJ was losing its *raison d'être*. As a result it abandoned the surrogate politics of socialist idealism for a more practical political activism based on confrontation - both rhetorical and violent - with the opponents of Social Democracy. The *Schutzbund* faced an analagous situation. It had trained for years for the task of defending the republican order in Steyr, and more broadly Austria as a whole. Yet neither local nor national party leadership were ever prepared to sanction the defence of the republican order despite the progressive degradation it suffered at the hands of *Heimwehr* and CSP in the 1930s. A defence organisation never allowed to defend was also, ultimately, engaged in a surrogate form of politics. This was gradually recognised in the *Schutzbund* after 1930. It too, as Chapter Eight shows, opted as a result for a strategy of open political confrontation which, supported by the 'post-surrogate' SAJ and under the leadership of what remained of the Steyr-Werke MAV, guided Social Democracy in Steyr into Civil War in 1934.

The use of the terminology of 'surrogate politics' in relation to the Social Democratic auxiliary organisations is not original. It has been used in a broadly similar way - to describe the 'negative returns' on the effort put into auxiliary activity - by both Rabinbach and Kulemann.[108] Rabinbach and Kulemann propose, though, in works focused on Vienna, that the 'surrogacy' in question resulted from an all-encompassing obsession with creating the future in the present: the Social Democrats lost touch with their immediate, concrete political problems through their quest to shape the nebulous 'new human being' of the future. This chapter has identified the same symptom - a loss of practical political 'touch' - but a different cause. The case of Steyr, in part supported by evidence from elsewhere, in particular Salzburg, presents the quest to shape the 'new human being' as marginal to an understanding of auxiliary activity. 'Surrogate' politics in Steyr was far more a from of defensive introspection which arose from the quest to express and defend a sense of separate social identity amid the intense political conflicts of the provinces, and which found its reflection in *Integration nach innen* and *Abgrenzung nach außen* through auxiliary activity.

The chapter has also made a number of observations about the traditional association of auxiliary activity with the 'new human being', both in the provinces and in the context of Red Vienna. These, drawing inspiration from Helmut Gruber and Josef Buttinger, pose a number of critical and sceptical questions about the imagery of the 'new human being' even in the Viennese heartland of Social Democracy. Unfortunately they can be taken no further here. A point which certainly can be taken further here, though, is the notion of organisation as *Selbstzweck*. As has been noted, Steyr was probably the most densely organised Social Democratic town in Austria. There existed an apparent obsession with organisation which, in some auxiliary activities at least, took on its own, inward-looking and blinkered momentum to the detriment of the movement's sensibility to the wider political situation. This tendency for organisation to become a *Selbstzweck* and to deepen the introspection of an already insular movement was, as the next chapter shows nowhere more clearly evident than in the lead Social Democratic organisation in Steyr: the SDAP.

Notes

1   Weidenholzer (1981), 89-91. It should be stressed that this figure is unavoidably exaggerated by multiple memberships of the same individuals in different organisations.

2   In an unfortunately unspecified year, the Viennese auxiliary organisations could, according to Gruber, boast a mass membership of some 400,000. This figure is of course again an aggregate figure containing an unknown number of multiple memberships. See Gruber (1991), 81.

3   See SPÖ Mauthausen (1989), 96-113.

4   See Bauer (1985), 63-81; Hans Burgstaller, Helmut Lackner, *Fohnsdorf. Erlebte Geschichte*, Verlag Erich Mlakar, Judenburg (1984), 164.

5   See Table 6.2 and note 43 below. The figures quoted for the national level, for Vienna and for Steyr have not been aggregated from the same selection of organisations, so should not be seen as fully comparable.

6   Ibid., 87-88.

7   Ibid., 88; see also Reinhard Kannonier, 'Arbeitswelt und Kultur', in Rudolf Kropf (Ed.), *Arbeit/Mensch/Maschine. Der Weg in die Industriegesellschaft*, Gutenberg, Linz (1987), 223.

8   The argument of the chapter is one designed to qualify the Renner view of the purpose of 'cultural' activity. From this point onwards, therefore, the less loaded adjective 'auxiliary' is preferred.

9   Most notably Max Adler, David Josef Bach, Otto Felix Kanitz, Otto Neurath, Josef Luitpold Stern and Richard Wagner. On their debates and disputes, see Gruber (1991), 83-87 and Weidenholzer (1981), 66-87.

10   So the SDAP prominent Julius Deutsch at the 1931 Party Conference. Quoted in Kulemann (1979), 324.

11   The analogy here is to the *'Hitlerwelle'* ('Hitler wave'), a series of biographies and 'psycho-histories' of Hitler which emerged contemporaneously in the 1970s. The analogy refers, of course, not to common subject matter, but to the obsessiveness with which the respective subjects were researched. On the *'Hitlerwelle'* see Eberhard Jäckel, 'Rückblick auf die sog. Hitlerwelle', *Geschichte in Wissenschaft und Unterricht*, **28** (1977).

12   Henriette Kotlan-Werner, *Kunst und Volk. David Josef Bach, 1874-1947*, Europaverlag, Vienna (1977); idem, *Otto-Felix Kanitz und der Schönbrunner Kreis. Die Arbeitsgemeinschaft sozialistischer Erzieher 1923-1934*, Europaverlag, Vienna (1982); Ernst K. Herlitzka, 'Josef Luitpold Stern (1886-1966). Versuch einer Würdigung', in Botz, Hautmann, Konrad, Weidenholzer (1978).

13   Weidenholzer (1981); Dieter Langewiesche, *Zur Freizeit des Arbeiters. Bildungsbestrebungen und Freizeitgestaltung österreichischer Arbeiter im Kaiserreich und in der Ersten Republik*, Klett-Cotta, Stuttgart (1979).

14   Pfoser (1980).

15   Neugebauer (1975).

16   Uitz (1975); Kordula Langhof, *Mit uns zieht die neue Zeit. Pädagogik und Arbeiterbewegung am Beispiel der österreichischen Kinderfreunde*, Geminal, Bochum (1983); Jakob Bindel (Ed.), *75 Jahre Kinderfreunde 1908-1983. Skizzen-Erinnerungen-Berichte-Ausblicke*, Jungbrunnen, Vienna (1983).

17   Krammer (1981).

18   Reinhard Kannonier, *Zwischen Beethoven und Eisler. Zur Arbeitermusikbewegung in Österreich*, Europaverlag, Vienna (1981).

19   Friedrich Scheu, *Humor als Waffe. Politisches Kabarett in der Ersten Republik*, Europaverlag, Vienna (1977).

20   Josef Außermair, *Kirche und Sozialdemokratie. Der Bund der religiösen Sozialisten, 1926-1934*, Europaverlag, Vienna (1979).

21   Wolfgang Speiser, *Die sozialistischen Studenten Wiens 1927-1938*, Europaverlag, Vienna (1986). Only in the early 1990s was the baton taken up again with new works on the Social Democratic 'festival culture' and the Socialist Students again. See respectively Béla Rásky, *Arbeiterfesttage. Die Fest- und Feiernkultur der sozialdemokratischen Bewegung in der Ersten Republik Österreich 1918-1934*, Europaverlag, Vienna (1992) and Helge Zoitl, *'Student kommt von Studieren!' Zur Geschichte der sozialistischen Studentenbewegung in Wien*, Europaverlag, Vienna (1992).

22   That is, Social Democratic 'culture'. There is a regrettable tendency in works on Social Democratic auxiliary organisations blithely to equate 'workers' with 'Social Democrats'. Despite considerable overlaps, the two groups were not, of course, mutually inclusive. This is indicated especially clearly in Gruber's comparison of 'Socialist Party Culture' with 'Worker Leisure' and the 'Worker Family'. See Gruber (1991).

23   Both were endowed with the evocative 'new human being' title: 'With us, the new age approaches'. See *'Mit uns zieht die neue Zeit': Arbeiterkultur in Österreich 1918-1934. Katalog zur Ausstellung*, Vienna (1981).

24 See e.g. the critical comments on the exhibition in Gruber (1983), 49-50, as compared to the rather misty-eyed recollections of Helmut Konrad, 'Zur österreichischen Arbeiterkultur der Zwischenkriegszeit', in Boll (1986), 89-90.

25 Gruber (1991), vii.

26 See the discussion in the Introduction to this book.

27 See Gruber's review of some of the products of this *'Kulturwelle'* in Gruber (1983), 52-57.

28 See the sources cited in footnote 23 of the Introduction of this book.

29 Gruber (1991), 112. For Gruber's full argument here, see the whole of Chapter Four, 'Socialist Party Culture' (81-113) and his Conclusion (180-186).

30 This question cannot, of course, be addressed fully here, although it is touched upon further below.

31 Dreier (1984), 190-193.

32 Weidenholzer (1981), 242-250.

33 Ibid., 253-267.

34 See e.g. Josef Weidenholzer (1988), 42-43, who includes a rather incredulous contemporary local press report of one of these festivals, *'Flammen der Nacht'*, 'flames in the night', in 1928.

35 See respectively SPÖ Mauthausen (1989), 96; Hummer (1984), 59; Christian Denkmaier, Siegbert Janko, 'Die Sozialdemokratie ist eine Kulturbewegung', in SPÖ-Bezirksorganisation Linz-Stadt (1988), 152.

36 Weidenholzer (1981), 253-267. The latter point is confirmed in the discussion of the 'new human being' in Steyr below.

37 See Bauer (1988a), idem (1988b), Bauer, Weitgruber (1985).

38 Ibid. c.f. Bauer (1988a), 205.

39 Bauer (1988e), 125.

40 Quoted in Bauer, Weitgruber (1985), 76.

41 Bauer (1988a), 205.

42 This point is illustrated rather touchingly in the following recollection by a First Republic Social Democrat from Hallein, as quoted in Bauer (1988e), 135:

> Our functionaries, who were supervising us at the time, always used to say: 'Kids, we are a Socialist Party, and Socialism means: help one another, because if you stand alone you can't help yourself'. We were something like a community of mutual aid. Yes, that's just how it seemed to me. Socialism according to Karl Marx ... - of course I've heard of Marx, but I've never read the book. For me, what I saw and heard, what the people around me showed me, was textbook enough.

43 The aggregate total membership of 17,190 must be treated with some caution, since the membership figures for the individual organisations - as far as they are available - are not all from the same year. However, it would be safe to assume that the total aggregate membership of the auxiliary organisations in the late 1920s actually reached around 20,000. The Consumer Cooperative alone had a membership in the Steyr District of 3,000 at the end of 1928; at least half of these could be assumed to live in Steyr. In addition, there are also some 26 organisations mentioned in Table 6.2 for which no membership figures are available. At least three of these (Abstinents, Cyclists and Footballers) had memberships running into hundreds.

44   These figures are collected from a diverse range of sources: STB 6-2-1927, 2-3; 5-2-1928, 11; 25-1-1929, 8; 9-2-1929, 10; 9-2-1930, 13; 14-2-1930, 7; 16-2-1930, 14; 11-6-1930, 10; 12-8-1930, 8; 17-2-1931, 11; OÖTB 1928, 57; 1929, 33, 56; 1930, 38, 51; *Rote Saat* 1929, 58; 1930, 88; Feuerbestattungsverein "Die Flamme" in Steyr, *Festschrift zur Feier der Eröffnung der Ersten Oberösterreichischen Feuerhalle in Steyr im Juni 1927*, Steyr, 1927, 27-29; AVA BKA Inneres 22/Oberösterreich Karton 5100: 103.821-30; 108.893-30; VGA Parteiarchiv Mappe 67/2.

45   STB 9-9-1927, 5; 1-2-1928, 2.

46   See e.g. STB 3-2-1929, 3; 9-2-1930, 13; 17-2-1931, 12. These presumably accounted for some of the *Bildungszentrale* lectures recorded in Upper Austria in Table 6.1.

47   Quoted in STB 9-11-1927, 7. See also 23-11-1927, 8; 16-10-1928, 10.

48   C.f. Gruber (1991), 81-102.

49   STB 26-11-1927, 5.

50   See e.g. STB 24-2-1929, 10.

51   STB 18-1-1928, 9.

52   See e.g. the lecture titles listed in STB 3-2-1929, 3.

53   STB 1-2-1928, 2.

54   STB 3-2-1929, 3.

55   See the annual reports of the activities of the Educational Committee in STB 9-2-1930, 13 (for 1929), 17-2-1931, 12 (for 1930), 23-2-1932, 10 (for 1931), after which there is no further mention in the *Steyrer Tagblatt* of party schools. It should be stressed that from 1930 the general level of activity in the Social Democratic movement was subdued by the ongoing economic crisis and growing state repression.

56   STB 18-1-1928, 9.

57   Ibid.

58   With the exception of a short period of enthusiasm which surrounded the launch of the Arts Centre. See STB 6-2-1927, 2; 9-11-1927, 7; 13-12-1927, 8; 5-2-1928, 10; 16-3-1928, 8; 27-4-1928, 8; 30-9-1928, 11.

59   STB 9-11-1927, 7. This sentiment had earlier been expressed by Alois Huemer at the 1927 convocation of Upper Austrian Social Democratic educationalists. See STB 14-10-1927, 3. Gruber suggests that Social Democratic educationalists faced just the same problem in Vienna, where, of course, the supply of such 'dubious' forms of entertainment was much larger. See Gruber (1991), esp. 116-141.

60   STB 3-2-1929, 3.

61   E.g. STB 24-1-1932, 12; 27-1-1934, 5.

62   STB 17-3-1928, 7.

63   So Josef Kirchberger, quoted in STB 23-11-1927, 8.

64   See, for example, Josef Buttinger's recollections of his time in Schneegattern in Upper Austria (Hummer (1984), 60), and, in particular, those of Peter Kammerstätter of his youth in Linz, in his 'Antifaschismus, Berge, Heimat, Politik. Kristallisationspunkte einer oberösterreichischen Arbeiterbiographie', in Hubert Hummer, Reinhard Kannonier, Brigitte Kepplinger (Eds.), *Die Pflicht zum Widerstand. Festschrift Peter Kammerstätter zum 75. Geburtstag*, Europaverlag, Linz (1986), 14-19.

65   So the title of Wolfgang Neugebauer's 1975 book on the SAJ. On the SAJ self-image in Steyr, see Interview with Josef Mayrhofer, 4-7-1986.

66   On SAJ collectivism see Interview with Josef Mayrhofer, 4-7-1986; Josef Mayrhofer, *Aus meinem Leben*, typewritten manuscript, Steyr (n.d.), 17-23; Stockinger (1988), 64-67; STB 27-5-1928, 12; 22-6-1928, 8; 5-5-1929, 11; 11-5-1930, 11; 22-6-1930, 12; 17-12-1930, 9; 13-12-1931, 11.

67   See ibid; STB 6-2-1927, 2; 22-6-1928, 8; 14-8-1928, 10; 6-6-1930, 10; 2-3-1932, 8.

68   See the discusson of youth *Wehrhaftigkeit* below, and in Chapter Eight.

69   For example, the income of the Steyr District SDAP in 1927 was 44,358.85 shillings,while that of the Steyr District *Kinderfreunde* was 123,550.96. STB 4-2-1928, 6; *Rote Saat* 1929, 61-62.

70   See the annual reports for 1927, 1928 and 1929 - the most active years for the organisation - in STB 5-2-1928, 10; 9-2-1929, 9-10; 11-2-1930, 9.

71   See e.g. STB 5-2-1928, 10.

72   See e.g. SZ 22-5-1927, 1; 5-6-1927, 5; 12-6-1927, 1; 14-6-1927, 6; 27-2-1931, 1.

73   STB 20-3-1929, 9.

74   Indeed, it could be argued in a broader sense that a number of other local Social Democratic auxiliary organisations performed similarly attractive service functions which may equally have helped to strengthen individuals' attachments to the movement. Most notable among these were the Consumer Cooperative, the Tenants' Association and the Crematorial Association. The Co-op gave rebates on goods sold to its members, while the Tenant's Association provided often invaluable aid at rent tribunals and other housing-related disputes. The Crematorial Association provided cremation, burial and grave-maintenance services for a small monthly fee. Other organisations which might be mentioned in this context of service-provision - although less information is available - are the Housing Cooperative and the local Social Democratic pensioners' and savers' groups.

75   See e.g. STB 25-4-1929, 12; 1-4-1931, 8; 2-4-1931, 9.

76   STB 15-2-1931, 11.

77   See the periodic reports of the activities of the Women's Organisation, as printed in STB 6-2-1927, 1; 4-2-1928, 7; 18-6-1929, 12; 7-11-1929, 10; 9-1-1930, 13; 29-10-1930, 9.

78   See STB 4-2-1928, 7; 10-5-1928, 9; 12-2-1930, 9. C.f. Franz Seibert, *Die Konsumgenossenschaften in Österreich*, Europaverlag, Vienna (1978), 90-91; Andrea Ellmeier, Eva Singer-Meczes, 'Modellierung der sozialistischen Konsumentin. Konsumgenossenschaftliche (Frauen)Politik in den zwanziger Jahren', *Zeitgeschichte*, **16** (1988-1989).

79   So STB 6-2-1927, 1.

80   Langewiesche (1979), 238-247.

81   See e.g. STB 15-2-1931, 11; 14-2-1932, 11. It is interesting to recall in this context the low participation rate of women in Steyr's party 'schools' of socialist education which was mentioned in above.

82   Josef Buttinger, *Das Ende der Massenpartei am Beispiel Österreichs*, Verlag Neue Kritik, Frankfurt (1972), 76-82.

83   Ibid., 76.

84   Ibid., 78.

85   Auxiliary organisation members need not, of course, necessarily have been members or voters of the SDAP. Instrumental motivations - for example to gain access to Social Democratic patronage, services or, in the case of many of the hobby clubs, facilities - will inevitably have extended the pool of auxiliary

organisation members beyond the 'core' supporters of the Social Democratic movement.

[86]   Buttinger (1972), 81.

[87]   See e.g. Kutschera (1972), 49-54; Salzer (n.d.), 161-2, 183

[88]   See e.g. STB 1-10-1929, 7.

[89]   Ritually condemned in the rival Social Democratic *Steyrer Tagblatt* as the 'black [i.e. clericalist] lying auntie on the Steyr town square'!

[90]   On the 'friendly' side, see Interview with Josef Mayrhofer, 4-7-1986 and Kotlan-Werner (1982), 252. On the 'hostile' side, see SZ 8-11-1927, 1; 3-4-1928, 1; Manfred Brandl, *Neue Geschichte von Steyr. Vom Biedermeier bis heute,* Ennsthaler, Steyr (1980), 274.

[91]   Entitled *Die Flamme.* This entered, it would seem, a macabre competition with the *Steyrer Zeitung* to make the other's preferred form of funeral/burial sound as revolting as possible! See e.g. SZ 4-9-1927, 14; 6-11-1928, 11; *Die Flamme,* January 1931, 13-14; March 1932, 4, April 1932, 6.

[92]   From the first cremation on 2 July 1927 onwards. See STB 20-8-1927, 7, and monthly thereafter through to 10-1-1934, 5.

[93]   On the broader relationship between *'Festkultur'* and religion, see Weidenholzer (1981), 183-188.

[94]   See e.g. SZ 17-6-1928, 1; STB 25-6-1930, 9-10; 26-6-1930, 10; 27-6-1930, 3; LTP 23-6-1930, 7; AVA BKA Inneres 22/Oberösterreich Karton 5100: 165.236-30; 165.832-30; Interview with Josef Mayrhofer 4-7-1986; Uitz (1975), 464.

[95]   See for Steyr Radmoser (n.d.), 39-61, and more generally Vincent J. Knapp, *Austrian Social Democracy 1889-1914,* University Press of America, Washington D.C. (1980).

[96]   STB 15-11-1928, 9.

[97]   STB 6-11-1928, 11.

[98]   The most comprehensive account of the Pfrimer Putsch in Upper Austria is given in Slapnicka (1975), 50-60.

[99]   Quoted in STB 15-11-1931, 11.

[100]   Military gymnastics consisted of marching, 'fully clothed running' (or yomping in modern terminology?), obstacle course negotiation, dummy hand-grenade throwing, and shooting practice.

[101]   For further details on the plans made for an *Ernstfall,* see the police files on prominent Social Democrats arrested in Steyr in the course of the Civil War of 1934, as collected in DÖW File 12202. See also Interview with Josef Mayrhofer, 4-7-1986.

[102]   Weidenholzer (1981), 94-95.

[103]   See e.g. STB 14-10-1927, 3; 14-10-1928, 11.

[104]   Quoted in W.L. Guttsman, *The German Social Democratic Party 1875-1933: from Ghetto to Government,* George Allen and Unwin, London (1981), 194, 203.

[105]   STB 22-6-1928, 8.

[106]   See DÖW File 12202a.

[107]   In this respect, it is worth noting that the Social Democratic reaction in Steyr to the events of 15 July 1927 in Vienna - a key event in the development of democratic politics in the First Republic - was muted, detached and tokenistic. See STB 20-7-1927, 8; 22-7-1927, 8; 28-7-1927, 8.

[108]   Rabinbach (1983), 79; Kulemann (1979), 326.

7 The SDAP in the Provinces: Bureaucracy, *Bonzen* and the Politics of Moderate Reform

Political parties normally possess mechanisms of intra-party democracy which, formally if not always in practice, offer their members opportunities to influence and shape their policies. The core argument of this chapter is that the formal mechanisms of intra-party democracy and the policies of the SDAP at the local level were circumscribed by the 'law' set out by Robert Michels in his seminal work on the sociology of political parties.[1] This 'iron law of oligarchy' states that large-scale party organisations are subject to tendencies to bureaucratisation and élite domination, and to a self-absorbed, organisation-centred political caution in the policies shaped by the party élite.

These, of course, are tendencies which were broadly evident, as Chapter Two has indicated, in the SDAP at the provincial and the Viennese/national[2] levels. The provincial- and national-level parties were very clearly large, bureaucratic, élite-dominated and highly self-absorbed organisations. It might plausibly be argued, however, that the local-level SDAP in the provinces lacked the largeness of scale for such tendencies to come clearly to the fore. This is a question addressed in section one of this chapter, which begins by summarising Michels' analysis of party organisation, and then measures up the available evidence from the provinces against that analysis. Of particular importance here is the drive for organisational penetration - the *Integration nach innen* - which was a core feature of Social Democratic *Hochburg* politics. It is proposed, although the supporting evidence is somewhat fragmentary, that this drive created an organisational structure large and diverse enough for the *Hochburg-*SDAP to be exposed to the oligarchical tendencies predicted by Michels.

Sections two and three test this proposition more fully in an examination of the SDAP in Steyr. Section two shows that the Steyr party had a large and ramified organisation with a three-level structure of ordinary members, activist members and leaders. The relationships between the three levels of the party were governed by a strong sense of hierarchy and discipline, and failed to provide opportunities for meaningful, 'bottom-up' democratic input by either ordinary or activist members. As a result, the party was dominated without challenge by a small élite of around twenty leaders. Section three examines the character and preoccupations of this leadership élite. It shows that its members developed an interest in and attachment to the organisation of Social Democracy for its own sake during the First Republic: most of them simultaneously held several different positions of authority in the Social Democratic movement, and most, crucially, were materially dependent in some way on one or other of the movement's organisations. This was a party élite which was deeply absorbed in the organisational life and well-being of the movement.

It is against this background that the development of SDAP policy in Steyr, discussed in section four, has to be seen. Party policy was much less a reflection of the concerns and interests of the party's supporters and members than a extension of the organisational mentality of the SDAP leadership. The party's strategy for power was, for example, mechanistically focused on organisational expansion; if it kept on recruiting voters and members, it would, *ipso facto*, one day find itself part of the governing party in Austria. A corollary of this gradualist strategy was the *de facto* acceptance of the social order into which the party was investing so much organisational effort. Notwithstanding occasional, platitudinous rhetoric about 'revolution' (and notwithstanding the outbursts of militant, territorial politics discussed elsewhere in this work), the Steyr SDAP was an unequivocally moderate, reformist party, firmly committed to working to improve the lot of its supporters within the existing framework of Austrian society. This was reflected in Steyr in the policy programme of pragmatic, ameliorative reform which was pursued by the SDAP-run municipal administration in the town. The final characteristic of SDAP policy addressed in section four is its unadaptability. The reformist politics of the Steyr SDAP became increasingly unworkable in the economic and political circumstances of the 1930s, yet the party leadership, bound up in its preoccupation with the organisational well-being of the party and the wider Social Democratic the movement, failed even to try to adapt them to the new situation, condemning the movement to a debilitating, introspective passivity.

Michels and the *Hochburg*-SDAP

Michels' classic work on political parties still contains, over eighty years after its first edition, 'some of the most intelligent and persuasive observations ... to be found'[3] about parties as organisational structures. This in part reflects the relative disinterest displayed by social scientists since Michels in examining parties explicitly as organisations.[4] More than this, though, it reflects the quality, logic and perceptiveness of Michels' insights. The outline of his argument is, consequently, well worth recalling here.

Michels on Political Parties

Michels was convinced of the inevitability of oligarchical rule in any expanding party (or, indeed, other) organisation. He pointed out that as the scale of an organisation expands, it becomes impossible for every member to oversee all its activities. A division of labour and a specialisation of function become an operational necessity. Representatives of the membership are thus entrusted with the direction of the organisation. An organisational hierarchy of directors and ordinary members is created, which becomes increasingly complex as functions are sub-divided and specialisations narrowed in the course of further organisational expansion. A bureaucratic superstructure thus develops which wrests effective control of the organisation away from the ordinary party members. Every division of labour represents a diminution of the control of the membership and, by implication, an accretion of power to those performing specialised functions:

> The more extended and the more ramified the official apparatus of the organisation ... the less efficient becomes the direct control exercised by the rank and file, and the more is this control replaced by the increasing power of committees.[5]

In theory, those delegated by the membership of a political party to direct the party organisation are usually subject to the criticism and democratic control of the membership. In practice, though, the membership is incompetent to perform these tasks; it does not possess the specialised knowledge and expertise necessary for effective criticism and control. Furthermore, with each division of labour and each incremental specialisation, the delegated party leaders become more and more indispensable. Logically, only a limited number of people is able to perform what have become highly specialised functions, so that ultimately the party cannot do without its leaders:

> This special competence, this expert knowledge, which the leader acquires in matters inaccessible to the mass, gives him a security of tenure which conflicts with the essential principles of democracy.[6]

In other words, no matter what formal arrangements are provided for the election and re-election of the leaders, their indispensability will more or less automatically secure for them an indefinite tenure. This indefinite tenure, combined with the inability of the rank and file effectively to criticise and control the leadership, means that any mechanisms of intra-party democracy which exist are a façade. For Michels there is a fundamental incompatibility between the specialisation of function and hierarchy inherent in any large-scale organisation, and effective democratic control by the rank and file. Intra-party power gravitates firmly and uncontrollably into the hands of the leadership.

Having attained this position of power, Michels asserts, the party leader undergoes a 'psychological metamorphosis'.[7] He who has attained power 'will not readily be induced to return to the comparatively obscure position which he formerly occupied'.[8] The experience of power encourages vanity and greed, which is reflected in the attempt to consolidate and extend further the basis of leadership power. Leaders, as a result, typically accumulate additional party functions and seek to give the party organisation an ever wider base and an ever increasing sphere of influence. New paths of activity are opened up and new specialisations taken on. In the process, sight of the 'immortal principles' of socialism is lost, and the 'fanatical advocates of the organisational idea' become 'stuck in a purely bureaucratic mode of thought, with no insight into wider political concerns.'[9] This narrow organisational mentality is compounded by the growing material dependence of the leadership on the party, as many of them assume paid employment in the party organisation. The result is a deep organisational conservatism. The leaders increasingly identify their personal interests with those of the party organisation; the organisation is their/the party's primary concern and must never be endangered in any way.[10] This organisational conservatism is reflected in the political arena in policies of exaggerated prudence and caution. Michels concluded:

> The party becomes increasingly inert as the strength of its organisation grows; it loses its revolutionary impetus, becomes sluggish, not in respect of action alone, but also in the sphere of thought. More and more tenaciously does the party cling to what it calls the 'ancient and glorious tactics', the tactics which have led to a continued increase in membership. More and more invincible becomes the aversion to all aggressive action.[11]

Michels' analysis of internal party bureaucracy inevitably has, in the 1990s, a somewhat dated feel. It would certainly display some glaring defects if applied to the hi-tech parties active in the mass information society of today. It retains, though, considerable explanatory power in the study of the inter-war SDAP. What Michels rather grandly assigns the status of a sociological 'law' is in reality little more than a series of generalised observations derived from an empirical examination of the German SPD in the years 1890-1915 (and spiced with less frequent references to other socialist parties in the same era). Seen in this less lofty light, Michels' work is close to the inter-war SDAP both in subject matter, where a Social Democratic 'family' resemblance to the SPD might be expected, and in historical era, where pre-war SPD and inter-war SDAP shared a broadly comparable 'technology' of party organisation and management. The remainder of this chapter therefore examines the local-level SDAP against the Michels model, focusing on the following criteria: the process of bureaucratisation and élite domination in the party organisation; the elevation of the party organisation from a means to an end of politics; and the neglect of the 'immortal principles' of the party in favour of a tactical caution reliant on tried and trusted methods.

Bureaucratisation in the SDAP: the Evidence from the Provinces

It might plausibly be assumed that political parties at the local level would lack the scale and diversity of function which promote a bureaucratic form of organisation. However, it has been a running theme of this work that Social Democracy at the local level in Austria was a movement which placed an unusually high premium on organisational penetration. The local-level Social Democratic movement was consumed in a drive for *Integration nach innen* which sought to establish for its followers a protected area, a *Schutzgemeinschaft, vis-à-vis* an otherwise dominant array of conservative forces in provincial politics. The premium placed on organisational penetration was seen most obviously in the wide range of auxiliary organisations which, as Chapter Six has shown, was established even in the smallest *Hochburgen*. In addition to these, though, each *Hochburg* could also claim some combination of Social Democratic FTUs (sectorally differentiated in line with the local economic structure) and, naturally, a number of SDAP sections gathered together into local and/or district party organisations. A clear impression of the end-result of this multi-faceted drive to organise is given by Weidenholzer in his listing of the different Social Democratic organisations in existence in 1930 in a provincial railway community (unfortunately unnamed) which had just 500 party members:

> 1. Train-drivers' executive. 2. Workshop executive. 3. Station executive. 4. Conductors' executive. 5. Signal-workers' executive. 6. Pensioners' group. 7. Political party. 8. Railworkers' FTU. 9. Building workers' FTU. 10. Gymnastics club. 11. Football club. 12. Athletics club. 13. *Naturfreunde*. 14. Cyclists' club. 15. Motorcyclists' club. 16. *Schutzbund*. 17. Railworkers' and telegraphers' [paramilitary] stewards unit. 18. *Kinderfreunde*. 19. SAJ. 20. Cremaforial association. 21. League of free thinkers. 22. Choral society. 23. Women's choral society. 24. Women's organisation. 25. Tenants' association. 26. Education committee. 27. Commercial employees' FTU. 28. Savings bank. 29. School council. 30. Municipal council party fraction. 31. Milk cooperative. 32. Radio hams' club.

33. House-building cooperative. 34. Bruckner society. 35. Consumer cooperative. 36. Music club. 37. Economic committee of the consumer coop. In addition various district and other committees not listed here.[12]

Although the SDAP figured in Weidenholzer's list only at number seven, it was unequivocally the most important organisation within the local Social Democratic movement. To it fell the responsibility for coordinating and giving overall leadership and direction to the extensive and diverse web of Social Democratic organisations. This leadership role applied, moreover, not only in the internal affairs of the movement, but also, especially after 1918, in the exercise of public functions, for example in the school council and municipal council activities noted above. In these senses the local-level SDAP stood, even in the smaller *Hochburgen*, at the head of what could certainly qualify, in Michels' terms, as a large-scale organisation.

No concerted attempt has yet been made in the literature to examine the implications of such large-scale organisation for internal party life. Occasional insights which hint at the existence of oligarchical tendencies can, however, be found. The SDAP in Linz, for example, is said to have undergone a process of 'professionalisation and bureaucratisation', linked to the increasingly frequent assumption of public functions in the early part of the twentieth century, which left the party with 'ossified structures'.[13] A number of authors point elsewhere to typical symptoms of organisational ossification. Karl Gutkas notes the high level of continuity among 'older', 'long-entrenched' (*alteingesessen*) party leaders in 'many local organisations' in Lower Austria.[14] An insight into this process of entrenchment in Lower Austria is given in Siegfried Nasko's chronicle of the Social Democratic movement in the St Pölten area when he discusses the 're-election of *the whole previous committee*' of the Neulengbach district party as a matter of routine at its annual district conference in 1928.[15] Karl Schiffer recalls in related vein having to fight as a young party member in Graz for opportunities to make constructive input into a party life which was 'boring' and dominated by 'worthy, [but] stolid' and, presumably, entirely uninspiring, long-serving, older party functionaries.[16]

These fragments of information are unfortunately too few to provide a fully satisfactory comparative context for the following case study of the internal organisation of the SDAP in Steyr. Incomplete as they are though, they do point, albeit impressionistically, to the existence of a Michelsian bureaucratisation process in the local-level SDAP in the provinces. This impression is given emphatic confirmation in the case of Steyr.

Intra-Party Democracy in the Steyr SDAP

The SDAP in Steyr was an organisation of considerable size and diverse function. It could rely on around 60% of the vote in elections locally and was the ruling party on Steyr's town council. It was also the centrepoint of a district-wide party organisation with 37 sections and almost 10,000 members in Steyr and its surrounding villages in the late 1920s. Of these, a core of ten sections[17] and around 5,000 members were situated in Steyr itself. In addition, the SDAP offered coordination and leadership to the fifty-plus auxiliary organisations discussed in the previous chapter, and to the eleven FTUs[18] which organised locally.

The party's extensive responsibilities were attended to through a pyramidal party structure of three organisational levels: the bottom (party section) level in which the party's ordinary members were organised; the intermediate level of party activists, who attended to routine organisational tasks; and the district level, the preserve of the party leadership. The following discussion analyses the relationships between these different levels, focusing in particular on the nature and extent of intra-party democracy in the Steyr SDAP.

At section level, party life consisted of a continuous round of procedural, informational and educational meetings and events, as well as some light entertainment. These meetings and events were organised by a network of party activists who were responsible for basic administrative tasks such as advertising meetings, collecting subscriptions, hawking the party press and so on. It is unclear how many activists there were. An informed estimate would be 150.[19] These met regularly in the section committees and in town-wide activist conferences. Moving up the pyramid, the sovereign body of the district-level party was the annual District Conference. This consisted of delegates - mainly activists - from the party sections and auxiliary organisations, and was numerically dominated by the ten party sections in Steyr itself. The District Conference held annual elections to the party leadership, composed as a District Committee of around 20 members which had responsibility for the day-to-day running of the party and the coordination of the whole district's activities.

On paper this party structure provided ample opportunity for influence to percolate up from ordinary members and activists to the party leadership. In reality, though, the level of ordinary member and activist participation in party affairs was low and the quality of this participation limited. At section level, for example, genuine participation was not encouraged or facilitated in the regular section meetings. These typically consisted of administrative routine (minutes, officers' reports etc.) followed by a lecture by one of the District Committee members. There was not much room for debate. As Josef

Mayrhofer, an active member of the SDAP in the First Republic, noted: 'If it was a purely informative meeting, inspired by some current event, then of course there was not much discussion'.[20] Of some 246 section meetings advertised in the *Steyrer Tagblatt* between 1928 and 1932, 155, or 63%, were of such an 'informative' nature, focused on current affairs.[21] This suggests that the role of the ordinary member at section meetings was purely receptive. S/he was there to hear and take in, but not discuss what a representative of the leadership had to say. Such was also the case, ironically, in special 'discussion evenings' which were also held in the sections. According to the *Steyrer Tagblatt*, these were instituted to provide occasions when current events in politics, economy and social policy could be discussed in the 'intimate' atmosphere of the section.[22] However, they distinguished themselves in practice from normal section meetings only in that the evening was begun and ended with some form of entertainment, and that two party notables instead of one gave a lecture. The two lectures were then summarised by the section leader. At no point were contributions sought from the floor. The impression left is that discussion evenings and section meetings alike were intra-party disciplining agencies, directed not at increasing popular participation, but at educating the rank and file in the views and outlook of the party leadership.[23]

In 1929 the style of party meetings was attacked (for the first and only recorded time) in a *Steyrer Tagblatt* article entitled 'Let's put an end to boring meetings!' In the article the (unnamed) author suggested a new format for Social Democratic meetings in the attempt to stimulate greater interest among the membership. S/he proposed a much less formal type of meeting which would abandon a fixed agenda and long, dry reports in favour of brevity, humour and entertainment.[24] The official party response to this call for innovation was vehemently negative. A counter-article, presumably written by the *Steyrer Tagblatt* Editor (and SDAP District Committee member) Josef Kirchberger, mounted an instructive defence of the traditional format of party meetings. In Kirchberger's eyes party meetings bore the major responsibility for the rise and successes of the SDAP. They were, he argued, the most effective means of 'proletarian education and enlightenment', and promoted 'class consciousness', 'iron discipline' and 'unconditional solidarity and party loyalty'.[25]

In other words, party meetings were viewed in the party leadership as means of educating the rank and file to the qualities of unity and discipline. They were clearly not thought of as a means to assess and take account of rank and file opinion in the development of party policies. Moreover, the virtues Kirchberger mentioned - unity and discipline - were regularly reiterated and reemphasised in the rhetoric of the Steyr SDAP, particularly when some kind of challenge to the party emerged.[26] The emphasis on intra-party discipline was further accentuated by widespread rhetorical use of militaristic terminology in describing party affairs: the SAJ was the 'cadet school of the party'; the tasks facing the party required a 'well-drilled and disciplined army of functionaries'; the activist dues collectors of the party were (more poetically) the 'unknown soldiers in the positional warfare of the proletariat, who conscientiously collected month after month the ammunition for the great army of class warriors'.[27] The emphasis on discipline in general and the allusions to military discipline in particular reinforce the impression of a local party which operated from the top level downwards and lacked opportunities for input and influence for its ordinary members.

The Social Democratic activists in Steyr had a far greater intensity of involvement in party life than the party's ordinary members, though it is doubtful whether this gave them any more influence over the policies and direction of the party. They were involved in two main activist forums: regular section committee meetings and periodic, town-wide activist conferences. The former reflected the function of activist work in the sections and concentrated exclusively on the central activist role of maintaining an ongoing link between organisation and members. This incorporated the advertisement of party meetings, the collection of membership subscriptions, the hawking of the party press, and the recruitment of new members. Available accounts of this link role do not suggest any wider function of sounding out, articulating and passing on ordinary members' concerns or grievances.[28] The district-level activist gatherings had a wider remit, taking in not only organisational matters, but also current affairs and Steyr's municipal politics. As at section level, though, the proceedings of these meetings were dominated by representatives of the district leadership to the exclusion of political debate. It appears that the function of these meetings was to secure formal activist acclamation for - and therefore lend legitimacy to - municipal policies decided at a higher level,[29] or to give the activists tactical instructions.[30] In other words, the SDAP activists in Steyr lacked the scope to play any genuinely creative role in intra-party life. They functioned merely as the organisational lubricants of the party and as the executors of policies laid down from above.

The limits of the activist role were clearly illustrated in the character of the annual SDAP District Conference. The formal tasks of the conference were to review the previous year's work whilst at the same time discussing 'thoroughly and profoundly' the tactical direction to be followed in the coming year.[31] Unsurprisingly, these tasks were in no sense fulfilled. The review of the past year took the form of a report by the full-time Party Secretary. The Secretary's report was invariably a dry, detailed, organisation-by-organisation listing of current membership figures, the frequency of meetings, special events held, and so on. There was no attempt to prescribe a future course from the experiences of the previous year or to seek suggestions for change or development. Characteristically, this entirely bland report was invariably accepted by the 150 or so assembled delegates uncritically, without debate, and even 'with great satisfaction'.[32]

Only in one field did genuine and lively discussion emerge in the conference: the annual party subscriptions debate. This debate was typically intense, heated and many-cornered. In 1928, for example, some 14 delegates, around a tenth of those present made some kind of intervention from the floor.[33] This level of involvement presented a marked contrast to the normally receptive and subordinate role of the party activists and was trumpeted by the *Steyrer Tagblatt* as an indication of the 'inner health' and freedom of expression which reigned within the party.[34] Seen realistically, though, it reflected little more than the discomfort the party activists felt about having to implement a higher subscription level in their day-to-day contact on the ground with the party's subs-paying ordinary members. More importantly, 'freedom of expression' did not extend beyond such essentially petty, organisational matters into issues of party tactics and policy, about which there was never open debate at the annual conference. Politically important issues were, in other words, decided within the ranks of a limited leadership circle and then transmitted, without discussion, to the lower levels of the party.

This clear leadership domination of the party organisation in Steyr compares well with the Michels model. So does its corollary: emerging leadership indispensability. The concentration of tactical and policy decision-making power in the hands of a small leadership group in the Steyr SDAP meant that the members of that small group were the only party members who were experienced in making tactical and policy decisions, and who were thus qualified to lead the party. There was no credibly qualified alternative to the existing leadership in a party which did not seek policy-related participation, criticism and debate from its members. The hierarchical structure of the party in Steyr became closed and ossified, assuring the leadership of a *de facto* indefinite tenure.

The process of ossification is clearly illustrated in the District Committee elections held annually at the District Conference. Between 1928 and 1933 there was no instance of controversy in the District Committee elections. No candidates put themselves forward to challenge the incumbents. The official slate, put forward by the conference elections committee, was the only slate to vote on. It was normally accepted either by acclamation or unanimous vote. 1928 provides the exception, when some of those on the official list attracted 'only' an overwhelming majority of the votes cast.[35] The elections were uncompetitive rubber stamps which, as Table 7.1 shows, confirmed in office a more or less unchanging élite. The only changes among the elected officers of the District Committee between 1928 and 1933 were the formal alternation of the two luminaries of the Women's Organisation, Erna Schwitzer and Fanny Pammer, and the departure (presumably the death) of Franz Huber. As Table 7.1. also shows, the

Table 7.1 The Stability of the Steyr SDAP District Committee 1928-1933

Year	Chair	Deputy Chair	Deputy Chair	Treasurer	Deputy Treasurer	Secretary	Deputy Secretary
1928	Schrangl	Witzany	Schwitzer	Tribrunner	Klement	Kirchberger	Huber
1929	"	"	Pammer	"	"	"	"
1930	"	"	Schwitzer	"	"	"	"
1931	"	"	Pammer	"	"	"	Roithner
1932	"	"	"	"	"	"	"
1933	"	"	"	"	"	"	"

Year	OM	OM	OM	OM	OM	OM	OM	OM
1928	Hafner	Russmann	Dedic	Fridrich	Sichlrader	Mitschko	Pfaff	Häuslmayr
1929	Moser	"	"	Roithner	"	"	"	"
1930	"	"	"	"	"	"	Schöner	"
1931	"	"	"	Sperl	"	Mellich	"	"
1932	"	Schopper	"	"	"	Mayrhofer	"	---
1933	"	"	"	"	"	"	---	---

Year	OM	OM	SM	SM	SM	SM	SM	SM	SM
1928	Azwanger	---	Dedic	Dressl	Huemer	Sieberer	Kohler	Hubmann	---
1929	"	---	"	"	"	"	Sippl	"	---
1930	"	---	"	"	"	"	"	"	Pammer
1931	"	Heumann	"	"	"	"	"	"	Schwitzer
1932	"	"	"	"	Konrad	"	"	"	"
1933	"	"	"	'	"	"	"	"	"

Note: *OM signifies 'Ordinary member', and SM 'Supervisory member'.*
Sources: *STB 12-2-1928, 11; 10-2-1929, 11; 16-2-1930, 14; 18-2-1931, 8; 23-2-1932, 10; 28-2-1933, 3.*

composition of the ordinary and supervisory members of the committee was only slightly less set in stone.[36] Intra-party power was thus concentrated in the hands of a leadership élite which was secure in its position, and which presided over a hierarchical, highly disciplined party structure which did not provide opportunities for democratic input by its lower levels. The SDAP in Steyr was manifestly a leadership-dominated party.

This conclusion does not, it should be stressed, automatically imply that there was any great frustrated demand in the party for more participation in internal party life and for more control over the leadership. The 'boring meetings' article discussed above is to my knowledge the only overt criticism of internal party life in Steyr to have been voiced before the disintegration of the party in 1933-1934.[37] As Michels noted in respect of the pre-1914 SPD, the great majority of party members seemed entirely indifferent to the decisions of the party leaders; in effect they voluntarily renounced their formal democratic rights in intra-party affairs.[38] In similar vein, Kulemann makes the point in his examination of Social Democratic party structures at the national level in Austria that the SDAP, as a mass party, was in theory prepared to accept anyone as a member as long as s/he was prepared to pay party dues.[39] Entrance into a party does not, in other words, automatically signify a commitment to participate and demand an active role in the intra-party decision-making process. This point is especially pertinent in the case of Steyr, particularly in the late 1920s when MAV control over access to local jobs attracted a large contingent of instrumentally motivated members to the Social Democratic movement (see Chapter Five). In this era some members joined the party purely for reasons of personal, material interest and not from any commitment to shape the character and policies of the party. Instrumentalists were essentially passive members, uninterested in intra-party democracy. Their passivity helped in a negative sense to reduce the potential for discussion and criticism in the party and thus, indirectly, to cement the leadership in its dominant position.[40]

The Character of the Party Leadership Élite

It is, for obvious reasons, difficult to establish the extent to which the party leadership élite in Steyr, once established in its dominant position, underwent the 'psychological metamorphosis' predicted by Michels. There is, though, plenty of evidence to suggest it had a certain 'greed' for power. The members of the Steyr party leadership were clearly concerned to broaden their intra-organisational power base through an accumulation of functions in the party, the MAV or other Social Democratic organisations. Of the 23 members of the District Committee in 1932, only one, to my knowledge, held no other Social Democratic office at the time. The remainder held at least two, and usually more, sometimes many more. The accumulation of functions in part reflected an incestuous process of mutual nomination to delegated positions in higher party bodies. An example would be the selection of delegates from Steyr to the Upper Austrian and national party conferences. Delegates - invariably members of the District Committee

- were elected (unanimously, as was the practice) at the District Conference 'according to the proposal' made by another member of the District Committee![41] Otherwise, accumulated functions traced the route of the individual's 'career' in the Social Democratic movement. For example, Julius Russmann was a 'local statesman', whose various functions derived primarily from his membership of the town council (see Table 7.2). August Moser, on the other hand, was first and foremost a trade unionist (Table 7.3), while Franz Sichlrader was a consummate bureaucrat whose interests were evenly spread across state, party and MAV (Table 7.4).

The apparent concern of the members of the party leadership to 'collect' functions suggests, in line with Michels, that they experienced some kind of personal benefit from performing the functions concerned and exercising the power that went with them. It indicates a blurring of personal and party interests in which the level of personal interest secured was broadly proportionate to the scale of - and number of functions available in - the organisation. This tendency towards a blurring of personal and party interests is given more direct confirmation in the material dependence of most of the party leadership on the organisations of the Social Democratic movement. Of the 23

Table 7.2 The Functions Held by Julius Russmann in 1930

Level	State Functions	Party Functions	Union Functions	Other Functions
National	---	---	---	---
Upper Austrian	---	---	---	---
Local	Vice-Mayor			
	Municipal Portfolio: Municipal Enterprises and Unemployment Office			
	President of the Welfare Committee			
	Chair of the Tourism Office			
	Member of the Municipal School Council			
	Councillor	District Committee	Leader of the Union of Industrial Employees	Chair of Football Club Vorwärts

Table 7.3 The Functions Held by August Moser in 1932

Level	State Function	Party Function	Union Function	Other	Functions
National			Austrian FTU Confederation Executive		
			MAV Executive		
	---	---	Delegate to MAV Congress	---	---
Upper Austrian	---	Delegate to Provincial Congress	Provincial MAV Executive	Provincial Health Fund Executive	---
Local			MAV Executive		
			Leader of Steyr-Werke Works Council		
	Councillor in St. Ulrich	District Committee	Works Councillor	Health Fund Executive	Schutzbund Executive

Table 7.4 The Functions Held by Franz Sichlrader in 1932

Level	State Functions	Party Functions	Union Functions
National	Parliamentary Candidate	---	MAV Executive
Upper Austrian		Provincial Executive	
	Member of Upper Austrian Parliament	Delegate to Provincial Congress	Provincial MAV Chair
Local	Mayor		
	Municipal Finance Portfolio		MAV Chair
	Councillor	District Committee	MAV Executive

members of the District Committee in 1932 (see Table 7.1), sixteen were in employment which was directly or indirectly dependent on the movement. Two, Hans Witzany, the local MP, and Franz Sichlrader, Steyr's mayor, owed their existences to Social Democratic votes. Five were employees of Social Democratic organisations: Karl Klement was the local, full-time SDAP Secretary, Josef Kirchberger the Editor of the *Steyrer Tagblatt*, Leopold Heumann the full-time Secretary of the local MAV, August Dressl a full-time representative of the local MAV on the

Upper Austrian Chamber of Labour, and Franz Tribrunner an employee of the local Social Democratic health insurance fund. Another five were secure in the MAV's closed shop at the Steyr-Werke (Franz Schrangl, August Moser, Emmerich Schopper, Michael Sieberer and Josef Sperl). Ferdinand Mayrhofer was an employee of the town council and three teachers - Hans Roithner, Anton Azwanger and Erna Schwitzer - worked under the administration of the SDAP council majority. This material dependence of over two-thirds of the local party leadership on the SDAP and the other organisations it led and coordinated further entwined personal with party interests. The result was that predicted by Michels: the emergence of a narrow and conservative, organisation-centred mentality among the party élite.

This conservative organisational mentality was expressed in a number of ways. It could be seen, for example, in a Michelsian 'tendency towards and exclusive and all-absorbing specialisation' in leadership functions.[42] For example, Franz Sichlrader, Mayor and holder of the municipal finance portfolio, presented the impression of complete self-immersion in the particular problems and details of municipal finance. He was the author of numerous articles on the Steyr council's financial situation in the local press and national journals. He gave regular speeches on the subject in the council chamber and the Upper Austrian *Landtag*, and was periodically involved in complex financial negotiations with the Upper Austrian and federal governments.[43] Anton Azwanger, Vice-Mayor after 1930, had a similarly intense preoccupation with his municipal finance portfolio.[44]

The organisational mentality of the party leadership was perhaps reflected most overtly, though, in the reports prepared by the full-time Party Secretary and District Committee member Karl Klement, for submission to the annual District Conference. In the late 1920s, a period of organisational growth, these reports were punctuated with calls to develop, extend and consolidate the organisation and to build on the advances being made.[45] In the decline of the early 1930s the emphasis changed to the attempt to establish - unconvincingly - the continued strength of attachment and commitment to the organisation and towards making good any losses which had been experienced.[46] The key point is that whatever the conditions, the *organisation* was always the centrepoint of the leadership's considerations. This syndrome of self-immersion in the intricacies of organisation had a decisive effect on the wider character of the SDAP in Steyr. It detached the party leaders from their members and supporters. The leaders became archetypal *'Bonzen'*, remote and self-important 'bigwigs' whose awareness of wider political concerns both within and without the party was blunted by an increasingly narrow-minded and rigid outlook, lodged in the minutiae of their particular organisational responsibilities.

Organisation had, in other words, become self-justification; it was no longer a means to secure political goals, but a *Selbstzweck*, an end in itself, for the party leadership in Steyr. This *Selbstzweck* terminology recalls of course the nature of commitment to the Social Democratic auxiliary organisations discussed in the previous chapter. In a sense, the party leaders in Steyr were 'Frau Meiers' writ large, who, like many of their followers, had lifted up 'organisation' to become their dominant political value and simultaneously narrowed their sense of political perspective. As the following section shows, this elevation of organisation to an end of politics had a decisive impact both on the character and the flexibility of SDAP strategy and policies.

SDAP Reformism in Steyr: the Politics of 'Small Steps'

The Steyr SDAP was clearly a party which conformed to Michels' 'law'. It lacked 'bottom-up' democratic input and participation, and was dominated by a small leadership élite of *'Parteibonzen'*. This section examines how the rigid organisational mentality of the party élite affected the policy priorities of the party. An initial indication is given in an emblematic clarion call for organisational consolidation made by Karl Klement in his Secretary's report to the 1928 District Conference:

> The more solidly we build up the organisations of the proletariat, the better each individual is integrated, the stronger we are, the better we can gather together the revolutionary energy and creative forces of the Austrian proletariat into a unified will ... The magic word for all progress is organisation![47]

A clearer expression of Klement's - and more broadly the party elite's - organisational mentality could hardly have been given. At no point did Klement elaborate on the goals to be striven for by the 'unified will' which would develop from stronger organisation. His 'revolutionary' and 'creative' phraseology was empty rhetoric. The party had lost touch with what Michels called the 'immortal principles' of Social Democracy. It had lost the radical, system-challenging impetus which, back in the nineteenth century, had originally created and driven the Social Democratic movement in Steyr.[48] Instead, the scope of its political horizons was bounded and defined by the desire to build up that 'magic word', the basis of 'all progress', organisation. The narrowness of these horizons was reflected in the formal public arenas of political life in Steyr - electoral competition and municipal policy-making - in a politics of 'small steps', or 'partial achievements',[49] a politics of cautious, moderate, incremental reform.

At first sight this image of caution and moderation might seem to contradict what has been written earlier in this work about *Abgrenzung nach außen*, the often incautious, militant commitment to defend Social Democratic 'territory' against the incursions of the Right. Cautious reformism and militant territorial self-assertion were, however, two sides of the same coin of *Hochburg* politics: the latter was part of the drive to demarcate the *Hochburg* and the community identity which could flourish within it from the 'outside world': and the former was a manifestation of the bureaucratic apparatus which had emerged from this drive for demarcation, from the quest to organise and structure the life of the Social Democratic community in Steyr. As the discussion below and in Chapter Eight suggests, the politics of cautious reformism and the politics of territory and identity did ultimately prove to be incompatible - and a source of growing tension within the Steyr Social Democratic movment - in the changed political circumstances of the 1930s. Before then, though, they stood as dual manifestations of the form of *Hochburg* politics which had entrenched itself in the town in the years after the First World War.

The SDAP and the Democratic Process

The narrow, organisation-focused horizons of the party leadership élite in Steyr were reflected most clearly and directly in the party's approach to the democratic process. The SDAP had an unambiguous commitment to democratic politics which was based in a highly mechanistic, essentially organisational conception of political power. Organisational advance was equated with political advance: the party would gradually approach 'power' in the Austrian state (i.e. control of national government) as they neared the critical point of 51% of the vote. The party's energies should therefore be consumed in increasing the size of the party organisation, in recruiting new members and voters, new councillors and MPs. A premium was placed on the sheer size of the party organisation; each incremental organisational advance was seen as a further step nearer state power. A crystal-clear expression of this incrementalist conception was given in a rallying cry issued in Steyr directly after the national election of April 1927, which saw the SDAP's national vote rise from 39.6% to 42.3%:

> An intensive recruitment of new members and subscribers to our press must be begun, so that we can achieve at future elections what was not yet possible in the election campaign which has just finished.[50]

The SDAP's commitment to the democratic process proved to be consistent and unbending, even in the face of the growing repression of the Social Democratic movement in Steyr by CSP-led national governments after 1930. A particularly telling example surrounded the searches for *Schutzbund* weaponry ordered by the then Interior Minister, the *Heimwehr* leader Starhemberg, in Steyr (and other centres of Social Democratic strength throughout Austria) on 4 November 1930. The searches were blatantly one-sided - the *Heimwehr's* arms caches were, naturally, left untouched - and were clearly intended to provoke Social Democratic retaliation and thus provide a pretext for suspending the national elections due to take place five days later.[51] The SDAP élite in Steyr appealed for discipline and the avoidance of confrontation, and that Starhemberg be answered in 'correct' manner on election day: 'All our forces must be gathered for 9 November, so we are able then to give the government the right answer'.[52] Indeed, throughout the strained circumstances of the early 1930s, the party élite in Steyr stubbornly retained its faith in the politics of incremental organisational advance, the attempt to amass sufficient support to gain influence over the state. The activities of the party remained firmly attached to the norms of the democratic process. Signatures were enthusiastically collected in support of initiative legislation on social insurance drawn up by the national party in 1930.[53] The coincident *Landtag* and municipal elections in April 1931 were approached with an unusual vigour,[54] as was a recruitment drive in October 1932, which was held with the following aims in mind:

> Every party comrade is to win a new fellow fighter! A battalion of Social Democratic party members ... means a regiment of Social Democratic voters. And more Social Democratic voters means successful defence against reaction, protection of the achievements of the revolution and a better future for the workers of Austria: Socialism![55]

This unswerving faith in incremental organisational advance within the democratic process - which survived even the elimination of parliament by Dollfuss in March 1933[56] - was, of course, ill-equipped to deal with the realities of Austrian politics in the early 1930s. As soon as the governments of the Right abandoned parliamentary politics for the gradual establishment of authoritarian dictatorship, the SDAP's commitment to the democratic process became increasingly irrelevant. As Otto Leichter aptly noted: 'the semi-visible battleground of illegality, of half- and three-quarters fascism, requires forces different from those the mass party would have been able to employ in the bright light of democracy.'[57] This, of course, raises the question of why the SDAP élite in Steyr failed to change its strategic tack in response to the twilight world of creeping authoritarianism. The inflexibility of political startegy in the Steyr SDAP is an issue the discussion returns to below. First though, an examination of Social Democratic municipal policies in

Steyr adds further insights into the SDAP's incrementalist approach to politics.

The Municipal Politics of Ameliorative Reform

Municipal politics was one of the areas identified earlier in this work where the SDAP could 'do something' for its supporters and help cement and strengthen the sense of community upon which the *Hochburgen* of the provinces were based. Steyr was no exception to this pattern. Where resources allowed - and this is a qualification addressed further below - the SDAP pursued policies directed firmly at improving the quality of life of its predominantly manual worker, and largely underprivileged and impoverished electorate.

The issue of interest here is the nature of those policies. They were unashamedly moderate. They revealed a clear acceptance of the existing bases of the Austrian economy, society and polity. Within that existing framework the SDAP municipal administration tinkered and finessed in order to ameliorate some of the most pressing problems facing its constituents; it never, though, even under what were at times extraordinarily difficult circumstances in Steyr, showed signs of rejecting the system which had generated those problems. This approach - which would place the Steyr SDAP firmly on the right wing of the reformist tradition of European Social Democracy - was, of course, a logical one considering the effort the party had put into building up an organisation capable of securing power bases within the existing system, such as the town council. Having made such an investment in the existing system, the SDAP was, naturally enough, thoroughly committed to that system.

The overriding problem facing the town council in Steyr was the economic dependence of the town, since the 1860s, on the often wildy fluctuating economic fortunes of the Steyr-Werke. SDAP municipal policies were primarily directed at countering economic instability and relieving its worst effects. This was reflected in a central emphasis in municipal policy on collective social responsibility. Private charity was rejected in favour of collective social welfare provision as a duty of the whole population. The council therefore provided (modest) aid, in the form of benefit payments, accommodation, health care, educational facilities and so on, as an explicit social right of the poor, the unemployed and the homeless.[58] The commitment to provide relief for the disadvantaged was complemented by the attempt to raise income through progressive taxation. Although the council had relatively little financial autonomy, it did have one locally set tax of financial significance at its disposal.[59] This, a property rate, was highly progressive. It was based on property values and split into twelve bands, each of which was taxed at a higher rate than the previous one. In addition, a 50% surcharge was added from the eighth band upwards. In these higher brackets, covering housing in the more affluent areas of the town, the property tax was up to eight times greater than its highly controversial equivalent in Vienna, and was the highest such tax in Austria. By contrast, in the lower bands, representing cheap, predominantly working class housing, Steyr's residents paid less than was charged in towns of similar size.[60] Seen in tandem with the sums raised by the property rate, the money spent on welfare provision represented a significant (if in absolute terms) small redistribution of income in Steyr.[61] The effect of redistribution was magnified when other municipal policies were taken into account. For example, the council provided incentives and subsidies for local housing cooperatives to build low-cost local housing,[62] and also ran a subsidised local bus service between 1927 and 1930.[63] SDAP policies were thus designed to secure from affluent taxpayers the means to ensure collective welfare and service provision for the economically disadvantaged in the town.

A further key area of council policy activity was in combatting the unemployment caused periodically by the economic cycle at the Steyr-Werke. If employment levels fell at the works, unemployment was increased both directly, by unemployed car workers, and indirectly, as a general reduction in local purchasing power 'knocked on' and plunged the whole local economy into recession. Lacking the financial resources to maintain a large unemployed population, the council's main concern was to support local economic diversification, with the aim of building up alternative local industries capable of providing an economic counterbalance to the Steyr-Werke. This it did in a number of ways. For example, it invested several hundred thousand shillings in shares in local 'lame duck' firms, which would otherwise have folded in 1926 and 1927.[64] It also invested considerable effort in an (unsuccessful) campaign to enlist federal support for major local public works schemes designed both to provide an immediate economic boost by activating the local building industry, and, through an improved economic infrastructure, to establish the basis for a more long-term upswing in local economic fortunes.[65] Another, equally long-term project was to support, in cooperation with the local private sector, the development and expansion of the local tourist industry in order to reduce the town's economic dependence on the car works.[66] The point to note about these diversification policies is that they were both pragmatic and highly eclectic, incorporating both direct state interventionism and a more indirect state role in stimulating private enterprise. This policy pragmatism reinforces the impression of the local SDAP as a system-supportive party, committed to working with, and making the best of the features of, the existing system.

The effect of the SDAP's anti-unemployment policy, and more broadly of its commitment to collective welfare and service provision financed by progressive taxation, was, however, always modest. And after 1929 it became utterly negligible. The depth of the local economic collapse in 1929-1930 caused in Steyr some of the worst poverty and social deprivation experienced in Central and Western Europe in the inter-war years.[67] At the same time it plunged the municipal administration in Steyr into a financial crisis so deep that it became impossible to fulfil even the basic statutory requirements of local government, let alone run a meaningful local policy programme.[68] The financial problem was, moreover, exacerbated by national funding policies for local government which favoured rural councils over urban ones with far greater policy obligations and which - deliberately - hit SDAP councils in urban, industrial communities most severely.[69] The SDAP council in Steyr was, in other words, faced by the impossible situation after 1929: it was, effectively, bankrupt, yet was supposed to provide for the one-third of the local population who were unemployed and often half-starved.

What was remarkable in these impossible circumstances was that the party did not give up. It did its best to ensure that the municipal administration continued to function, and doggedly sent delegation after delegation to the national authorities to beg - unsuccessfully - for additional financial support. Only once did the SDAP councillors consider - and reject - laying down their mandates in protest at the severity of conditions in Steyr and the funding policy of the national government.[70] Ultimately, though, their commitment to the system and procedures of the First Republic ruled out such a course of action. They were unwilling - or perhaps unable - to relinquish either what had become an impotent position of power or a misplaced faith that their case for additional financial aid could be won by force of persuasion.

This dogged commitment to established methods underlines the credentials of the Steyr SDAP as a classically reformist Social Democratic party. It displayed an unwavering faith in and commitment to the democratic process and sought to use the procedures of the democratic process to introduce, where appropriate, limited and moderate change - 'small steps' - to and within a socio-economic system with which it had fully come to terms. The attachment to established methods in conditions in which they were manifestly not effective also, though, reinforces the impression noted earlier of an inherent inflexibility and unadaptability of party tactics.

The Party Élite and the Politics of Inflexibility

In the early 1930s the reformist politics of the SDAP in Steyr had manifestly become anachronistic and ineffective. They were attuned to the greater economic and political stability of the 1920s and proved unworkable in the vastly changed circumstances of the 1930s: Economic collapse and the financial restrictions of central government scuppered the ameliorative reform programme run by the SDAP council in the 1920s; and the creeping authoritarianism of the CSP-led governments of the early 1930s made increasingly irrelevant the democratic process - in particular the electoral cycle - to which the Steyr SDAP was so deeply committed. The questions remain then: Why did the party not change tack? Why did it not even reconsider its strategic options? The explanation lies in the character of the party leadership in Steyr.

As discussed above, the reformist politics of the Steyr SDAP were shaped by a party leadership élite imbued with an intense organisational mentality. This mentality laid out a strategy for the party based in the 'small steps' of incremental organisational advance and incremental policy change. Just like the leadership itself, this strategy had become firmly entrenched and unchallenged by the end of the 1920s, especially since the leadership's personal interests were so heavily bound up with the scale and well-being of the party organisation. The party leadership was inherently unwilling to endanger the organisation it had so painstakingly built up, and with which its own interests were so closely associated, by changing course and embarking on a different, perhaps more confrontational form of politics. This clearly recalls the analysis of Michels which suggested the emergence of an increasingly tenacious adherence to the 'ancient and glorious' tactics of the past alongside a growing 'aversion to all aggressive action' in the present:[71]

> The sentiment of tradition, in cooperation with an instinctive need
> for stability, has as its result that the leadership represents always
> the past rather than the present.[72]

Applied to the situation in Steyr from 1929, the 'sentiment of tradition' was reflected in an intense leadership preoccupation with the avoidance of any controversy which might be detrimental to the organisation. This initially became apparent in late 1929, when the *Heimwehr* was first trying to establish a foothold in 'red' Steyr. On the one hand, confrontation with the *Heimwehr* within Steyr was tolerated, even encouraged. This was 'safe', since the municipal police force could be relied upon to favour the Social Democrats. On the other hand, when the *Heimwehr* held parades in nearby villages, or when it was merely travelling through Steyr, the party leadership ordered the avoidance of confrontation.[73] In these situations, security was the responsibility of the provincial gendarmery, a force broadly sympathetic to the *Heimwehr*. Confrontation in these circumstances would most likely have led to the partisan intervention of armed and unfriendly gendarmes. The intervention of Mayor Sichlrader to prevent the *Schutzbund* from confronting the *Heimwehr* in Steyr on 2 February 1930 (see Chapter Five) should be seen in the same light. Any violence on 2 February would have provoked the intervention of the outside police presence ordered into Steyr, whose political sympathies would have ensured that the Social Democrats bore the brunt of their 'peace-keeping'.

The SDAP leadership would not risk bringing the wrath of the state down on the party organisation. Party discipline, 'the strongest dam, the safest stronghold of the proletariat'[74] was the central theme of party rhetoric in the 1930s, especially after the installation of an anti-Social Democratic federal police force in Steyr in July 1930. Thereafter the party leadership issued the order 'Do not let yourselves be provoked!' with monotonous regularity whenever political tensions rose in the fraught political atmosphere of the early 1930s. Faced by the regular provocations of the *Heimwehr* and the central government, the SDAP leadership withdrew timidly and introspectively into its organisational shell. In doing so it condemned the party to a tactical inflexibility and an ultimately fateful political passivity in an era of far-reaching political change.

The SDAP in Steyr had all the hallmarks of an oligarchical party. It lacked effective mechanisms of intra-party democracy, was élite-dominated, pursued a brand of cautious and moderate politics, and proved to be highly inflexible when faced with changed political circumstances. Two questions raise themselves, in conclusion, about this unequivocally Michelsian party. First, how representative was it of the SDAP elsewhere in the *Hochburgen* of the provinces? And second, what were the implications of inflexibility for provincial Social Democracy? The former question cannot be definitively answered. As was noted earlier, there is some evidence of an incipient process of Michelsian bureaucratisation and leadership entrenchment elsewhere in the provinces. In addition, there is a wealth of published material which locates the local-level SDAP as a *'staatstragend'*, 'state-supportive' party fully committed to the democratic process in the First Republic, and fully immersed in the minutiae of municipal administration.[75] Local-level parties were almost without fail engaged in a politics of moderate and gradualist reform, adapting existing institutions and practices in the interests of their supporters in the fields of housing, public health, welfare, public transport and education policy. Robert Schediwy even goes so far as to suggest that the adoption of an unambiguously reformist policy platform by the post-1945 SPÖ can be traced back to the pioneering work of the reformist 'godfathers' active in inter-war provincial Social Democracy.[76] This must remain a matter of conjecture. What is clear, though, is that the reformist policy programmes of these 'pioneers' were, again almost without fail,[77] financially undone by the onset of economic crisis. Stripped by the crisis of the financial means to pursue their programmes, local-level reformism slipped into a period of policy stagnation and immobilism which was cut off only by the civil war in 1934.[78]

There exist, in other words, broad parallels between the experience in Steyr and that in other provincial *Hochburgen*. A tentative conclusion would be that Steyr's experience, while perhaps not entirely typical, would have been at the very least recognisable from experience elsewhere. This conclusion is given more weight when one looks at the second question raised above: the implications of political inflexibility for provincial Social Democracy. The emphasis on tried and trusted methods was, to say the least, an unpromising recipe for meeting the challenges of politics in the early 1930s. It merely compounded the inward-looking, self-referenced mentality of an already insular, fragmented and isolated movement, heightening its vulnerability to its opponents. It was clearly inadequate to the task of protecting the democratic process to which the party was committed. More importantly, it offered inadequate protection for the community and the community identity from which the party had emerged. This failing was recognised by an emergent opposition faction in the Social Democratic movement which gained strength in Steyr and in other centres of Social Democratic strength in the provinces in 1933-1934. This opposition faction rejected the authority and policies of the local, and indeed provincial and national, party leaderships, and pushed for a politics of active resistance to creeping authoritarianism which culminated in some *Hochburgen* at least in armed resistance in the Civil War of February 1934. The genesis and evolution of this opposition are the subject of the next chapter.

Notes

[1]   Robert Michels, *Zur Soziologie des Parteiwesens in der Modernen Demokratie*, Klinkhardt, Leipzig (1911). A second edition was published in 1915. The English translation from which all references in this book are culled is of the second edition and was published as *Political parties. A sociological study of the oligarchical tendencies of modern democracy*, Dover, New York (1959).

2   Indeed, as noted in Chapter Two, the most important work hitherto on the organisational structure of the national-level SDAP - Peter Kulemann's masterly analysis - is very clearly influenced by Michels' work. See Kulemann (1979), 295-332.

3   Angelo Panebianco, *Political parties: organisation and power*, Cambridge University Press, Cambridge (1988), 3.

4   The preference has been to examine parties through their function of representing social interests and through their ideological positions. For a discussion, see ibid., 3-6.

5   Michels (1959), 33.

6   Ibid., 83-84.

7   Ibid., 205-215.

8   Ibid., 206.

9   Ibid., 187-188.

10   An attitude Michels described with the phrase *'le parti c'est moi'*! Ibid., 226.

11   Ibid., 372.

12   Weidenholzer (1981), 89.

13   Weidenholzer (1988).

14   Gutkas (1983), 862.

15   My italics. Quoted in Nasko (1986), 303.

16   Karl Schiffer, 'Die Linke in der steirischen Sozialdemokratie während der Ersten Republik. Ein autobiographischer Bericht', in Hinteregger, Müller, Staudinger (1984), 270.

17   The number fell to nine after June 1930, when the federalisation of the municipal police force on 1 July led to the dissolution of the section of the municipal police force. See AVA BKA Inneres 22/Oberösterreich Karton 5100: 165.832-30. Early in the 1920s, twelve sections had existed. For a full list of these see Radmoser (n.d.), 87.

18   Commercial employees, industrial employees (white-collar workers), public employees, food industry workers, building workers, print workers, railworkers, timber industry workers, metalworkers, soldiers, and postal workers.

19   Activist contact with ordinary members was always at a personal level. With such intimacy of contact, it is unlikely that each activist would have had more than fifty members on his or her personal list. With around 5,000 members in the late 1920s, this reasoning would imply roughly 100 activists. To these must be added the six members of each of the ten section committees, giving a rough total of 150-160 activists.

20   Interview with Josef Mayrhofer, 4-7-1986.

21   These figures are derived - imperfectly - from a survey of the meetings advertised in the *Steyrer Tagblatt* column 'party and club news' between 1928 and 1932. Only 246 of these advertisements also contained information on the lecture subject. Of these, and alongside the 155 focused on current affairs, 59 (24%) dealt with organisational matters, 23 (9%) with some form of entertainment and 9 (4%) with matters of socialist theory. Although these figures cannot claim to be comprehensive, they do give a solid general impression of the content of party section meetings.

22   STB 9-4-1930, 10.

23   This of course echoes the paternalism which was evident in the activities run by the party's Educational Committee, as discussed in the previous chapter.

24   'Schach den langweiligen Versammlungen!', in STB 18-4-1929, 7.
25   STB 21-4-1929, 11.
26   E.g. by the German Gymnastics Festival of 1928, the *Heimwehr* campaign in
Steyr in 1929-1930, and subsequent surges of strength of the local Communists (in
1931) and the National Socialists (in 1932). See e.g. STB 12-7-1928, 10; 17-10-1929, 7;
7-12-1929, 9-10; 6-2-1930, 8; 20-8-1931, 8; 28-10-1931, 1; 25-10-1932, 3.
27   See STB 4-2-1928, 7; 9-2-1930, 13.
28   See for example the descriptions of activist work in STB 12-5-1927, 1; 4-2-
1928, 6; 3-2-1929, 2; 30-7-1929, 6; 9-2-1930, 13; 16-2-1930, 14; 14-2-1932, 11.
29   For example, the *unanimous* decision by the activists *to agree to* the
municipal austerity programme drawn up by the town council finance
committee in November 1928. See STB 27-11-1928, 9. The legitimisation function
of the activists in municipal policy matters was expressed even more forcefully
in January 1933: ' ... the attitude of the Social Democratic fraction in the town
council was approved wihtout reservation, and it was voiced that the whole
working class stands, now as before, behind its municipal representatives'. See
STB 8-1-1933, 5.
30   On one occasion, for example, the SDAP District Leader, Franz Schrangl,
spoke about recent political developments and then 'set out the tactics for the
activists of our party to follow in this district'. Quoted in STB 9-4-1920, 10. See
also STB 20-10-1929, 10.
31   Quoted in STB 14-2-1932, 11.
32   Quoted in STB 16-2-1930, 14. See also STB 19-5-1927, 8; 24-9-1927, 8; 12-2-1928,
11; 2-9-1928, 11; 10-2-1929, 11; 23-2-1932, 10; 2-3-1933, 4.
33   See STB 12-2-1928, 11, and also 11-2-1929, 11 and 16-2-1930, 14.
34   STB 16-2-1930, 14.
35   STB 12-2-1928, 11; 10-2-1929, 11; 22-2-1932, 10; 2-3-1933, 4.
36   Especially if one considers that the turnover of Mitschko, Mellich and
Mayrhofer was a formal alternation of successive military leaders of the
Schutzbund and that of Pammer and Schwitzer a formal alternation of the
women's organisation leaders. In addition, Roithner was replaced by Sperl only
because of his elevation to the 'inner' committee of elected officers, and
Rußmann by Schopper only because he moved away from the town.
37   See further on this theme in Chapter Eight.
38   Michels (1959), 50-53.
39   Kulemann (1979), 301.
40   On this point, but focused on the more fully researched Second Republic
experience in Austria, see Müller (1988), 479.
41   See e.g. STB 16-2-1930, 14; 23-2-1932, 10.
42   Michels (1959), 188.
43   See for example STB 14-5-1927, 1; 20-12-1927, 1-2; 15-4-1928, 9; 1-1-1929, 5-7;
15-9-1929, 13-14; 30-3-1930, 8; 22-12-1930, 1-4; 17-6-1931, 3; 3-1-1932, 1-2; 31-12-1932,
1-2; 30-4-1933, 7; 3-1-1934, 5; *Illustrierter Steyrer Geschäfts- und
Unterhaltungskalender 1933*, 292; OÖTB 1932, 21-22; Franz Sichlrader, 'Das
Schicksal der Stadt Steyr', *Arbeit und Wirtschaft*, 1-2-1930, 99-102; OÖLA
Landtagsakten Nachtrag, Schuber 34: 5. Sitzung 15-12-1931, 90-92.
44   See STB 1-1-1932, 6; 1-1-1933, 1-2; 2-1-1934, 6; *Illustrierter Steyrer Geschäfts-
und Unterhaltungskalender 1933*, 307-308.

45   See STB 4-2-1928, 6-7; 5-2-1928, 10; 3-2-1929, 2-3; 9-2-1929, 9-10; 9-2-1930, 13-14; 11-2-1930, 9-10; 12-2-1930, 9.

46   STB 14-2-1931, 7; 15-2-1931, 11; 14-2-1932, 11.

47   Quoted in STB 5-2-1928, 10.

48   On nineteenth century Social Democracy in Steyr, see Gerhard Baron, *Der Beginn. Die Anfänge der Arbeiterbildungsvereine in Oberösterreich*, Oberösterreichischer Landesverlag, Linz (1971); Konrad (1981); Radmoser (n.d.).

49   C.f. Kulemann (1979), 324.

50   As expressed at the District Conference of May 1927 and quoted in STB 19-5-1927, 8. In similar vein, see further STB 4-2-1928, 6; 20-4-1929, 8; 9-2-1930, 13; 26-3-1931, 8.

51   As Starhemberg himself admitted: 'I entered the Cabinet with the intention of carrying out a coup. I had very little interest in new elections as I was convinced that they would hardly bring about a change in the parliamentary balance of power, and that Austria's fate would never be decided in parliament'. Quoted in Ernst Rüdiger Starhemberg, *Memoiren*, Amalthea, Vienna (1971), 84-85.

52   STB 7-11-1930, 10; 9-11-1930, 11; 11-11-1930, 11; AVA BKA Inneres 22/genere Karton 4867: 214.660-30.

53   See STB between 7-9-1930 and 8-10-1930.

54   See STB 5-4-1931, 11; 8-4-1931, 9; 9-4-1931, 11; 11-4-1931, 9; 13-4-1931, 1; 15-4-1931, 1; 16-4-1931, 1; 17-4-1931, 1.

55   STB 1-10-1932, 1. On the progress of the recruitment drive, see STB throughout October 1932.

56   See e.g. STB 3-5-1933, 3.

57   Otto Leichter, *Glanz und Ende der Ersten Republik. Wie es zum österreichischen Bürgerkrieg kam*, Europaverlag, Vienna (1964), 204.

58   See e.g. STB 29-7-1927, 7; 11-4-1931, 9; 27-10-1931, 10; 1-1-1932, 6; 31-3-1932, 8; 1-1-1933, 1-2.

59   The main source of muncipal income was, however, a local income tax whose rate was set nationally.

60   See STB 11-4-1928, 9; 2-12-1928, 1.

61   Receipts from the property tax accounted for 105% of municipal welfare expenditure in 1929, 97% in 1930, 73% in 1931, 61% in 1932 and 50% in 1933. The proportional decline reflects increasing welfare expenditure at a time of mass unemployment rather than any reduction in tax receipts. See OÖLA Bezirkshauptmannschaft Steyr Präs. Faszikel 8: 'Die Finanzlage der Stadt Steyr' von Dr. Josef Walk, 21, 23.

62   See STB 20-12-1927, 2; 14-2-1928, 10; 28-7-1928, 8; 17-3-1931, 11; 4-5-1933, 8.

63   See STB 29-5-1927, 11; 15-7-1928, 10; 19-7-1930, 9.

64   OÖLA Bezirkshauptmannschaft Steyr Präs. Faszikel 8: 'Die Finanzlage der Stadt Steyr' von Dr. Josef Walk, 3-4; STB 15-7-1928, 10.

65   STB 17-4-1931, 1.

66   See Julius Rußmann, 'Kann Steyr eine Stadt des Fremdenverkehrs werden?', in Erwin Stein (Ed.), *Die Städte Deutsch-Österreichs. Band II. Steyr und Bad Hall*, Deutscher Kommunalverlag, Berlin (1928); Zentralstelle des Fremdenverkehrs in Steyr und Umgebung, *Stadt Steyr. Die alte Eisenstadt in Oberösterreich 980 bis 1930*, Steyr (1930); STB 15-7-1927, 11.

[67] This was true in particular after the collapse of the Steyr-Werke in 1929. See STB 23-4-1930, 2; 7-1-1932, 5; 1-1-1933, 1-2; 2-1-1934, 6; *Der österreichischer Metallarbeiter*, 19-4-1930, 1-2; *Der Kuckuck*, 12-1-1930, 1, 8-9; 17-1-1932, 3; *Arbeiter-Zeitung* 1-1-1932, 1; Hans Habe, *Leben für den Journalismus. Band 1: Reportagen und Gespräche*, Knaur, Munich (1976), 33-40.

[68] The best account of the financial situation of the town council is OÖLA Bezirkshauptmannschaft Steyr Präs. Faszikel 8: 'Die Finanzlage der Stadt Steyr' von Dr. Josef Walk. See also STB 22-5-1928, 11-12; 30-3-1930, 8; 21-7-1931, 9-10; 19-6-1932, 13-14; 31-12-1932, 1-2; 30-12-1933, 8.

[69] See e.g. Schediwy (1990), 373-374.

[70] See AVA BKA Inneres 22/Oberösterreich Karton 5101: 234.634-31; STB 1-11-1931, 12; 31-12-1931, 1.

[71] Michels (1959), 372.

[72] Ibid.,

[73] See e.g. STB 27-9-1929, 8; 17-10-1929, 7.

[74] STB 5-2-1928, 10.

[75] See Bauer (1988e); Bauer, Weitgruber (1985), 62-63; Burgstaller, Lackner (1984), 162-166; Flanner (1983), 46; Kaut (1982), 123; Lewis (1991), 134, 171; Johann Mayr, '100 Jahre - 10 Bürgermeister. Die Linzer vertrauen den Sozialisten', in SPÖ Bezirksorganisation Linz-Stadt (1988), 79-86; Nasko (1986), 133-139; SPÖ Mauthausen (1989), 93-94; Weidenholzer (1988), 34-40

[76] Schediwy (1990), 364-365. See also Pferschy (1983), 956.

[77] The exception which proves the rule is the SDAP council in Wörgl, Tirol, which, against all economic policy orthodoxy (and technically illegally), issued its own local currency in a renowned job creation experiment in 1932-1933. This radical policy initiative is uncharacteristic of the local-level SDAP and can be traced to the maverick ideas of the Wörgl Mayor, Michael Unterguggenberger, which were gleaned from the unorthodox theories of the economist Silvio Gesell. See Franz Baltzarek, 'Das Schwundgeldexperiment von Wörgl 1932/33', in Fröschl, Mesner, Zoitl (1990).

[78] See Schediwy (1990), 373-374.

8 Decline, Disintegration, Destruction: Provincial Social Democracy 1930-1934

By late 1933 the local-level Social Democratic movement in the provinces had all but disintegrated. In the face of mass, long-term unemployment and intensifying state repression, many Social Democrats had withdrawn from political life. Many others, dismissive of the acquiescent and fatalistic attitude of the movement's leadership, had defected to the Communists or the National Socialists. Of those who remained attached to the movement, most had slipped into a resigned and fearful passivity. The only dynamic force left at the local level was a small, loosely organised, but vocal and militant, left-wing opposition. Centred mainly in Styria and Upper Austria, but represented also in Lower Austria, Salzburg and Tirol, this opposition demanded, and, in February 1934, led active resistance in the provinces to the emerging Dollfuss dictatorship.

The purpose of this chapter is to examine the process of decline and disintegration which spawned this militant opposition, and which culminated in the destruction of the Social Democratic movement in the Austrian Civil War. The argument revisits an enduring theme of this book: the politics of territory, community and identity on which the Social Democratic *Hochburgen* of the provinces were based. It has a twofold thrust: first that the Social Democratic *Hochburgen* were ultimately unsustainable; and second that militant opposition can be understood as the vehement reflex of a community under threat, of a community whose vulnerable position on the 'front-lines' of a deeply divided provincial society had, by the early 1930s, been starkly exposed by the unsustainability of *Hochburg* politics.

Section one of the chapter begins with a review of some of the key themes developed so far in this work, focusing initially on the roots of the *Hochburg* in the pattern of social segmentation in the provinces and on the form of territorial, identity-based politics this produced. This form of politics suffered a number of inherent, 'pathological' weaknesses which meant that none of the *Hochburgen* proved able in the long run to reproduce themselves, and consequently collapsed. At the same time, no Social Democratic leadership group - local, provincial or national - proved able to respond effectively to this process of collapse. The result was a process of disillusionment and demoralisation throughout the provinces which led at least some to move into internal opposition to the movement's established leaders and policies.

Existing accounts of this opposition have tended to focus on the national-level spokespersons of opposition politics.[1] Insufficient attention has been given to the grass roots disaffection in the provinces which, arguably, gave the opposition the vitality and drive to give it a profile of national significance. The final part of section one attempts to rectify this problem by setting out the main characteristics of opposition politics across the provinces. The remainder of the chapter builds from this to discuss in depth the emergence and politics of the opposition in Steyr. Section two starts by recalling the bases, scope and, in 1929-1930, the collapse of the Social Democratic *Hochburg* in Steyr and the inability of an inflexible local leadership to generate effective strategic responses to the post-1930 situation. The result was a burgeoning sense of disaffection which was reflected both in a pattern of defection from the movement, but also, as section three shows, in the emergence of a number of focal points of intra-movement opposition - situated in the MAV, the *Schutzbund* and the SAJ - which began to demand a more aggressive and innovative response to the problems of the early 1930s.

The opposition of MAV, *Schutzbund* and SAJ was motivated by a shared sense of anger which was focused on the loss of the powers and privileges of the *Hochburg*, on the debilitating process of state repression the movement was forced to endure in the 1930s, but also on the incapacity of the leaders at all levels of an ostensibly powerful movement to halt the process of decline and debilitation. This anger was expressed in the emergence of a local opposition strategy which rejected the political tradition of reformist Social Democracy on which the Austrian movement was based. Instead, it opted for a crude Bolshevism which, as section four shows, inspired and spurred on Social Democratic resistance in Steyr in the Austrian Civil War of February 1934.

The concluding section reflects on the nature of the resistance launched in Steyr and elsewhere in the provinces in February 1934. This resistance was, in military terms, hopeless and doomed to failure. The commitment nevertheless to embark on it therefore had tremendous, if largely symbolic significance. It symbolised most immediately a potent and definitive rejection of a repressive regime. But it also symbolised a definitive rejection of reformist Social Democracy. Violent resistance was the ultimate negation of the reformist tradition. The decision for violent resistance was, the conclusion suggests, a final, elemental outburst of disaffection on the part of a community which had for so long sustained, but had now been decisively failed by, the Social Democratic movement.

The Opposition in the Provinces

The Pathology of Hochburg Politics

The emergence of the opposition in the provincial movement can be traced to what might be termed the 'pathology' of *Hochburg* politics, a distinctive pattern of structural peculiarities which conditioned and shaped Social Democratic politics in the 'red islands' of the provinces. As the early chapters of this work stressed, the Social Democratic movement in these 'red islands' was rooted in the strong sense of separate social identity which had emerged in the dense manual worker milieux of a deeply segmented provincial society. This sense of identity was simultaneously a reflection of the intense social inter-relationships and community solidarity which formed within these milieux and of the 'front-line' confrontation of manual worker milieux with the rural-conservative milieux which typically surrounded them. The form of Social Democratic politics which arose in this social context was intensely territorial. Political energies were consumed in the defensive drive to organise, shape and control political and social relationships within the *Hochburg* and simultaneously to insulate the *Hochburg* as extensively as possible from the rural-conservative milieu which lay beyond it. Each *Hochburg* thus provided a 'safe haven' in which an embattled community identity could be expressed, through the Social Democratic movement, without the hindrances and hostility it would otherwise have faced.

Seen against this background, *Hochburg* politics were, above all, a politics of insularity, of restricted perspective. Their focus was restricted to the territory of the 'safe haven' and immersed in what were essentially local problems. This localisation of political perspective has been a central theme throughout this work, particularly in the discussion of the characteristic features of *Hochburg* politics, *Integration nach innen* and *Abgrenzung nach außen*. *Integration nach innen*, the drive for an ever more cohesive and solidaristic Social Democratic community, underpinned by as extensive as possible a network of Social Democratic organisations, was a defensive reaction to the threat posed by *local* enemies. And *Abgrenzung nach außen*, the commitment to mark out and defend the *Hochburg* as inviolable Social Democratic territory was, again, focused on those same *local* enemies. Importantly, both these features of *Hochburg* politics were also responses to the place of the local level in the internal politics of the Social Democratic movement. The local level had, as Chapter Two argued, effectively been abandoned to its own devices as a result of the preoccupations of the provincial and national levels with, respectively, *Landtag* politics and Red Vienna. The lack of support from 'above' effectively condemned the local-level movement to political self-reliance, intensifying the inward-looking momentum established by the *Integration* and *Abgrenzung* processes.

The result of this exaggerated localisation of perspective was the organisational and political fragmentation of the provincial Social Democratic movement. Social Democrats within individual *Hochburgen* were far more concerned with their own local problems of *Integration* and *Abgrenzung* than with making common cause with other *Hochburgen* faced by similar problems. In particular, they placed an exaggerated emphasis on organisational penetration and expansion which led 'the organisation' ultimately to become a *Selbstzweck*, an end of participation in political life, rather than a means to secure wider political goals. This process was illustrated especially clearly in Steyr, both in the effort put by countless petty functionaries into consolidating the Social Democratic network of auxiliary organisations, and in the absorption of the SDAP leadership in the bureaucratic intricacies of its stewardship of the movement's organisational structures. The end result was an impressively large, but deeply self-absorbed and inherently unwieldy organisation which proved incapable of adapting to new situations and new challenges. The *Hochburg* movement was, in its local setting, a 'giant with feet of clay', remarkably big, but ponderous and cumbersome, too consumed in itself to be able to respond to wider changes in the path and pattern of politics in Austria. The unfortunate outcome of this pathological syndrome of isolation, insularity and inflexibility was a heightened vulnerability to precisely those anti-Social Democratic forces against which *Hochburg* politics were supposed to be directed.

The political vulnerability of the local-level movement was gradually exposed as two, complementary factors combined to undermine the sense of community which sustained its *Hochburgen*: Austria's feeble economic performance throughout the First Republic; and the persistent sniping of an anti-Social Democratic coalition of 'bourgeois' parties, employers, the *Heimwehr*, the Catholic Church, the security forces and the provincial authorities. Economic weakness allowed employers to marginalise the FTUs as defenders of Social Democrats' interests and as dispensers of political patronage at the workplace. It also shrank the financial base for the policy programmes and patronage of Social Democratic municipal administrations across the provinces. The Social Democratic movement became less and less able to maintain the allegiance of its supporters by 'doing something' for them. The result was a decline in the cohesion of the Social Democratic community which in turn opened up opportunities for the anti-Social Democratic coalition to reclaim the political preeminence it had enjoyed until the 'revolution' of 1918-1919. Unable to call on effective support or intervention from the provincial or national levels of the movement, the local-level movement was by and large helpless to prevent the resurgence of the conservative Right. By 1930, as a result, all the provincial *Hochburgen* had symbolically 'fallen' to their local enemies, many in high-profile 'surrenders' of Social Democratic territory to the ostentatious bombast of *Heimwehr* parades.

With the onset of the depression in 1929-1930, the fall of the *Hochburg* revealed itself to be only the starting point of a long period of decline. The mass, long-term unemployment of the depression years debilitated the movement, causing dramatic falls in membership. To give just two examples, SDAP membership fell by 13% in Linz between 1930 and 1931 and by 18% in Wiener Neustadt from 1932 to 1933.[2] The organisational impact of mass unemployment was felt in two ways. First, unemployment heightened the propensity of individuals to defect to more radical, activist movements. In Styria in particular, where unemployment had been a severe problem throughout the First Republic, the further deterioration experienced in the depression years weakened allegiances to the Social Democratic movement sufficiently for the unemployed to become fertile ground for Communist Party agitation and recruitment.[3] After 1932, when the Hitler bandwagon began to gather pace in Germany, the Nazi Party became a further beneficiary of such defections.

A second - and contrasting - effect of unemployment was exemplified in the classic study by Jahoda, Lazarsfeld and Zeisel of extreme, near-100% unemployment in the predominantly Social Democratic Lower Austrian village of Marienthal.[4] In line with a number of other, similar, first-hand studies of the inter-war era,[5] their work on Marienthal showed that, in the face of mass unemployment, politics lost at least some of its power to shape the content and relationships of everyday life. For many individuals the experience of unemployment ushered in a process of gradual social and personal disintegration which saw a loss of self-confidence and the progressive withdrawal of the individual from social relationships outside the family.[6] This process of withdrawal had an especially severe impact on a local-level Social Democratic movement which had drawn much of its solidaristic strength from the comprehensive range of social and leisure activities which were run under its aegis. The organisational commitment which had sustained these activities ebbed away amid the high unemployment rates of the 1930s, further weakening the movement's fabric and cohesion.

A final, and ultimately decisive problem which confronted the provincial Social Democrats in the early 1930s was central government repression. For a short period in the autumn of 1930, when the *Heimwehr* made its first, brief appearance in central government, and more or less continuously from the beginning of 1932, the Social Democratic movement throughout Austria was subject to official, state-led discrimination and repression. The tempo was stepped up after March 1933, when Chancellor Dollfuss' 'salami-tactic' systematically eliminated remaining Social Democratic positions of strength in state and economy, muzzled the Social Democratic press, confiscated *Schutzbund* weapons, and progressively restricted the range of permissible Social Democratic activities.[7] The measures of the Dollfuss government were in one sense no great novelty in a provincial environment in which (provincial) state repression had long been a feature of political life (particularly in Vorarlberg, Tirol and Styria). In other senses, though, they had a deep and novel significance for the provincial movement. The fear of central government sanctions acted, especially for those employed in the public sector, as an additional deterrent to continued participation and membership, accelerating the spiral of organisational decline which was noted above. Moreover, the experience of routinised repression made it crystal clear to Social Democrats at the local level that no authority existed within the movement - either locally, provincially or nationally - which was capable of lending them effective support or protection.

Disaffection and Opposition

The realisation that the movement at all levels was impotent to combat the problems of the 1930s compounded the sense of helplessness felt at a local level already deprived of its *Hochburgen*. It promoted as a result a growing disaffection among (what remained) of the membership. This grass roots disaffection was a deeply felt expression of anger at the loss of the 'safe haven', the loss of the powers and privileges so painstakingly built up after 1918, and with them the progressive loss of freedom to express and develop without hindrance a distinctive manual worker identity through the Social Democratic movement. It was projected at the perceived inadequacy of (SDAP) leadership at all levels in the movement. Disaffection focused locally on the inability of the SDAP to adapt tactically to creeping authoritarianism in the way that its competitors in opposition, the Communists and Nazis, did, with their dynamic methods of mobilisation, protest and direct action. The local-level 'giant with feet of clay' had begun to reveal itself as an inflexible and increasingly irrelevant force in local politics, and was, as a result, increasingly dismissed, rejected and ignored.

The provincial-level SDAP also felt the ire of grass roots disaffection, above all because provincial party leaderships across Austria still broadly adhered, even in the face of the intense repression of the movement on the ground, to the politics of accommodation and conciliation outlined in Chapter Two. This was justified as the best way of retaining some kind of role for the Social Democratic movement in the emerging authoritarian state and, in particular, of combatting the threat of the Nazi Party, which had shot to prominence in Austria in a series of provincial and local elections in 1932. The sudden emergence of the Nazis in 1932 led the SDAP in a number of provincial capitals to enter or renew close links with the 'bourgeois' parties of the Right. A notable example was the arrangement struck by the SDAP with the CSP in the Styrian *Landtag* in 1933 in order to pursue a constructive 'politics of the lesser evil' which could fend off the danger presented by the province's burgeoning Nazi Party.[8] Another was the establishment in May 1933 of the so-called 'Carinthian Committee' of SDAP-CSP conciliation, again designed to head off the threat posed in Carinthia by what was the fastest growing provincial Nazi Party in Austria.[9] More broadly, those in the Social Democratic movement who most forcefully pressed in national-level debate in 1933-1934 for some wider form of constructive accommodation with the Dollfuss regime were representatives first and foremost of the provincial parliamentary élites of the SDAP, for example Oskar Helmer and Heinrich Schneidmadl from Lower Austria, and Matthias Zeinitzer from Carinthia.[10] These various instances and plans of political cooperation with parties whose representatives in Dollfuss' government were at the same time issuing anti-Social Democratic decrees were, however compelling the reason, quite predictably opposed at the local level. They caused, for example, a deep 'loss of trust'[11] at the grass roots of the Styrian party. A similar picture existed in Salzburg and Upper Austria, where the conciliatory politics of the provincial party leaderships met with incredulity, 'deepest dissatisfaction',[12] and, on at least one occasion in Upper Austrian Attnang-Puchheim, near-violent rejection[13] at the local level.

The groundswell of disaffection at the local level was also fed by the perceived inadequacies of the national-level SDAP's response to growing state repression. This response was conditioned by the increasingly fatalistic and pessimistic outlook of Otto Bauer. In a series of articles grounded in a deeply deterministic Marxism, Bauer developed the thesis that Austria had entered a 'pause' between the revolutionary events of 1918-1919 and the next, future revolutionary crisis. Moreover, the revolution of 1918-1919 had been merely a 'bourgeois revolution' in that it had not changed the pattern of ownership of the means of production. This meant that the role of the SDAP in government in 1918-1920 had been an inevitably temporary phenomenon which necessarily gave way to the restoration of bourgeois power in what Bauer termed 'the bourgeois republic', as the Austrian 'political superstructure became adjusted to the economic basis'.[14] Such a resigned analysis allowed no scope for an offensive strategy for the SDAP; that would have to wait until the next revolutionary crisis. In the meantime, the party could only sit tight and defend as best it could the achievements of the previous revolutionary crisis, in particular the democratic constitution, the social legislation passed by the 1918-1920 government, and, of course, Red Vienna.

This was a depressingly downbeat message. It was also - confirming the impression given in Chapter Two - very much Vienna-centred and ignorant of conditions in the provinces, where the defence of Red Vienna was far from uppermost in everyday concerns, and where the democratic constitution and post-war social legislation had often long been abandoned in political practice. A predictable consequence was the projection of local-level disaffection - with growing vehemence and bitterness - onto a national leadership which had no evident understanding of provincial politics. Karl Flanner writes, for example, of Wiener Neustadt Social Democrats threatening a 'day of reckoning' on which the national leadership would pay for its failures.[15] Richard Bernaschek, the Upper Austrian party functionary who sparked the Civil War, recalled a similar mood among the 'party faithful' in Upper Austria during 1933: 'If the party capitulates to this miserable, treacherous ... enemy, then we will spit in the faces of the leaders responsible [when we meet them] in the concentration camps'.[16]

The result of the burgeoning disaffection at the local level was twofold. Many left the movement, sometimes withdrawing into political passivity, but often reappearing in the ranks of the Communists[17] or, particularly after their electoral breakthrough in 1932, the Nazis.[18] Others, though, chose to remain within the movement but to press, in opposition to its leadership, for a more activist policy of resistance to the emergent dictatorship in Austria. A full and detailed picture of this opposition is difficult to give. It was mainly active in conditions of semi-legality from 1932-1934 and therefore led a rather subterranean existence which is not extensively recorded in available source materials. Moreover, past writing has tended to focus on the role played by the national 'leadership' of the opposition, centred around the *Arbeiter-Zeitung* editor Ernst Fischer, rather than the situation on the ground.[19] Fischer was the most prominent member of a group of leftist intellectuals situated mainly in Vienna, but also in Graz, which pushed - in dispute with Otto Bauer and the SDAP Executive - for a radical change of party tactics in response to the Dollfuss regime. According to Anson Rabinbach Fischer's group also had links with a 'network of militant activists in all parts of the country'.[20] Some care needs to be taken here. While a variety of such links did exist (extending for example into Steyr)[21] the cohesion of the provincial opposition 'network' should not be overestimated. In the provinces, the opposition was far from being a cohesive political force.

Its scale and profile varied widely from one centre of Social Democratic strength to another, and, most importantly, it lacked the formal organisational and communication structures which could have facilitated coordinated opposition activities. The provincial opposition is therefore best understood as an essentially disparate collection of like-minded individuals, motivated by the same broad concerns, but acting more or less in isolation from one another.[22]

Fischer and his colleagues in other words did not so much *lead* the opposition throughout Austria as provide national-level *articulation* of the concerns of the disaffected at the grass roots of the Social Democratic movement. These disaffected elements - drawn primarily from the paramilitary *Schutzbund*, the increasingly militant party youth movement, the SAJ,[23] and those FTU branches still active on the shopfloor - were drawn together and mobilised by a deep and bitter anger at the loss of what had been gained after the First World War and a bitter resentment at the passive acquiescence of Social Democratic leadership groups to intensifying repression. Their concern was to make some kind of stand in defence of their 'territory' and of the social identity and community solidarity which had been able to develop within it. This mood of defiance fed into an unsophisticated actionism which, by early 1934, had stiffened into a resolve to mount what was acknowledged to be hopeless, violent resistance to the Dollfuss regime. The emergence of what Richard Bernaschek aptly called the 'courage to commit political suicide'[24] is examined below in a discussion of the opposition in Steyr.

Steyr and the Pathology of *Hochburg* Politics

The Social Democratic movement in Steyr has revealed itself throughout this work to be an extreme case. As such, it provides a crystal clear illustration of the 'pathology' of *Hochburg* politics. The movement was rooted in the dense manual worker milieu of a town with a long-standing industrial tradition, and revelled in the opportunity given after 1918 to structure and shape social and political life in Steyr in the image and interests of the manual worker community which inhabited that milieu. In the late 1920s in particular, boosted by the local boom which resulted from the expansion of production at the Steyr-Werke, the movement succeeded in establishing for itself hegemonic status. Allegiances to the movement were secured by the effectiveness of the MAV in industrial relations at the Steyr-Werke, the reformist social policies of the SDAP-run town hall, and by the control of both town hall and, in particular, MAV over extensive patronage resources in the town. In addition, a vast range of auxiliary organisations criss-crossed local society to buttress a cohesive Social

Democratic community whose breadth and solidarity both metaphorically and, at times, physically kept at bay a hostile 'outside world'. The 'bourgeois' parties within Steyr had, as a result, minimal room for manoeuvre in political life in the town. And those external, anti-Social Democratic forces which attempted to establish a presence in the town - e.g. the German Nationalist and Nazi 'gymnasts' in July 1928 or the *Heimwehr* in late 1929/early 1930 - were rebuffed by intimidation and violence. Steyr was, as both Social Democratic leaders and rank and file proclaimed during the anti-*Heimwehr* campaign, an *Arbeiterstadt*,[25] a place where a dominant manual worker community could express - and defend - its identity openly and freely through a hegemonic Social Democratic movement. As a result, the Steyr *Hochburg* was arguably the safest haven for Social Democrats which existed in the provinces.

However, Social Democratic hegemony within this extraordinary *Hochburg* was shattered during 1930. The collapse of car production at the Steyr-Werke in August 1929 whipped away the material foundation of the *Hochburg* and set in motion a process of political collapse which was complete just twelve months later. Effective trade unionism, municipal policies and political patronage all fell victim, directly or indirectly, to the effects of mass, local unemployment. The impact on the organisational cohesion of the movement was rapid. There was, as Chapter Five showed, a marked decline in the willingness to demonstrate public allegiance to the movement.[26] There was also a rapid fall in membership. As Table 8.1 shows, the party had lost around

Table 8.1 The Decline in Social Democratic Membership in Steyr, 1928-1931

Organisation	1928/1929 membership	1930/1931 membership	Decrease %
Steyr SDAP	*ca.* 5,000 (1929)	3,837 (1931)	*ca.* 23.3
SDAP Section 9	1,471 (1929)	1,157 (1931)	21.3
SDAP Section 5	737 (1928)	596 (1931)	19.1
SDAP Section 6	393 (1928)	263 (1931)	33.1
Women's Organisation	1,582 (1929)	1,055 (1931)	33.3
Kinderfreunde (Children)	2,046 (1929)	1,762 (1930)	13.9
Naturfreunde	817 (1929)	662 (1930)	19.0

Sources: *STB 2-2-1929, 7; 22-2-1929, 9; 7-2-1930, 10; 16-2-1930, 14; 3-2-1932, 10; 13-2-1932, 8; 13-2-1933, 3; VGA Parteiarchiv Mappe 67/2; Rote Saat 1929, 58; Rote Saat 1930, 60; OÖTB 1929, 56; OÖTB 1930, 68.*

a quarter of its 1929 membership by 1931, while a number of the leading auxiliary organisations similarly lost at least a sixth and up to a third of their members around the turn of the decade. This emergent disintegration of the Social Democratic movement, due in part to the withdrawal of former instrumentalist members, widened the scope for anti-Social Democratic politics in the town. It was reflected in a new assertiveness of the local 'bourgeois' parties and in the growing confidence of the *Heimwehr* in its campaign to 'conquer' Steyr. The right-wing backlash reached an interim highpoint when the *Heimwehr*, with local 'bourgeois' party support, won access to Steyr's streets in February 1930. It culminated in the mass *Heimwehr* rally held with the cooperation of the new federal police force, on the town square, in front of the 'red' town hall, on 31 August 1930. The *Heimwehr* rally had a deep, symbolic significance. It was a public humiliation which signified the capitulation of Social Democratic 'territory'. It proclaimed the loss of the 'safe haven' within which the sense of shared social identity based in the manual worker milieu in the town, and developed through the organisational framework of the Social Democratic movement, could be freely and fully expressed.

The loss of hegemony during 1930 was the starting point of a period of continuous organisational decline, which persisted - with the exception of a temporary upswing late in 1932 following an intensive recruitment drive - through to the dissolution of the movement in February 1934. Its primary cause was the scale of unemployment in Steyr. On a rough measure, local unemployment rose from a lowpoint of just over 5% in June 1929 to 21% by the end of that year, and continued to rise until its peak of 33% at the end of 1932. The decline in unemployment levels thereafter was very slow, and had fallen only to 28% by the start of 1934.[27]

There is considerable evidence to suggest that high, long-term unemployment weakened the Social Democratic movement in the sense suggested by the study of Marienthal by Jahoda, Lazarsfeld and Zeisel. Available sources suggest a high degree of hopelessness and resignation among the local unemployed,[28] which, to use the local SDAP's own, euphemistic term, contributed to a 'weariness' among supporters hitherto highly active in Social Democratic organisational life.[29] The decline in political participation caused by unemployment was compounded by a wave of unemployment-driven emigration from the town. The *Kinderfreunde* in the Steyr district claimed to have lost around a thousand members to emigration by the end of 1930, and the district party almost 500 in 1931. Although these figures seem a little on the high side, they do point to an important problem which had not just quantitative, but also qualitative significance for the Social Democratic movement. Emigrants tended to be composed disproportionately of the young[30] and of skilled workers[31] - some of the most vital groups in any party organisation.

The broad impact of unemployment on political participation and emigration rates presented problems for the Social Democratic movement which were inherent in the local economic situation after 1929. These were compounded, though, by the 'home-grown' problem of tactical inflexibility. By the end of 1932 the astonishing figure of over 70% of the District SDAP membership was unemployed.[32] The party leadership in Steyr was, however, unable to devise coherent and attractive policies capable of articulating and addressing the particular problems of the unemployed and - therefore - of maintaining their interest and participation. This is perhaps the clearest example of the political inertia, discussed in the previous chapter, which befell a party leadership whose ideas, horizons and, indeed, personal interests, were bound up in the organisation-centred strategies of the 1920s. The leadership remained immovably fettered to the politics of the 1920s, continuing to pursue policies for the unemployed which remained bound within the established, orthodox parameters of a democratic process through which, in the 1930s, Austrian politics was no longer being conducted.

Leading Steyr Social Democrats helped, for example, to formulate a series of eloquent, if largely futile, resolutions for debate in the Upper Austrian *Landtag*, which condemned cuts in state unemployment support.[33] They also collected signatures with great enthusiasm for popular initiative legislation - which stood no realistic chance of enactment - designed to improve social insurance provision.[34] Such tactics had no immediate relevance to the day-to-day concerns of the average unemployed person, and clearly overestimated the potential of traditional democratic methods when the national government was in increasingly anti-democratic hands. They left the Steyr SDAP increasingly remote from the unemployed majority of its members. This remoteness was something the Communist Party in Steyr capitalised on by addressing the concerns of the unemployed in a much more direct way. They carried out campaigns for the unemployed as it were *on the streets*, in direct contact with those who were out of work. They focused on the integration of the unemployed into mainstream party activities in the attempt to retain the sense of political purpose and involvement which otherwise - as in Marienthal - tended to evaporate in the face of long-term and mass unemployment.[35] The emphasis on participation was supported by the provision of material relief which, although modest, proved to be an important mobilisational tool. Between 1930 and 1932 the Communists made repeated gains in membership, presumably from the Social Democrats, and due, according to police reports, to the effectiveness of their agitation among the unemployed.[36] These successes highlighted the limitations of the SDAP as a party of innovation and mobilisation. It remained a slow-changing, bureaucratic organisation stubbornly attached to the tried and trusted methods of a bygone era, despite their manifest ineffectuality in dealing with the problems of the present. As a result, it lost both support and credibility.

The SDAP also lost, in a similar process, support and credibility among both younger members and *Schutzbündler*, this time to both the Communists and National Socialists. The attractiveness of extremist movements to younger people in the inter-war years has typically been interpreted as a consequence of youth unemployment.[37] The defection of young former Social Democrats to the Nazis and Communists in Steyr may well have had an element of this kind of unemployment-driven impetus. Defections to KPÖ and NSDAP were, however, in most cases traceable to the attitude of the SDAP leadership, at all levels in the party, to the intensifying anti-Social Democratic repression of the early 1930s. The formulaic responses of the party to growing persecution - which focused on the potential of the democratic process or the possibility of accommodation with the CSP, or which simply advised 'don't be provoked', or 'wait and see' - were both patently ineffective in protecting the movement and profoundly depressing for many younger Social Democrats. Such responses merely legitimised political passivity. They allowed the surrender of position after position of strength and, thereby made defunct the professed rationale of the Social Democratic youth movement: to prepare for and practice in the 'culture' of the society which would emerge following the SDAP's 'inevitable' ascent to power. As this future function became more and more obviously unachievable, growing numbers of younger Social Democrats defected to movements which were more prepared to take action in support of their aims.[38] The regular defection in the early 1930s of groups of Steyr's *Schutzbündler*, at first to the Communist *Arbeiterwehr*,[39] and later to the National Socialist SA and SS[40] should be seen in a similar light. They were expressions of growing *Schutzbund* alienation from a party which refused to use the *Schutzbund* to fulfil its proclaimed rationale of *Wehrhaftigkeit*: to defend the movement and its achievements from the anti-Social Democratic Right.

The Components and Strategy of the Opposition in Steyr

The deep disillusionment felt in Steyr in the early 1930s about the ineffectiveness and passivity of the SDAP was, as elsewhere, expressed not only in defection, but also in the development of intra-movement opposition. The opposition in Steyr had three pillars. It drew in part from the disaffection noted above among the Social Democratic youth and the *Schutzbund*,[41] and had as its third focal point the MAV's organisation within the Steyr-Werke. What united these three focal points of opposition was a deep and growing sense of anger that all the advances won after 1918 were being reversed. For many, a *Lebenswerk*, their 'life's work', and the accumulated investment of time, energy and pride they had put into it were being undermined. The privileges and power they had enjoyed in the *Hochburg* had been destroyed and the political freedom of manoeuvre and self-expression won by their intense efforts were steadily being whittled away by economic crisis and repression. At the same time, the wider Social Democratic movement - at the provincial and national levels - seemed unable to buck the trend and do anything about it. The causes and the path of the welling anger this situation produced are illustrated in Table 8.2, which pinpoints the key issues which provoked, along with the organisations which expressed,[42] opposition between 1930 and 1933.

Table 8.2 The Incidence of Intra-Movement Opposition in Steyr, 1930-1932

Cause and Date of Opposition	Source of opposition	Cooperation with the Communists?	Defection to the Communists?
Loss of 'monopoly' of the streets to the *Heimwehr* : January/February 1930	Schutzbund	No	Yes
	SAJ	Yes	No
MAV Negotiations at the Steyr-Werke: October 1930	MAV	No	No
Arms search: November 1930	Schutzbund	No	Yes
Heimwehr Putsch: September 1931	Schutzbund	Yes	No
Acquittal of *Heimwehr* Putschists: December 1931	Schutzbund	Yes	No
	MAV	No	Yes
Fear of Nazi Putsch: June/July 1932	Schutzbund	Yes	No
	MAV	Yes	No

Sources: *AVA BKA Inneres 13/6 Karton 2382: 195.315-30; 238.347-31; 22/genere Karton 4867: 214.060-30; Karton 4868: 230.754-31; Karton 4873: 145.062-32; 22/Oberösterreich Karton 5100: 180.710-29; 110.119-30; 110.946-30; 111.425-30; 111.427-30; 111.430-30; 121.881-30; Karton 5101: 190.931-31; 199-871-31; 220.723-31; 106.243-31; Karton 5102: 190.484-32; STB 18-12-1932, 10.*

    An important initial point to note about Table 8.2 is that expressions of opposition were increasingly shaped by events of national rather than local provenance and significance. At the same time and as a result, the SDAP at national level gradually overtook the local party as the primary focus of opposition sentiment. This indicates two things. Firstly, it shows that the context for Social Democratic politics in Steyr was becoming 'de-localised' as local Social Democrats became increasingly subject to the repressive measures of national government, and as the insulating effect of the now fallen *Hochburg* ebbed away. Secondly, it also denotes that the opposition in Steyr was developing, in response, a wider perspective on the problems facing the movement than had hitherto been the case. In this respect, the emergence of opposition from 1930 onwards signified a growing openness to adopt new ideas, approaches and solutions to the problems the movement and its supporters faced. These themes are explored further in the discussion below of emergent *Schutzbund*, MAV and SAJ opposition.

The Sources of Opposition: Schutzbund, MAV and SAJ

The waves of opposition emanating from the ranks of the *Schutzbund* were generally directed against the - in the *Schutzbund* view - excessively quiescent response of both the local and the national party leaderships to the provocations of *Heimwehr* and central government. The starting point here was the surrender by Mayor Sichlrader of the Social Democratic 'monopoly' of the streets in Steyr in February 1930 (see Chapter Five). Sichlrader's actions overrode the determination of the *Schutzbund* (and elements of the SAJ) to uphold the monopoly by force in a violent showdown with the *Heimwehr*. Sichlrader's part in the humiliating incursion of the *Heimwehr* arch-enemy into Social Democratic 'territory' caused such dissent, according to police reports, that 130 men - around a fifth of the total membership[43] - left the *Schutzbund* by the end of February to join the Communist's paramilitary unit, the *Arbeiterwehr*.[44] The dissenting *Schutzbündler* were unwilling to see such a clear expression of the integrity of the *Hochburg* as their control over the local streets to be surrendered without a fight. The attitude shown by the *Schutzbund* in February 1930 revealed an emerging commitment to confront and resist - if necessary violently and in defiance of the party - those forces which were hostile to the Social Democratic movement. It was illustrated repeatedly over the following years in an impatience and deep irritation about the non-confrontational passivity of the national party leadership.

Otto Bauer's deterministic and passive 'wait and see' response to state repression amounted, for the Steyr *Schutzbündler*, to weak and humiliating capitulation. It allowed the movement gradually to be robbed, without resistance, of its political strength. It allowed the CSP, *Heimwehr* and security forces to subvert the democratic order the *Schutzbund* was supposed to be protecting. Crucially, it also allowed them to strip the *Schutzbund* of the ultimate means of protecting that order and the place the local Social Democratic movement had carved out for itself within it: weapons. Between November 1930 and February 1934, some 588 guns and gun-stands of various kinds, 20,475 rounds of ammunition and eight hand grenades were confiscated in arms searches in Steyr.[45] This passive surrender of weaponry in the course of the increasingly frequent police arms searches of the early 1930s caused a festering resentment in *Schutzbund* ranks in Steyr and, indeed, as Ilona Duzsynska has argued, throughout Austria:

> With every search for weapons, with every confiscation grew the rancour, the suppressed anger with a government infested with *Heimwehr* influence and with a party and *Schutzbund* leadership which silently put up with every provocation. Many *Schutzbündler* entered a state of dangerous instability which swung between not wanting to bother any more and wanting to take to arms immediately.[46]

Between November 1930 and February 1932 *Schutzbund* opposition in Steyr was always concerned with weapons: either the confiscation of their own, or the ability of the *Heimwehr* to use theirs, even to putsch with them, with apparent impunity. The *Schutzbündler* condemned the inaction of the national Social Democratic leaders over arms searches and the *Heimwehr* threat and even called for their deposition. Equally, they were deeply embittered by the preferential treatment accorded to the *Heimwehr* by the government, and demanded offensive action against the government and violent resistance to future arms searches.[47]

As Table 8.2 shows, *Schutzbund* opposition was always expressed between 1930 and 1933 in connection with the Communist *Arbeiterwehr*. During 1930, the pattern was one of defection, and after 1930 of cooperation,[48] of which the most extraordinary product was the composition in July 1932 of a detailed battle plan for the occupation of Steyr, designed to be put into effect in the event of a National Socialist putsch in Austria.[49] This evident closeness of the *Schutzbund* to the *Arbeiterwehr* gives an indication of the trajectory of its opposition. It was increasingly willing to abandon the politics of the democratic mass party to act, in line with the Leninist conception which underlay the KPÖ, as a vanguard for radical change. In doing so it was heading broadly in the same direction as the opposition forces in the MAV.

The opposition in the MAV centred around the Chair of the Works Council at the Steyr-Werke, August Moser, and Moser's fellow Works Councillor and the SDAP District Leader, Franz Schrangl. Moser and Schrangl emerged as the leaders of a wider opposition grouping in Steyr during 1933 which incorporated MAV, *Schutzbund* and SAJ militants. Significantly, although Schrangl was the local SDAP leader and Moser a member of its Executive Committee, their opposition was never conducted through *party* structures. This may have been a comment on the incapacity for tactical renewal in an unwieldily bureaucratic party. More concretely, it reflected the roots of the Moser-Schrangl opposition in the MAV-management dispute at the Steyr-Werke in the first half of 1930. As Chapter Four showed, management was determined to impose working conditions on the planned resumption of car production in July 1930 which would have eliminated the MAV's raft of extra-statutory rights on the shopfloor. The MAV Works Council, under Moser's leadership, was equally determined to defend those rights, which had formed the backbone of Social Democratic hegmony in Steyr. The Works Council was, however, undone when the national MAV Executive went over its head to deal directly with management and accept its terms.

Moser and Schrangl reacted with anger at the 1930 MAV National Congress, accusing the National Executive of succumbing to an undue pessimism and determinism in the face of economic crisis and the accelerating rationalisation process. Their bitterness at the loss of the major source of Social Democratic power in Steyr was expressed vehemently. Schrangl condemned the (national) union for using the vision of crisis too often as a feeble excuse for neglecting its responsibilities to its members.[50] Moser saw no reason why the union could not still mount an aggressive industrial relations policy despite the economic situation. Although the chances of success may have been limited, the membership still needed to see that the union was working on its behalf.[51] Both called for a more innovative and flexible approach to industrial relations, better adapted to the new, post-1930 situation, arguing, for example, that rationalisation should not seen be seen simply as a portent of shopfloor impotence, but a new opportunity for the union. It meant, among other things, that more women and younger workers would be employed in place of the traditional MAV constituency of skilled, male workers. The union should therefore move with the times and begin to address the concerns of these new workforce groups in order to retain its influence on the shopfloor. [52]

Moser and Schrangl clearly rejected the pessimistic and fatalistic attitude which had begun to afflict their national union executive and which, in their view, had lost them their shopfloor powers. While the national MAV lapsed, alongside the local and national SDAP, into a debilitating passivity, they moved towards the adoption of an innovative and offensive stance. This presumably brought them into touch with like-minded Social Democrats elsewhere in Austria, since by the autumn of 1932 they were identified as adherents of the Ernst Fischer opposition.[53] It seems likely that Moser and Schrangl sought over the next eighteen months to 'spread the word' of opposition within the Works Council and remaining workforce at the Steyr-Werke.[54] There is certainly strong evidence to support this view in the increasing militancy of the workforce in the last few weeks before the Civil War (see below), along with at least some indication of a radical potential on the shopfloor before 1933. For example, the Communist 'Revolutionary Trade Union Opposition' received 191 votes in the Steyr-Werke Works Council elections in December 1931.[55] In addition, the local police reported in June 1932 that Social Democrats and Communists were conducting talks on the establishment of 'surveillance committees' in important firms which would observe local Nazi activities in the event of a Nazi putsch in Germany during or after the *Reichstag* election of July 1932. At least one such committee was established in the Steyr-Werke.[56] The manual workforce at the Steyr-Werke thus emerged as a further locus of opposition to the passive aquiescence of the SDAP.

The third component of the emergent opposition in Steyr was the SAJ. Throughout Austria the Social Democratic youth movement emerged to prominence in 1931 and 1932 as a critical and militant force. In Vienna and Styria in particular, a new, semi-autonomous organisation of younger Social Democrats, the *Jungfront*, had sprung up as a focus both for dissatisfaction with the SDAP national leadership and for militant anti-fascist activism. In many respects it was a forerunner of the Fischer opposition of 1932.[57] Although there was no *Jungfront* organisation in Steyr, the SAJ developed a similar militancy in the early 1930s. It is possible that Franz Schrangl played a significant role here. He was a recent Chair of the Steyr SAJ and still exerted a strong influence over the youth organisation.[58] His influence may have encouraged the adoption of new, more confrontational political activities by the SAJ from 1932 onwards. For example, satirical humour, based on the political cabarets of the Viennese *Sozialistische Veranstaltungsgruppe*, was exploited with considerable success as a mobilisational tool.[59] Moreover, the SAJ engaged the local opponents of the Social Democratic movement both in energetic public debate, and, if the intellectual 'battleground' failed to win the day, in straightforward street violence. A first indication that violence was being adopted as a political tactic had been given early in 1930, when Social Democratic youths, in cooperation with their Communist counterparts, were active in defending the territory of 'red Steyr' from the *Heimwehr*.[60] Subsequently violence and disruption also formed part of the SAJ's portfolio of anti-Nazi tactics in 1932-1933.[61] More broadly, the SAJ began after 1930 to play an increasingly important role in the Social Democratic paramilitary organisations. This was seen both in the increased levels of activity of the youth-based *Wehrturner* (Military Gymnasts') organisation, and also in the fact that many *Schutzbund* members reappeared in the ranks of the SAJ after the formal dissolution of their own organisation at the end of March 1933.[62]

The new-found activism of the SAJ, which contrasted starkly with its previous preoccupation with the detached, 'surrogate' politics of cultural preparation for the future, represented an implicit rejection of the SDAP's passivity in the face of continued repression and of its inability to maintain a realistic prospect of the future the SAJ had been committed to. The SAJ thus joined the *Schutzbund* and the MAV as a third opposition force.

The Opposition Strategy in Steyr

The intra-movement opposition of MAV, *Schutzbund* and SAJ remained sporadic and uncoordinated before 1933. However, the events surrounding the parliamentary crisis of 4-15 March 1933 signalled a turning point. The parliamentary crisis proved for many to be the final straw of disillusionment with the SDAP and ushered in a period when these three components of opposition cohered to form the most vital, driving force in the Social Democratic movement in Steyr, the *Schutzbund* contributing the deep resentment it felt over its frustrated role as the defence organisation of the movement, the MAV the offensive and innovative drive it had developed after the loss of its shopfloor powers in the Steyr-Werke, and the SAJ its new-found spirit of aggression and confrontation towards the movement's opponents.

On 4 March 1933 the work of the Austrian parliament became deadlocked on a procedural technicality. Dollfuss exploited the deadlock as a pretext for abandoning 'unworkable' parliamentary government and commencing rule by emergency decree. Initially the SDAP National Executive displayed a determination to mobilise the membership and take up battle in defence of the parliament and the constitution.[63] However, this uncharacteristic commitment to face the full consequences of confrontation soon weakened. On 13 March the party executive began to prevaricate, alleging the unreadiness of the masses for battle. The showdown scheduled for 15 March then became a 'great evasion', as the SDAP MPs (accompanied by their German Nationalist counterparts) crept into parliament before the announced time, thus avoiding the police who were to have prevented the sitting. The sitting was formally opened and immediately closed again. The party leadership then loudly proclaimed in supposed triumph that a genuine parliamentary sitting had taken place.[64]

The events of 15 March were, in the words of one national party executive member 'tragicomical'.[65] After preparing its followers for decisive confrontation, the SDAP executive contented itself with a near-farcical evasion of conflict and even claimed 'victory' for ensuring that parliament did indeed 'sit'. The disappointment and disillusionment felt throughout the movement was palpable. Almost everywhere the movement had been ready - both mentally and logistically - to fight and be fought. The *Schutzbund* in Steyr and throughout Upper Austria was mustered, weapons at hand, ready to act: 'The working class waited for the signal which would announce the general strike. The *Schutzbündler* for the call to support the general strike with armed force'.[66] The news that the national leadership of the SDAP had at the last minute evaded the confrontation was received in Steyr with anger, indignation and derision.[67] This was the point at which the national leadership lost all remaining credibility in opposition circles in Steyr. It revealed unequivocally that the national leadership's predominant instinct was prevarication and not action, and gave a decisive impetus to the emergent opposition in Steyr.

At the same time, the established SDAP leadership in Steyr became increasingly marginalised as it continued - in line with the discredited example of the national leadership - to preach a local politics of conflict-avoidance at all costs.[68] Its own tired brand of passive acquiescence was, in the process, shunted aside by a new, unsophisticated, but radical opposition strategy which was articulated by Moser and Schrangl. This strategy encompassed a fundamental rejection of the democratic reformism which had hitherto held sway in the SDAP, and which had patently failed in the 1930s to serve the movement's supporters effectively. Instead Moser and Schrangl opted for an offensive and activist strategy, which would be pursued by a more dynamic organisational apparatus, and which would, supposedly, culminate in a 'social revolution'. This strategy was based not only on an analysis of the failings of Austrian Social Democracy at the local and national levels, but also compared these with the fate of German Social Democracy in the 1930s. This led Moser and Schrangl to draw conclusions not just about the role of Social Democracy in Austrian politics, but also about the character - and apparent failings - of Social Democracy as a broader political tradition.

A central problem for Moser was the determinism of the national SDAP leadership. He was deeply critical of its insistence that the party should sit tight in the expectation that a policy of negotiation and restraint, or perhaps even the intervention of foreign powers, would solve the political crisis in Austria. He dismissed this argument as 'just a hope, and even a very vague hope', and referred to the fate of the German labour movement under Hitler as a logical consequence of such a 'wait and see' attitude.[69] The reference to Hitler indicated the profound influence the situation in Germany had on the opposition in Steyr. Knowledge of Nazi crimes against the German labour movement was widespread and produced a determination to avoid the same fate.[70] Schrangl emphasised the need to learn from mistakes which had been made in Germany. He argued that the Social Democrats had to grasp that a politics of the 'lesser evil' - i.e. of appeasing the Dollfuss regime in the hope of preventing a Nazi takeover in Austria - was fundamentally misconceived. Seeking compromise with the 'lesser evil' was one of the main reasons for the current predicament of the German working class. Schrangl then widened his attack to reject the underlying principles of Social Democratic reformism. Reformism for him had revealed itself to be wholly impracticable. It was, after all, through the pursuit of a reformist philosophy of achieving socialism by 'occupying legislative and administrative positions' that German Social Democracy had 'fallen into the abyss'.[71]

The repudiation of a reformist strategy for power was confirmed in the emphatic rejection by Moser and Schrangl of the methods of parliamentary politics and the nature of the Social Democratic party organisation.[72] Only a broad front of extra-parliamentary actions - protests, demonstrations, strikes and so on - was felt to be suitable as a method with which to break the dictatorship. These were gradually to be escalated, with the mobilisation of the whole working class, into the general strike which would signal the battle for power in the state.[73] The existing type of party organisation, the classic mass party, could never be the instrument of such violent, revolutionary change. The internal machinery of the party was far too cumbersome to be able to reach and take responsibility for speedy decisions. This latter point was held to be partly responsible for the prevarication of the national leadership on 15 March 1933.[74] The nature of its leadership was a further problem: it was unrepresentatively over-aged, far too dependent for its material existence on the party organisation,[75] and as a result far too remote from the concerns of the average member, and in particular from those of younger members.[76] The instrument for change would, by implication, instead be a younger, more dynamic, ruthless and selfless vanguard.

This strategy for power was complemented by a vision of 'social revolution' which remained only hazily defined, but whose model was the Russian Revolution of 1917. Schrangl attacked the restraint the SDAP had exerted on the working class in the revolutionary upheaval of 1918 to prevent the establishment of an Austrian soviet republic. If the 'methods of the Russian proletariat' had been used throughout Central Europe after the war, there could never have emerged such a brutal fascist regime as now existed in Germany, and which threatened to take hold in Austria. Austrian Social Democracy needed to embrace 'Russian methods', the violent and total overthrow of the existing system, and thus ensure the 'social revolution' in Austria.[77]

The Opposition and the Civil War in Steyr

However unsophisticated their terminology may have been, it is clear that Moser and Schrangl had decisively rejected the principles on which Social Democracy - in Steyr, Austria, Germany and everywhere else - was based. They had abandoned the principle of reforming the existing system from within, and now sought its complete abolition and substitution with a revolutionary order inspired by Soviet-style Bolshevism. This emphatic rejection of reformism was given additional momentum in the months following the 'great evasion' of March 1933 by two factors. The first was the continuing comparison between the intensifying persecution of the labour movement in Germany during 1933 and the 'salami-tactic' repression of Austrian Social Democracy by the Dollfuss regime, in particular the regular confiscation of *Schutzbund* arms. These confiscations were steadily reducing the ability of the Social Democrats to take to arms to resist a 'German' fate. Opposition figures in Steyr therefore called for the national SDAP leadership to move towards armed resistance quickly before that ability was completely obliterated:

> We can no longer 'wait and see' any more, otherwise we will be unarmed and at the mercy of the enemy. Without weapons we are helpless, and then the same will happen to us as happened to the workers in Germany.[78]

The continuing inaction of the national SDAP, however, exacerbated the sense of disillusionment felt about the leadership and policies of the Social Democratic movement. This growing disillusionment was reflected in Steyr in an accelerated trend of defection to the Nazi Party, whose dynamism, radical policies and willingness to take direct action against the Dollfuss regime had obvious attractions when compared to the constant prevarication and passivity of the SDAP.[79] The accelerating rate of defection to the Nazis was the second factor which lent urgency to the opposition debate in Steyr: put bluntly, the Social Democratic movement was falling apart. Although no exact figures are available, police reports showed that a 'quite considerable' proportion of local Social Democrats had shifted its allegiance to the Nazi Party during 1933.[80] This high rate of defection confirmed the impression that if the remaining Social Democrats did not undertake decisive action soon to resist Dollfuss and halt the disintegration of the movement, there would be nothing left to fight back with. This was an attitude expressed forcefully by August Moser in a presentation to the national SDAP Executive late in 1933:

I said [to the Executive] 'haven't you read about what is going on out there, did nobody talk of the mood in the party? The people are already running away from us. The party does nothing, it's not even alive any more. When will the party finally issue a call for resistance? ... Don't you see the dangers as they smash our great movement to pieces? There is no longer much left, just like it happened in Germany.[81]

The accelerating disintegration of the movement towards the end of 1933 led opposition circles in MAV, *Schutzbund* and SAJ in Steyr to prepare concrete plans for violent resistance to the Dollfuss regime.[82] There was, however, no move to implement those plans until January 1934. Between 1 December 1933 and mid-January 1934 the government proclaimed a 'Christmas peace' which was modelled on the 'civil peace' (*Burgfrieden*) of the First World War: all parties were, at least temporarily, supposed to suspend their partisan interests and activities. Predictably, while the 'Christmas peace' was being observed by an acquiescent SDAP, the Dollfuss government issued a further series of decrees directed against remaining remnants of Social Democratic influence in state and society: social insurance programmes were cut, the budget of Red Vienna was slashed, and moves were made to eliminate Social Democratic influence in Chambers of Labour and Works Councils throughout Austria.

The decrees issued during the Christmas peace were evidently the last straw for Moser, Schrangl and their colleagues on the Works Council of the Steyr-Werke. MAV control over the Steyr-Werke Works Council was effectively the last vestige of the Social Democratic *Hochburg* in Steyr. The latest decrees threatened even that. The Works Councillors became determined not to accept this final humiliation in the style which had become usual since March 1933:

We asked ourselves how much longer are we going to sit by and watch this situation? There was one day [around 20 January 1934] when we distributed 25 rounds of ammunition to the leading committee members of the Works Council ... and to reliable *Schutzbündler* who were still employed at the works ... We also told them that if the party ... does not make a response to all the events of the past weeks, then we will attack ourselves, and hope for solidarity and support.[83]

The determination to fight - even to spark civil war - rather than relinquish a final position of strength was again illustrated a few days later. As was discussed in Chapter Four, the Steyr-Werke management, encouraged by the latest series of decrees, chose to ignore the MAV and conduct negotiations on a new collective agreement for the works with the Viennese Christian Metalworkers' Union. The Works Council responded, with the full support of the workforce, with the promise of a strike if management should go ahead, along with the thinly veiled threat that the picket line would be defended by armed force, even if that should lead to wider hostilities.[84]

The confrontational attitude of Moser and his colleagues was a clear reflection of the mood which prevailed throughout the opposition in Steyr. Feelings of desperation and indignation about the continuing passivity of the SDAP were widespread, and many continued to press for violent action.[85] The commitment to confrontation was intensified by extensive arms searches in Steyr on 8 and 10 February, which were accompanied by on-the-spot searches of passing pedestrians and vehicles.[86] It was further stoked up by the demands made by the *Heimwehr* in the same week for the installation of a *Heimwehr*-nominated government commissioner to take over the administration of Steyr's 'red' town hall.[87]

This atmosphere of heightening tension in Steyr provides an important backdrop to the meeting called by Richard Bernaschek, the Upper Austrian *Schutzbund* leader, on 11 February 1934 in Linz. Among those called to attend were Moser, Schrangl, Mayor Sichlrader and the military leader of the Steyr *Schutzbund*, Ferdinand Mayrhofer, along with a number of Social Democratic functionaries from elsewhere in Upper Austria. The purpose of the meeting was to discuss the threat posed in the statement made by Dollfuss' *Heimwehr* Vice-Chancellor, Emil Fey, earlier the same day that: 'I have seen Dollfuss and I can tell you quite definitely that he is now our man. Tomorrow we shall go to work, and we shall make a thorough job of it.'[88] Bernaschek wanted to discuss Fey's statement, assess the mood of the Social Democrats in Upper Austria and plan a response in case Fey carried out his lightly veiled threat. He himself felt that any provocation on the following day - for example arrests or arms searches - should be resisted and that Social Democratic forces should be mobilised to escalate this active resistance into a wider offensive against the dictatorship.[89] His proposal received unanimous support, and a letter was drafted to be sent to the SDAP Executive in Vienna to inform it of the Upper Austrians' decision. The meeting then discussed what would happen if the SDAP Executive tried to deflect the Upper Austrians from their commitment to resist. August Moser predicted this was indeed what the Executive would do, but proposed that the Upper Austrians should simply ignore any Executive order to back down. Moser's proposal was also accepted unanimously.[90] Subsequently, despite Otto Bauer's last-minute attempt to intervene, civil war was sparked on the morning of 12 February 1934 when *Schutzbündler* in Linz followed Bernaschek's orders and resisted an attempt by the police to enter the local SDAP headquarters by force.

It is not the intention here to discuss the course of events in Steyr during the Austrian Civil War. The two days of battle which commenced in the town in the late morning of 12 February, and which were fought by a heavily outnumbered and underarmed Social Democratic force, have been extensively discussed and analysed elsewhere.[91] The intention here and in the concluding section below is rather to dwell on the reasons why Social Democrats took to arms. Obviously, resistance on 12 February was on one level a desperate protest against repression and dictatorship. But it was also the climax of a politics of opposition and protest *within* the Social Democratic movement which had flared sporadically in MAV, *Schutzbund* and SAJ between 1930 and 1933, and which coalesced during 1933 into a coherent political force. The decision for civil war embodied for these groups the final rejection of the constitutionalist, parliamentary orientation and mass party organisation of reformist Social Democracy for the rudimentary Bolshevik strategy of Moser and Schrangl. The participation of Moser and Schrangl in the Bernaschek meeting on 11 February, and the subsequent armed resistance - largely led by August Moser[92] - of around 600 Social Democrats in Steyr on 12-14 February represented, in effect, the Steyr opposition strategy put - unsuccessfully of course - into action.[93]

This is not to say, though, that the decision for civil war in Steyr simply represented some kind of localised triumph of Bolshevism over a rejected Social Democracy. A distinction needs to be made between the *form* of rejection and its underlying *source*. The opposition strategy of Moser and Schrangl certainly provided the dominant (but not sole)[94] form of rejecting Social Democracy in February 1934. The source of rejection was, however, rather more fundamental. The Civil War in Steyr was a vehement, final outburst of indignation at the failures of leadership which had prevented the movement from adjusting itself to the new political rules laid down after 1930 by a resurgent Right, and which had allowed the erosion of the movement in Steyr, its positions of strength, the *Lebenswerk* of its supporters. The violent resistance of February 1934 was the climax of the sense of anger which had been progressively stoked up since 1930 by the inability of the movement to shield the manual worker community from which it had emerged and drawn its strength from its opponents. It was, in a sense, a last, definitive expression of the politics of territory and identity which had shaped the Social Democratic movement in Steyr. This was aptly, if brutally symbolised in the conduct of hostilities in Steyr. After a number of small, offensive skirmishes the Social Democratic forces fell back to be besieged, and ultimately defeated in the Ennsleite, the manual worker housing estate next to the Steyr-Werke which represented the core of the manual worker milieu in Steyr. The unsustainable, if heroic defence of this core area under persistent artillery bombardment by the army provided a poignant metaphor for the experience of the wider local-level movement in the First Republic: abandoned by the higher levels of the movement, the local level was condemned to fight a losing battle against the overwhelming forces which surrounded it.

Conclusions: The Civil War and the Politics of Identity

The process of decline, disintegration and - in the Civil War - destruction experienced by the Social Democratic movement in Steyr in the early 1930s was certainly extraordinary. It nevertheless provides a number of exemplary and emblematic insights into the wider experience of the local-level movement in the First Republic. First and foremost, the experience in Steyr in many respects exemplified the wider pathology of *Hochburg* politics in the provinces. The central problem shared by Steyr and all the other *Hochburgen* was that they by definition stood alone. They were the inward-looking product of a multi-faceted experience of geographical, socio-political and intra-movement isolation and proved, unsurprisingly, to be unsustainable in the long-run. Viewed in their isolation they were a stark and clear expression of the fragmentation and weakness of the provincial Social Democratic movement. Buffeted by the vagaries of an endemically weak economy and by the enduring hostilities of provincial conservatism, they proved unable to reproduce the inward *Integration* and outward *Abgrenzung* on which they had been founded, and gradually toppled.

The emergence of opposition in the Steyr and elsewhere was one form of Social Democratic response to the realisation that *Hochburg* politics were unsustainable. Like the other forms of response touched on in this chapter - withdrawal into political passivity or defection to other movements - the move into internal opposition incorporated a rejection of the leaders and policies which had failed to secure a more enduring basis for Social Democratic self-assertion and self-expression in local-level provincial politics. Unlike the other forms of response, though, intra-*movement* opposition by definition combined a rejection of established leaders and policies with a form of continued attachment to the Social Democratic movement. The reasons for this continued attachment are not easy to pin down. It may have reflected in part an apparent ambiguity in the organisational conception of left-opposition politics throughout Austria. While the opposition tended towards, and professed the necessity of, a tightly organised, Leninist vanguard organisation, it also sought to remain within the SDAP, presumably because the SDAP was the only party which was capable of mobilising popular support behind any prospective opposition actions.[95]

Continued attachment may also have reflected a belief that the SDAP held within it a latent potential for the violent and revolutionary tactics proposed by the opposition. The SDAP's Linz Programme of 1926 had set out the course to be followed in the case of a bourgeois counter-revolution which destroyed democracy (a condition which the Dollfuss regime arguably fulfilled): '... then the working class could only win power through a civil war'.[96] With the Linz Programme in mind, the left-opposition could argue that in demanding active, and ultimately violent resistance to dictatorship, they were upholding party policy. As one prominent member of the Steyr opposition noted: 'These people were merely adhering consistently to the party programme and its decisions';[97] the leadership of the movement was out of step with the established aims of the Social Democratic movement in the particular circumstances of the early 1930s, not the opposition.

It seems doubtful, though, that the mass of rank and file opposition members in Steyr and elsewhere sought to express their disaffection from within the movement for such reasons of strategic foresight or programmatic rectitude. A more convincing reason for continued attachment amid deep disillusionment lies in the sense of shared, community identity which had emerged in the manual worker milieux of the provinces, and which allegiance to the Social Democratic movement had helped to consolidate and express *vis-à-vis* other, generally hostile groups in Austrian society since the latter quarter of the nineteenth century. To recall the words of the Salzburg Social Democrat Karl Steinocher:

> You have to have experienced it, this feeling of being a 'second-class person'. But this feeling was completely offset by the movement, by our community. It was something like a *Heimat* that we had there, and that had a profound influence on me.[98]

In similar vein, the movement simultaneously represented 'home, fatherland and religion' for Buttinger's *'Frau* Meier'.[99] For the countless Steinochers and *'Frau* Meiers' in the provinces, the Social Democratic movement had provided a realm of personal and community freedom and opportunity in which common identity and background could be fostered and enjoyed. In this way, it had provided a sense of purpose for rank and file Social Democrats, without which their lives would have been significantly less fulfilled. It was this experience of purpose and fulfilment above all else which kept intact the ties between opposition and movement until 1934.

These are issues the discussion will return to below. First, though, it is important to note that the contradictory combination of growing disaffection and continued attachment created a powerful tension in opposition groups, a tension which increased with each instance of perceived inadequacy and prevarication on the part of the movement's leadership. Accounts of grass roots opinion in the provincial movement in 1933-1934 are peppered with reports of intensifying protest at the ongoing politics of Social Democratic acquiescence, of growing embitterment and discord about the humiliation of 15 March 1933, of the 'ferment in the factories' unleashed by the lack of response to the central government ban of the *Schutzbund* later in March 1933, and so on.[100] The tension, frustration and pressure for action which enveloped the opposition steadily rose until the release came in the form of the explosions of violence ignited first in Linz, then in Steyr and other former *Hochburgen* in the provinces on 12 February 1934.

The release of opposition pressure in Steyr in the violence of the Civil War was in two respects emblematic of the wider character of Social Democratic resistance to the Dollfuss regime throughout the provinces: It was both *hopeless* but also, for those involved, absolutely *necessary*. It was hopeless because the Social Democrats were vastly outnumbered and outarmed by the coalition of police, army and *Heimwehr* ranged against them. It was hopeless because the fabric and cohesion of the movement had been decimated by unemployment, repression, defection and demoralisation; as Moser and his colleagues in Steyr had warned, there was, by February 1934, simply nothing much left to fight back with. Resistance, finally, was hopeless above all because of the scattered character of the movement in the provinces. This was a problem vividly exemplified by the *Schutzbündler* who mustered, ready for action, in industrial communities throughout the provinces on 12 February 1934, or the workers who similarly obeyed the call for a general strike, only to find that once assembled and once on strike they had no instructions to follow, no clear plan of action to carry out, no way of communicating effectively with their counterparts in the next industrial community a few miles away.[101] 12 February 1934 definitively exposed the weaknesses inherent in a movement characterised by geographical and organisational fragmentation.

In the light of the above, it is unlikely that many of those who struck, mustered or fought on 12 February 1934 thought they had any chance of winning. Most fully realised that they had no realistic hope of victory. A particularly striking and prophetic expression of the simultaneous acceptance of hopelessness alongside the commitment nevertheless to resist was that given in February 1934 by the standard bearer of the Upper Styrian Social Democratic grass roots, Kolomann Wallisch, just days before his execution under the orders of Dollfuss: 'I am convinced that, at a time when the government is so strong, it [civil war] is organised suicide. I also know that after the battle I will be one of the victims.'[102] Similarly, Richard Bernaschek was 'conscious of the hopelessness of what he was planning' when he called the decisive meeting of Upper Austrian functionaries on 11 February.[103] Despite this, Bernaschek, Wallisch and thousands of others across the provinces still retained an unwavering commitment to present some kind of resistance to the regime. There was a feeling that an act of defiance unconditionally *had* to be launched. In the words of a leaflet in Bischofshofen in Salzburg: 'We would rather fight with the most extreme means than let ourselves be finished off without fighting back and without honour'.[104] The commitment to launch resistance to Dollfuss was exactly this: a matter of honour. This honour was not attached to Social Democracy *per se*, as some have written.[105] Indeed, the broad thrust of the opposition politics which spurred on resistance in February 1934 was one which rejected the Social Democratic tradition. Honour was attached far more to the milieu, the community, the sense of shared social identity from which the Social Democratic movement had sprung. In an otherwise pettily personal condemnation of Richard Bernaschek, the Upper Austrian historian Harry Slapnicka made the shrewd comment that Bernaschek's actions on 11 and 12 February were 'the outcry of a minor, tortured functionary' about the prospective loss of the 'project' (*Aufbauwerk*) in which he had invested so much effort and purpose in his life.[106] Bernaschek's actions were driven by the destruction of his 'project', by the sense of loss his community had had to endure, by the degradations to which his community's identity had been exposed. The resistance he launched along with Moser, Schrangl and the other Upper Austrian functionaries, and which other provincial Social Democrats took up was a defiant assertion of the community and identity which had hitherto sustained the movement. It was directed simultaneously against the repeated violations of that identity experienced at the hands of a repressive regime and the inability of the movement to give adequate protection to it.

Seen in this light, the Civil War in the provinces was conducted not *in honour* of the Social Democratic movement but *in exasperation* with it, and, ultimately and above all, with its leadership in Vienna. The Social Democratic leaders in Vienna stood at the helm of (in relative terms) the strongest party organisation in the world, yet had failed to make any significant, effective contribution to the protection and defence of the movement's achievements at the local level. Mired in their deterministic passivity and acquiescence, they had done nothing, it seemed, to prevent the loss of the *Hochburg* or the debilitating 'torment'[107] of the arms searches, the *Heimwehr* parades, and all the other instances of repression and humiliation which followed. The decision to resist in February 1934 was an act of definitive disillusionment and emancipation directed against the passivity, acquiescence and, ultimately, inadequacy of the Social Democratic leadership and its policies. To embark on violent resistance was to reject the political tradition which the leadership represented. It broke the ties of community and identity between movement and supporters which had endured hitherto. It was, as August Moser put it in Steyr, 'like being freed'[108] from a profoundly unsatisfactory Social Democratic past.

Notes

1   Above all Ernst Fischer. See below.
2   SPÖ-Bezirksorganisation Linz-Stadt (1988), 329; Flanner, (1983), 10.
3   Hinteregger (1978), 277, 285; Peter Wilding, " ... *Für Arbeit und Brot" Arbeitslose in Bewegung. Arbeitslosenpolitik und Arbeitslosenbewegung in Österreich*, Europaverlag, Vienna (1990), 256, 280.
4   Jahoda, Lazarsfeld, Zeisel (1960).
5   See e.g. E. Wight Bakke, *Citizens without work. A study of the effects of unemployment upon the workers' social relations and practices*, Archon, New York (1969). See also Dieter Stiefel, *Arbeitslosigkeit. Soziale, politische und wirtschaftliche Auswirkungen am Beispiel Österreichs 1918-1938*, Duncker und Humblot, Berlin (1979), 136-144.
6   Jahoda, Lazarsfeld, Zeisel (1960), 42-44; c.f. Bakke (1969), 46-72.
7   For a typically exhaustive account of the Dollfuß 'salami-tactic', see Gulick (1948), 905-921, 951-1265.
8   Hinteregger (1978), 288.
9   See Steinböck (1983), 817-818.
10   See e.g. Rabinbach (1983), 154-180. On Zeinitzer see Gerd Schindler, 'Der 12. Februar in Kärnten', *Zeitgeschichte*, 1 (1973-1974), 32-34; Wilhelm Wadl, Alfred Ogris, *Das Jahr 1938 in Kärnten und seine Vorgeschichte. Ereignisse - Dokumente - Bilder*, Verlag des Kärntner Landesarchivs, Klagenfurt (1988), 108-109. On Schneidmadl, see Nasko (1986), 180, 200. The provincial-level commitment to accommodation is addressed again in the Conclusion.
11   Ibid.
12   Hanisch (1983), 927.
13   An exchange between Ernst Koref, acting leader of the Upper Austrian SDAP in early February 1934, and the leader of the SDAP railwaymen's militia in the town of Attnang-Puchheim, Karl Sulzberger, is worth recalling in this respect: 'Dr Koref came to the SDAP District Secretariat in Attnang a week or a few days before 12 February to stop us ... to use his expression, from doing something stupid if things got difficult ... I was already extremely nervous and there was a danger that I couldn't hold myself back any more, so I interrupted him and told him to leave the Secretariat immediately, because otherwise I couldn't guarantee that I wouldn't get violent with him. He went.' Quoted in Erich Treml, Christian Hawle, *Der Widerstand in Attnang-Puchheim 1934-1945. Eine Dokumentation*, Österreichischer Gewerkschaftsbund Bezirksbildungsausschuß Vöcklabruck, Timelkam (1988), 21.
14   Otto Bauer, 'Hoppla, wir leben!', *Der Kampf*, 21 (1928); Otto Bauer, 'Die Bourgeois-Republik in Österreich', *Der Kampf*, 23 (1930). Cited in Gulick (1948), 1393-1394.
15   Flanner (1983), 8.

[16] Richard Bernaschek, 'Die Tragödie der österreichischen Sozialdemokratie', in *Österreich, Brandherd Europas*, Genossenschaft Universumsbücherei, Zurich (1934), 265.

[17] The pattern of defection to the Communists was widespread, with examples recorded in Tirol (Oberkofler (1986), 225, 228), Salzburg (Ingrid Bauer, 'Im Würgegriff der Krise. Die 1930er Jahre', in: Bauer (1988b), 160), Upper Austria (Helmut Ettl, 'Vorwärts, und nicht vergessen. Die sozialistische Jugend in Linz', in SPÖ-Bezirksorganisation Linz-Stadt (1988), 194; Treml, Hawle (1988), 19-20), and Styria (Pferschy (1983), 955).

[18] The literature is rather more coy on this issue, although Bernaschek was refreshingly candid about the situation in Upper Austria. See Bernaschek (1934), 264.

[19] See in particular Rabinbach (1983) and - unsurprisingly - Ernst Fischer's own *An opposing man*, Allen Lane, London (1974).

[20] Rabinbach (1983), 85.

[21] See below.

[22] No one work examines the emergence of opposition in the provinces in any great depth, but the following all touch on it: Flanner (1983), 37; Hanisch (1983), 914, 927; Hinteregger (1978), 281-288; Hinteregger, Schmidlechner, Staudinger (1984), 208, 213-214; Lewis (1991), 185-196; Nasko (1986), 195; Schiffer (1984); Treml, Hawle (1988), 19-21, 27. Bernaschek (1934) also provides a vivid and powerful account of his experience in Upper Austria, with often dramatic insights into the disintegration of the movement and his own decision for active resistance to the Dollfuß regime.

[23] Youth contributions to the left-opposition were in part an extension of the activities of the *Jungfront*, a semi-autonomous youth group which emerged at the fringes of the formal structures of the Social Democratic movement in 1932. Although the *Jungfront* was situated mainly in Vienna and Styria, it pioneered a new brand of activist and non-conformist youth politics which stood at least in part in conflict with the SDAP leadership, and which filtered through into SAJ activities throughout Austria, even where no *Jungfront* organisation existed. See Rabinbach (1983), 72-78 and on the Styrian *Jungfront* Schiffer (1984) and Lewis (1991), 185-189.

[24] Bernaschek (1934), 272.

[25] See Chapter Five.

[26] See Chapter Five.

[27] These figures are measured against the size of the workforce as cited in the census of 1920. The stated unemployment rates are inaccurate to the extent that the size of the workforce was obviously not static from 1920. However, an increase in workforce size during the 1920s was balanced by a fall in the 1930s caused largely by emigration. Also the rates for before 1930 are underestimates in that they refer only to those unemployed who were in receipt of state unemployment support. See Statistische Zentralkommission, *Beiträge zur Statistik der Republik Österreich. 6. Heft. Ergebnisse der außerordentlichen Volkszählung vom 31. Jänner 1920. Alter und Familienstand, Wohnparteien*, Verlag der österreichischen Staatsdruckerei, Vienna (1920), 42-43; STB 4-7-1929, 11; 11-1-1930, 7; 7-1-1933, 1; 10-1-1934, 5.

[28] See e.g. Magistrat der Stadt Steyr, Registratur Faszikel J/o 2731-31 Arbeitsamt; AZ 1-1-1932, 1.

29 STB 29-3-1931, 9.

30 Evidence on emigration from Marienthal in the early 1930s suggests that younger people were over-represented among those who emigrated. The village lost, as a result, some of its most energetic and vital forces. See Jahoda, Lazarsfeld, Zeisel (1960), 59. Although there is no direct evidence, it is probable that the same applied in Steyr. Emigration involved considerable material and mental rigours which younger people were far more likely to undergo than their older colleagues.

31 In an earlier wave of emigration (during the Steyr-Werke lockout of 1925), the bulk of the emigrants had been skilled workers, traditionally among the most active and loyal members of the movement (see *Bericht des Vorstandes des österreichischen Metallarbeiterverbandes* (1927), 160; STB 31-10-1925, 2). Despite the absence of an occupational breakdown of post-1929 emigrants, it would be a fair assumption that the same type of workers was involved. Rationalisation at the Steyr-Werke had created a surplus of skilled labour, and workers with transferable skills were more likely to find work elsewhere. See Magistrat der Stadt Steyr, Registratur, Faszikel J/o 2731-31 Arbeitsamt. Stiefel underlines this point in his assessment of emigration throughout Austria during the First Republic. The labour market was 'denuded' of its 'best and most productive elements': the qualified, skilled workers who constituted the bulk of the emigrants. See Stiefel (1979), 110-116.

32 Sozialdemokratische Partei Oberösterreichs. Tätigkeitsbericht 1932, Gutenberg, Linz (1933), 13.

33 See OÖLA Landtagsakten Nachtrag Schuber 34: 2. Sitzung, 19-5-1931, 6; Schuber 35: 11. Sitzung, 3-6-1932, 7-8; Schuber 36: 12. Sitzung, 8-6-1932, 7-9; 15. Sitzung 16-12-1933, 5.

34 See STB throughout October and November 1930.

35 See the guidelines issued by the KPÖ National Executive and confiscated by the federal police in Steyr in AVA BKA Inneres 22/genere Karton 4872: 142.966-32.

36 AVA BKA Inneres 22/genere Karton 4872: 142.882-32; Karton 4873: 145.912-32; 22/Oberösterreich Karton 5100: 136.833-30; Karton 5101: 112.721-31; 117.661-32; Karton 5102: 147.226-32.

37 Studies of Germany in the depression years have shown that young people tended to be less easily 'broken' by unemployment and were less likely than older colleagues to fall into political passivity. In these circumstances, the Communist and Nazi Parties, especially their activist paramilitary wings, provided meaningful structure for the daily lives of youthful recruits. They also provided a sense of comradeship and belonging and, perhaps most importantly, a sense of mission directed against the system which had, so far, failed them. See e.g. Conan J. Fischer, 'Unemployment and left-wing radicalism at the end of the Weimar Republic', in Peter D. Stachura (Ed.), *Unemployment and the Great Depression in Weimar Germany*, Macmillan, London (1986); Detlev Peukert, 'The lost generation: youth unemployment at the end of the Weimar Republic', in Richard J. Evans and Dick Geary (Eds.), *The German Unemployed. Experience and consequences of unemployment from the Weimar Republic to the Third Reich*, Croom Helm, London (1987).

38 AVA BKA Inneres 22/Oberösterreich Karton 5101: 189.504-31; 5104: 245.705-33; 249.793-33; 22/genere Karton 4879: 241.658-33.

39 AVA BKA Inneres 22/Oberösterreich Karton 5100: 121.881-30; Karton 5101: 189.504-31; 190.931-31; 199.871-31.

40 AVA BKA Inneres 22/Oberösterreich Karton 5104: 245.705-33; 22/genere Karton 4879: 241.658-33.

41 Indeed, as the discussion below suggests, there was a thin and fluid line between defection and intra-movement opposition which at times was bridged by cooperation between the SAJ or the *Schutzbund* and the equivalent Communist youth and paramilitary organisations.

42 Although the Social Democratic youth movement, the SAJ, appears only once as a source of opposition in Table 8.2, it did in fact play a much more prominent role. It was the proponent of a new, aggressive activism after 1930 which saw a new emphasis on methods of direct action and, increasingly, paramilitary activities. Much of its opposition was, as a result, identical to and subsumed in that of the *Schutzbund*.

43 See Table 6.2.

44 AVA BKA Inneres 22/Oberösterreich Karton 5100: 121.881-30.

45 Stockinger (1988), 147.

46 Duczynska (1975), 184.

47 AVA BKA Inneres 22/genere Karton 4867: 214.060-30; Karton 4872: 129.456-32; 22/Oberösterreich Karton 5101: 106.243-31; 190.931-31.

48 AVA BKA Inneres 22/genere Karton 4869: 230.754-31; Karton 4873: 145.062-32; 22/Oberösterreich Karton 5101: 106.243-31; 220.723-31.

49 AVA BKA Inneres 22/Oberösterreich Karton 5102: 190.484-32.

50 *Verhandlungen des 15. Verbandstags der österreichischen Metallarbeiter* (1931), 157-158.

51 Ibid., 147.

52 Ibid., 144-148; 156-159.

53 See Rabinbach (1983), 85.

54 Alois Zehetner, a former Works Councillor, recalled, for example, the 'decisive political influence' that Moser had over the Steyr-Werke workforce. See Zehetner's letter to the author, 19-11-1987. C.f. Kammerstätter (n.d.), 1116.

55 See STB 18-12-1932, 10; AVA BKA Inneres 13/6: 238.347-31.

56 AVA BKA Inneres 22/Oberösterreich Karton 5102: 174.258-32.

57 See Rabinbach (1983), 66-86.

58 See Interview with Josef Mayrhofer 4-7-1986; DÖW File 12202.

59 See STB 24-10-1930, 8; 1-12-1931, 8; 11-10-1932, 10; OÖTB 1932, 29-30; Interview with Josef Mayrhofer 4-7-1986. On the Viennese political cabarets, see Scheu (1977).

60 See AVA BKA Inneres 22/Oberösterreich Karton 5100: 111.430-30.

61 See e.g. STB 16-6-1932, 1; Interview with Josef Mayrhofer 4-7-1986.

62 AVA BKA Inneres 22/Oberösterreich Karton 5105: 113.970-34.

63 See Leichter (1964), 170.

64 Ibid., 157-182; Rabinbach (1983), 86-92.

65 Leichter (1964), 179.

66 Quoted in Bernaschek (1934), 266-267. On the situation in Steyr see SZ 19-3-1933, 6; AVA BKA Inneres 22/Oberösterreich Karton 5103: 129.522-33; 133.037-33.

67 As expressed by August Moser at the Extraordinary Party Conference of April 1933. See VGA Parteiarchiv Mappe 65. C.f. Bernaschek (1934), 268-269.

68   The most vivid illustration of the non-confrontational politics of the local party leadership was when SDAP Vice-Mayor Anton Azwanger attempted to lock up August Moser in January 1934 in order to prevent him from coordinating resistance to the Dollfuß dictatorship. See Kammerstätter (n.d.), 1116-1117.

69   Quoted in VGA Parteiarchiv Mappe 65, 9-10.

70   See Letter to the author by Alois Zehetner, 19-11-1987.

71   See STB 21-6-1933, 2; AVA Sozialdemokratische Parteistellen Karton 175a: Antrag Schrangl und Genossen.

72   For example, according to the testimony of Dr Franz Jetzinger, member of the Upper Austrian SDAP Executive, Schrangl recommended in 1933 that all Upper Austrian *Landtag* deputies should lay down their mandates and relinquish all associated responsibilities. See DÖW File 12200a.

73   AVA Sozialdemokratische Parteistellen Karton 175a: Antrag Schrangl und Genossen.

74   See VGA Parteiarchiv Mappe 65, 9a.

75   Ibid.; STB 18-6-1933, 2. This may also have been a sideswipe at the local party leadership, most of which was, as the previous chapter showed, in some form materially dependent on the Social Democratic movement.

76   STB 18-6-1933, 2.

77   Quoted in: AVA BKA Inneres 22/genere Karton 4878: 222.549-33; 22/Oberösterreich Karton 5104: 225.559-33.

78   Thus Alois Zehetner's recollection of his intervention at a meeting of Social Democratic activists addressed by Otto Bauer in October 1933. Quoted in Letter to the author by Alois Zehetner, 19-11-1987; see also Kammerstätter, (n.d.), 1121.

79   See AVA BKA Inneres 22/genere Karton 4879: 241.658-33; 22/Oberösterreich Karton 5104: 245.707-33; 249.793-33; VGA Parteiarchiv Mappe 65, 10.

80   See DÖW File 12202.

81   Quoted in Kammerstätter (n.d.), 1118, 1121.

82   See e.g. Letter to the author by Alois Zehetner, 19-11-1987; Kammerstätter, (n.d.), 1116-1135; Interview with Josef Mayrhofer, 2-7-1986; DÖW File 12202.

83   So August Moser, as quoted in Kammerstätter, (n.d.), 1116.

84   Ibid., 1127. See also STB 6-2-1934, 5, and Chapter Four of this work.

85   See e.g. Kammerstätter, (n.d.), 1119-1121.

86   AVA BKA Inneres 22/Oberösterreich Karton 5104: 119.651-34; 121.580-34.

87   See Francis L. Carsten, *Fascist Movements in Austria*, Sage, London (1977), 234.

88   Kammerstätter, (n.d.), 1131. Fey is quoted in Rabinbach (1983), 189.

89   Kammerstätter, (n.d.), 1132.

90   Ibid., 1132-1134.

91   See especially Stockinger (1988), 155-178. See also Brigitte Perfahl, 'Linz und Steyr - Zentren des Kampfes', in Stadler (1984).

92   See Kammerstätter, (n.d.), 1136-1143; DÖW Files 12200a and 12172. Many of those arrested during and after the Civil War also talked of the prominent role played by Moser. See especially OÖLA Kreisgericht Steyr Politische Strafakten 1934-1941 Karton 1.

93   The participants in battle in Steyr were largely drawn from ranks of the Social Democratic youth, paramilitaries and metalworkers. Available police and court records show that of 174 people arrested for participation in the Civil War,

over 40% were under thirty years of age, 70% were *Schutzbündler*, and around 60% were metalworkers. See IFZ Microfilm A/259; DÖW Files 12160-12172, 12174, 12196, 12200a, 12201, 14520 and 17112; OÖLA Bezirkshauptmannschaft Steyr Faszikel 112 and 117; OÖLA Kreisgericht Steyr Politische Strafakten Karton 1; Kammerstätter (n.d.), 1344-1347, 1353-1354.

94   While a number of leading Social Democrats reemerged after the Civil War as Communists (e.g. Moser, Alois Zehetner and Ferdinand Mayrhofer), others switched to the Nazi Party (e.g. Schrangl and Mayor Sichrader) or the clericalist Fatherland Front (e.g. *Steyrer Tagblatt* Editor Josef Kirchberger).

95   Rabinbach (1983), 101-102.

96   Quoted in Berchthold (1967), 253. C.f. Rabinbach (1983), 117.

97   Quoted in Zehetner's letter to the author, 19-11-1987.

98   As discussed at fuller length in Chapter Three. Quoted in Bauer (1988e), 126.

99   Buttinger (1972), 81.

100   See for example Hanisch (1983), 914, 927; Hinteregger, Schmidlechner, Staudinger (1984), 208; Hinteregger (1978), 281, 286-288; Treml, Hawle (1988), 21, 27; Oberkofler (1986), 218.

101   See e.g. the accounts of events in: Itzling and Salzburg in Bauer, Weitgruber (1985), 91-92; in Hallein in Bauer (1988a), 209-210; in Mauthausen in SPÖ Mauthausen (1989), 130; in rural areas in Upper Austria in Hummer (1984); in the St. Pölten area in Nasko (1986), 205-214, 320-321; in Wiener Neustadt in Flanner (1983), 89-90; in Carinthia in Schindler (1973); in Burgenland in Schlag (1983), 784; and in Tirol in Oberkofler (1986), 240-241

102   Quoted in Hinteregger, Schmidlechner, Staudinger (1984), 213-214.

103   So Helmut Fiereder, 'Der Republikanische Schutzbund in Linz und die Kampfhandlungen im Februar 1934', in *Historisches Jahrbuch der Stadt Linz* 1978, 209.

104   As expressed in a leaflet found in Bischofshofen in Salzburg in autumn 1933. Quoted in Hanisch (1983), 914.

105   E.g. Fiereder (1979), 209.

106   Slapnicka (1975), 129-130.

107   So Paula Wallisch, wife of Kolomann Wallisch, in regard to the arms searches the Social Democrats were forced to endure in the 1930s. Quoted in Hinteregger, Schmidlechner, Staudinger (1984), 208.

108   Ibid., 1136.

Conclusions

The purpose of this conclusion is not to present a summary of the content and argument of this work, but rather to return, in the broad light of the findings of the previous chapters, to some of the issues raised in the Introduction of the book. The central premiss put forward in the Introduction was the need to look beyond Red Vienna, beyond traditionalist, 'top-down' methodologies, and beyond party-political partisanship in order to provide a fuller and more balanced assessment of interwar Social Democracy in Austria. One book, especially one whose empirical core is a case study of a single town, can, of course, make only a limited contribution to meeting this need. The following discussion nevertheless highlights some of the areas in which that contribution has been made: in helping to understand the character and function of the Social Democratic movement at the local level; in highlighting the intra-movement dynamics which contributed to the destruction of the movement in 1934; and, more broadly, in raising new questions about, and suggesting new avenues for research on both Social Democratic Red Vienna and the movement in the provinces.

Failure and Success at the Local Level

In the course of this work I have been highly, at times perhaps over-critical of the failings of what one might call the 'high' politics of Social Democracy at the local level - the character of the local movement's leadership, its élitist stewardship of the SDAP, its self-absorption, the limited perspective and inflexibility of its policies and strategies, and so on. These criticisms may at times have appeared rather harsh towards a group of local politicians which was faced by extraordinarily difficult circumstances on the 'front-lines' of provincial politics. The harshness of my criticism may in part be a somewhat exaggerated by-product of the methodological route I have taken. Working deliberately from the 'bottom upwards', I intended to make possible a fuller understanding of the political behaviour of the individuals who constituted the movement, focusing above all on the factors which influenced, inspired and mobilised their engagement in political life as Social Democrats. This approach has perhaps tempted me to internalise and represent their interests and, in particular, the frustrations they felt when the local-level movement began to lose the positions of strength it had won after 1918, and when its leaders proved incapable of adapting effectively to the new situation in which they found themselves. To be fair to the local-level leaders, though, it ought to be remembered that for however short a time - perhaps just two or three years in the small and far-flung *Hochburgen* of, say, Tirol, or up to a decade or more in some of their larger and stronger counterparts in Styria, Lower Austria and Upper Austria - they did preside over a set of organisational structures which met important needs of the rank and file supporters of the movement. Party, trade unions and auxiliary organisations in their various ways helped to keep a hostile and intimidating 'outside world' at bay and offered possibilities for personal and collective development which would have been impossible before 1918. This was a success of the local-level movement and its leadership which should not be underestimated: it created the space - both in territorial and metaphorical terms - in which a despised and disadvantaged manual worker community for the first time had a genuine freedom for self-assertion and self-realisation.

From *Hochburg* to Civil War: the Local Level and the Destruction of Austrian Social Democracy

The fact that this freedom could not be sustained was in part a reflection of the tendency to introspection in the local-level movement, and in particular its leadership. The inadvertent result of this tendency was the scattering of forces at the local level. It produced a pattern of horizontal fragmentation which left an outnumbered movement, isolated in its various *Hochburgen*, vulnerable to a coalition of far more powerful opponents. The local level was the 'soft underbelly' of Austrian Social Democracy, exposed invitingly by its own insularity to the gamut of anti-Social Democratic forces which surrounded it. The existence of this 'soft underbelly' is, of course, one part of the answer to the central question raised in the Introduction of this book: How and why did a movement which had the largest per capita membership in the world, and which had an unrivalled position in left-wing politics in Austria, come to disintegrate and be destroyed so quickly after so successfully leading the transition to democratic government in Austria after the First World War? The existence of the soft, provincial underbelly certainly throws light on *how* the process of disintegration and destruction could happen. It says less, though, about *why* it happened. The answer to this part of the equation requires a look beyond the local level at some of the wider characteristics of the Social Democratic movement.

The first is the vertical fragmentation of the movement. Austrian Social Democracy was extraordinarily ill-coordinated, riven by a pattern of self-absorption at all of its vertical levels. The provincial level was consumed in its commitment to parliamentary cooperation and accommodation with the CSP, and the national-cum-Viennese level in the magnificence of its project for Red Vienna. The inter-relationships between these different organisational levels of the movement were minimal and, where they did exist, were restricted to a ritualism and formalism which precluded any genuine exchange of views. This pattern of vertical fragmentation was, of course, part responsible for the introspection of *Hochburg* politics and the pattern of horizontal fragmentation at the local level: Unable to secure support or even consideration from the higher levels of the movement, the local level had little choice but to turn in on itself and make the best, however temporarily, of the bad lot it had been dealt. The vulnerable soft, provincial underbelly of Austrian Social Democracy was, in effect, a by-product of the flawed internal dynamics of the movement.

These flawed internal dynamics - and especially those within the SDAP - point to a second characteristic of Austrian Social Democracy which helps explain *why* the movement came to be destroyed. The local, provincial and national levels of the SDAP all lacked genuine intra-party debate and were all subject to a Michelsian syndrome of élite domination and ossification. As a result there was little scope for 'bottom-up' input into the formulation of party strategy and priorities. There was negligible opportunity for the ordinary membership to have significant input into shaping the priorities of the leadership at the local level, or for the local level to influence the cooperative and accommodationist strategies of the provincial leaderships, or for either the local or provincial levels to modify the Vienna-centred vision of the national leadership. This was a party within which there was no tradition of discussion or consultation. In this situation, there was little possibility of combining the efforts and resources of the whole movement to develop a coordinated and effective response to the rapidly changing context of Austrian politics during the First Republic, and in particular in the early 1930s.

This limited potential for a concerted mobilisation of party forces was, perhaps somewhat paradoxically, confirmed as soon as a genuine strategy debate finally did emerge after 1932. This debate arguably occurred too late for the movement to recover from the advanced state of disintegration into which it had by then fallen. More importantly its protagonists, lacking the experience of a debating tradition, unsurprisingly displayed an inability to reconcile their divergent positions and choose - and unite behind - a single, effective course of action. The debate revolved around whether to seek accommodation with the nascent 'Austro-Fascist' regime, or whether to embark on active resistance against it. Significantly, the conduct of the debate confirmed the pattern of vertical fragmentation which had weakened the movement. Its protagonists were drawn not so much from ideologically driven factions represented throughout the movement, as some have argued,[1] but largely from the different vertical organisational levels of the movement. The debate reflected the divergences of mentality and experience which had arisen in the different contexts of Social Democratic politics at the local, provincial and national/Viennese levels. The accommodationists had their centre of gravity among the provincial parliamentary élites who were steeped in a cooperative and conciliatory approach to politics. The insurrectionists, though nominally led by the group of leftist intellectuals around Ernst Fischer, were based in those rank and file groups at the local level - both in the provinces and in Vienna - which were disaffected by the passive acquiescence of the movement in its own disintegration. Neither had time or understanding for the views of the other. This left the National Executive around Otto Bauer, with one eye on preserving something of Red Vienna, the hopeless task of trying to hold the accommodationist and insurrectionist wings together - a task which plunged it into a debilitating, dithering paralysis, a politics of 'neither-nor',[2] neither committed to credible accommodationism, nor capable of a decision for active resistance. This paralysis at the highest level did little but stoke up yet further the centrifugal tensions within the movement until they reached bursting point in February 1934, when the forces for insurrection, inspired by Richard Bernaschek, led the movement into destruction in the Austrian Civil War.

Looking Beyond Red Vienna - and Back Again

As noted above, the central premiss underlying this work was the need to look beyond Red Vienna in order to provide a fuller and more balanced assessment of inter-war Social Democracy in Austria. At this point it seems worth turning this premiss on its head and asking what new insights into Red Vienna might be gained by employing the 'bottom-up' methodology and the analytical concepts developed in this work. A full answer to this question cannot, of course, be given in a work which has deliberately adopted a non-Viennese focus, so the following comments necessarily have to remain speculative. Nevertheless, Vienna does raise some striking parallels to the situation in the provinces. In the national-level context Vienna was - like Steyr, or Bruck an der Mur, or Hallein were locally - a *Hochburg*, a place of Social Democratic refuge and safety, 'fortified' against the intrusions of an antagonistic 'outside' world. Vienna was a nationwide focal point for the suspicion, hostility and hatred of anti-Social Democrats in inter-war Austria, with a negative resonance just as strong in in anti-Social Democratic circles in distant Vorarlberg as it was in neighbouring Lower Austria. For Social Democrats within Vienna, though, the city was equally a safe haven which insulated them from these external hostilities. This was, after 1918, *their* territory. The SDAP city government enacted welfare and housing policies directed at their interests. Social Democratic FTUs, empowered by post-war employment legislation, extended the representation of those interests into the workplace. In addition, both city government and FTUs may well have developed patronage strategies to give further rewards to the membership of the movement: through the allocation of city housing, municipal jobs and other benefits, and through the distribution of private sector employment through closed shops. Finally, while the network of Social Democratic auxiliary organisations may not have contributed as much as their leaders would have liked to the development of 'new human beings', they certainly provided opportunities for individual and collective fulfilment in social and leisure activities which would otherwise not have been available.

It would be both fascinating and highly instructive to find out more about what this vast *Hochburg* meant both for the leaders who attempted to direct it, and for the ordinary members who enjoyed its safe haven and the benefits - material or otherwise - it provided. A whole range of questions, drawn from the experience of provincial *Hochburgen*, raise themselves: To what extent did the organisational logistics and effort involved in running Red Vienna contribute to a Michelsian bureaucratisation process at the highest levels of the SDAP? To what extent was a bureaucratic preoccupation with the problems of running Red Vienna responsible for the self-absorption and inflexibility of the national SDAP leadership? How much did Social Democratic policies and organisations build on and consolidate the sense of community and identity based in the manual worker milieux scattered around Vienna's *Gürtel* (outer ring road)? What did the erosion of the *Hochburg* mean for rank and file Social Democrats: the events of July 1927, the restriction of trade union rights from 1930, the gradual curtailment of the Vienna city budget and the onset of wider central government repression from 1932, the emergence of a right wing challenge on the streets of Vienna, and so on? To what extent was the inability of the movement to halt the process of erosion reflected in a determination among elements of the rank and file to make at least a symbolic stand of resistance to the Dollfuß regime in honour of their *Lebenswerk* in the movement? Can the growing dissatisfaction and intra-movement opposition evident[3] in the Social Democratic strongholds of the Viennese suburbs in 1933-1934 be explained, as in the 'red islands' of the provinces, as the expression of a community under threat? To what extent was the decision for civil war 'like being freed' from a Social Democratic experience which had gone sour, from a movement which, despite the grandeur of the Viennese experiment in the 1920s, had ultimately failed its supporters?

Towards a 'New History' of Austrian Social Democracy

These are questions which I hope will come to be addressed in research on Social Democracy in Vienna in the coming years. To answer them fully would require a concerted pursuit of the 'new history' outlined in the Introduction, a history which places a stronger research emphasis on the individuals who constituted and shaped the character of the movement in Vienna, and which consciously detaches itself from the iconography which has traditionally pervaded the study of Red Vienna. I equally hope that similar questions will continue to be asked of the local-level movement to supplement the rather meagre ration of 'bottom-up' studies currently available.[4] This work, with its primary focus on Steyr, can only offer a limited addition to this genre. Even for Austrian standards, Social Democracy in Steyr had an extreme experience during the First Republic. No other 'red island' can match the extraordinary combination of factors which shaped the politics of this town: the starkness of the social divide between the town and the surrounding countryside; the local economic structure dominated by one, highly unstable enterprise, the Steyr-Werke; the unparalleled range of non-statutory rights enjoyed by the MAV in the Steyr-Werke; the scope of Social Democratic patronage; the scale and variety of the network of cultural organisations; the depth of the bureaucratisation process in the SDAP; and the vehement rejection of the Social Democratic tradition in the opposition of MAV, *Schutzbund* and SAJ in 1933-1934. Nevertheless, in all these respects Steyr displayed clear parallels to the situation in the other *Hochburgen* of the provinces. The findings from the Steyr case study can therefore provide crucial, general insights into the broader possibilities and problems of *Hochburg* politics. They cannot, though, provide a full and rounded picture. That will have to await further, 'bottom-up' research in the provinces.

A final issue to raise is that of partisanship. No work can ever be free of partisanship. One person's attempt at detached, critical analysis is another's partisan bias. My own partisan bias is for the individuals who made up the Social Democratic movement, and who the movement was intended to serve. The adoption of their perspective on political life, as exemplified in the mythical *Frau* Meier - a new icon for the grass roots? - remains for me, however, a more acceptable form of partisanship than that which shaped a historiographical tradition of subservience to the interests of party politics in Austria.

Notes

[1]   The fullest discussion of this period of intense debate is given in Rabinbach (1983). Rabinbach tends, though, to present the debate in rather simplistic terms

as one between a group of 'rightists' in the Lower Austrian SDAP, and a coherent 'left-opposition' centred initially on Ernst Fischer and then boosted by a 'united' Upper Austrian SDAP under the influence of Richard Bernaschek and, through him, committed to active resistance. As Chapter Eight argued, though, the drive for 'rightist' accommodation was widespread among provincial SDAP parliamentarians, and the Fischer opposition lacked any noticeable organisational coherence outside the immediate realm of Fischer influence in Vienna and Graz. And Fischer's group, without a recognisable nationwide organisation could and did not *lead*, but rather *articulated* the burning resentments of the various activists around the country who, like Bernaschek and the group around August Moser in Steyr, were committed to making at least a symbolic stand in defence of, in many cases, their life's work. An insight into the geographical breadth of this activist resentment is given in the roll call of speeches critical of the national leadership in the Extraordinary Party Conference of April 1933, in VGA Parteiarchiv, Mappe 65.

2   C.f. Leser (1968), 332.

3   E.g. Rabinbach (1983), 130-132.

4   Most notably those of Ingrid Bauer (1988a-f), Elisabeth Dietrich (1991), Kurt Greußing (1989), Hubert Hummer (1984, 1989) and Jill Lewis (1991).

Bibliography

Primary Sources

Unpublished Documents

a) Allgemeines Verwaltungsarchiv (Vienna):

Bundeskanzleramt Inneres 13/6 Kartons 2380-2383.
Bundeskanzleramt Inneres 22/genere Kartons 4865, 4867-4869, 4871-4881.
Bundeskanzleramt Inneres 22/Oberösterreich Kartons 5100-5106.
Sozialdemokratische Parteistellen Kartons 24, 27, 36, 42, 54, 175a.

b) Dokumentation der Kammer für Arbeiter und Angestellte in Wien (Vienna):

Lohnbewegungen/Streiks/1925.
SP: Kinderfreunde.
Zusammenstoß 15/10/1929 Steyr.
Heimwehr Oberösterreich.
Kommunalpolitik 1928-1932/33.

c) Dokumentationsarchiv des Österreichischen Widerstandes (Vienna):

Files 2733, 5684, 5980, 10705, 12090, 12160-12172, 12174, 12196-12199, 12200a, 12200b, 12201-12202, 13151, 13339, 14520, 16462, 17039, 17112.

d) Institut für Zeitgeschichte (Vienna):

Microfilms A/258, A/259, A/334, A/335, A/336.

e) Kammerstätter, Peter (Ed.) (n.d.), *Der Aufstand des Republikanischen Schutzbundes am 12. Februar in Oberösterreich. Eine Sammlung von Materialien, Dokumenten und Aussagen von Beteiligten.* Band II, unpublished manuscript, Linz.

f) Magistrat der Stadt Steyr (Steyr):

Sitzungsniederschriften des Gemeinderates der Stadt Steyr 1932-1934.
Registratur Faszikel B/a 1926-1934; E/a 1925, 1930-1934; E/c 1927-1934; G/a 1919; G/a Städtische Unternehmungen; G/g 1928; H/g 1916, 1931-1932; J/d 25-45 Vereine; J/d 50-299 Vereine; J/o 1920-; J/0 Arbeitsamt; J/o Kollektivverträge; M/c 1927; M/g 1927-1934.

g) Oberösterreichisches Landesarchiv (Linz):

Bezirkshauptmannschaft Steyr Faszikel 108b, 111-112, 114-115, 116a, 117.
Bezirkshauptmannschaft Steyr Präs. Faszikel 5-11.
Kreisgericht Steyr Politische Strafakten 1934-1941 Karton 1.
Landtagsakten Nachtrag Schuber 34-36.

h) Verein für Geschichte der Arbeiterbewegung (Vienna):

Sacharchiv Lade 5 Mappe 56; Lade 6 Mappe 54; Lade 16 Mappe 34.
Parteiarchiv Mappen 65, 67/2.

Newspapers and Periodicals.

Arbeiterzeitung (Vienna, 1925).
Die Flamme, (Steyr, 1930-1934).
Illustrierter Steyrer Geschäfts- und Unterhaltungskalender für Stadt- und Landleute (Steyr 1928-1935).
Der Kuckuck (Vienna, 1930-1932).
Linzer Tagespost (Linz, 1927-1934).
Linzer Volksblatt (Linz, 1927-1934).
Linzer Volksstimme (Linz, 1925, 1927-1934; 1932-1934 as *Volksstimme*).
Oberösterreichische Arbeiterzeitung (Linz, 1925-1934).
Oberösterreichische Tageszeitung (Linz, 1929).
Der österreichische Metallarbeiter (Vienna, 1925-1934).
Der österreichische Volkswirt (Vienna, 1927-1934).
Der österreichische Volkswirt. Bilanzen (Vienna, 1927-1934).
Der Starhemberg-Jäger (Linz, 1930-1931).
Steyrer Tagblatt (Steyr, 1920-1934).
Steyrer Zeitung (Steyr, 1925-1934).

Reports and Conference Minutes of Social Democratic Organisations

Bericht des Vorstandes des österreichischen Metallarbeiterverbandes über seine Tätigkeit, 1926-1932 editions (1927-1933), Verlag des österreichischen Metallarbeiterverbandes, Vienna.
Jahrbuch der österreichischen Arbeiterbewegung, 1926-1932 editions (1927-1933), Verlag der Wiener Volksbuchhandlung, Vienna.
Jahrbuch des Bundes der Freien Gewerkschaften Österreichs, 1928-1932 editions (1929-1933), Arbeit und Wirtschaft, Vienna.
Protokoll der Verhandlungen des Parteitages der Sozialdemokratischen Arbeiterpartei Deutschösterreichs, 1919-1932 editions (1920-1932), Verlag der Wiener Volksbuchhandlung, Vienna.
Rote Saat. Bericht des Sozialdemokratischen Erziehungs- und Schulvereins 'Freie-Schule-Kinderfreunde', 1926-1932 editions (1927-1933), Verlag des Vereins, Vienna.
Sozialdemokratische Partei Oberösterreichs. Tätigkeitsbericht, 1923-1932 editions (1924-1933), Gutenberg, Linz, 1924.
Verhandlungen des Verbandstages der Metallarbeiter Österreichs, 1924-1933 editions (1924-1933), Verlag des österreichischen Metallarbeiterverbandes, Vienna.

Other Contemporary Reports and Official Publications

Bericht über die Wirtschaftlichen Verhältnisse in Oberösterreich im Jahre 1926 (1927), Verlag der Kammer für Handel, Gewerbe und Industrie in Linz, Linz.

Bundesamt für Statistik (1923), *Beiträge zur Statistik der Republik Österreich. 12. Heft. Vorläufige Ergebnisse der Volkszählung vom 7. März 1923,* Verlag der österreichischen Staatsdruckerei, Vienna.

Bundesamt für Statistik (1927), *Statistische Nachrichten. Sonderheft. 'Wahlstatistik'. Nationalratswahlen vom 24. April 1927. Einzeldarstellung nach Gemeinden und Geschlecht,* Überreuter, Vienna.

Bundesamt für Statistik (1932), *Gewerbliche Betriebszählung in der Republik Österreich vom 14. Juni 1930. Ergebnisse für Oberösterreich,* Verlag der österreichischen Staatsdruckerei, Vienna.

Bundesamt für Statistik (1935a), *Die Ergebnisse der österreichischen Volkszählung vom 22. März 1934. Bundesstaat Textheft,* Verlag der Österreichischen Staatsdruckerei, Vienna (1935).

Bundesamt für Statistik (1935b), *Statistik der Republik Österreich. Heft 5. Die Ergebnisse der österreichischen Volkszählung vom 22. März 1934. Oberösterreich,* Verlag der österreichischen Staatsdruckerei, Vienna.

Statistische Zentralkommission (1920), *Beiträge zur Statistik der Republik Österreich. 5. Heft. Vorläufige Ergebnisse der Außerordentlichen Volkszählung vom 31. Jänner 1920 nebst Gemeindeverzeichnis,* Verlag der österreichischen Staatsdruckerei, Vienna.

Verzeichnis jener Betriebe, welche über fünf Kammerumlagepflichtige beschäftigen, 1927-1933 editions (1927-1933), Kammer für Arbeiter und Angestellte in Linz a. Donau, Linz.

Wirtschaftsstatistisches Jahrbuch, 1927-1934 editions (1928-1935), Verlag der Kammer für Arbeiter und Angestellte in Wien, Vienna.

Other Primary Sources

Interview with Josef Mayrhofer, 4/7/1986.
Letter to the author from Alois Zehetner, 19/11/1987.

Secondary Sources

Ardelt, Rudolf G. (1990), 'Arbeiterschaft und Nationalsozialismus - ein Thema zwischen Legende und Realität', in Ardelt, Hautmann (1990).

Ardelt, Rudolf G., Hautmann, Hans (Eds.) (1990), *Arbeiterschaft und Nationalsozialismus in Österreich. In Memoriam Karl R. Stadler,* Europaverlag, Vienna.

Ausch, Karl (1968), *Als die Banken Fielen. Zur Soziologie der Politischen Korruption,* Europaverlag,Vienna.

Außermair, Josef (1979), *Kirche und Sozialdemokratie. Der Bund der religiösen Sozialisten, 1926-1934,* Europaverlag, Vienna.

Bakke, E. Wight (1969), *Citizens without work. A study of the effects of unemployment upon the workers' social relations and practices,* Archon Books, New York.

Baltzarek, Franz (1990), 'Das Schwundgeldexperiment von Wörgl 1932/33', in Fröschl, Mesner, Zoitl (1990).

Barnay, Markus (1989), '"Echte Vorarlberger" und "fremde Bettler". Bildung von Landesbewußtsein und Ausgrenzung von Zuwanderern in Vorarlberg im 19. und 20. Jahrhundert', in Greußing (1989).

Baron, Gerhard (1971), *Der Beginn. Die Anfänge der Arbeiterbildungsvereine in Oberösterreich,* Oberösterreichischer Landesverlag, Linz.

Bauer, Ingrid (1988a), 'Tschikweiber haum's uns g'nennt ...' Frauenleben und Frauenarbeit an der 'Peripherie': Die Halleiner Zigarrenfabriksarbeiterinnen 1869 bis 1940, Europaverlag, Vienna.

Bauer, Ingrid (1988b), Von der alten Solidarität zur neuen sozialen Frage. Ein Salzburger Bilderlesebuch, Europaverlag, Vienna.

Bauer, Ingrid (1988c), 'Zu diesem Buch', in Bauer (1988b).

Bauer, Ingrid (1988d), '"Uns das Bißchen nackte Leben erhalten ..." Die Jahre 1918 bis 1920', in Bauer (1988b).

Bauer, Ingrid (1988e), 'Zwischen konkreter Utopie und den Zwängen der Realität. Die 1920er Jahre', in Bauer (1988b).

Bauer, Ingrid (1988f), 'Im Würgegriff der Krise. Die 1930er Jahre', in Bauer (1988b).

Bauer, Ingrid, Weitgruber, Wilhelm (1985), Vom Dorf zur Vorstadt - Ein Spaziergang durch Itzling. Arbeiteralltag und Arbeiterkultur in Itzling: 1860-1945, SPÖ-Sektion Itzling, Salzburg.

Benedikt, Heinrich (Ed.) (1954), Geschichte der Republik Österreich, Oldenbourg, Munich.

Berchthold, Klaus (Ed.) (1967), Österreichische Parteiprogramme 1868-1966, Oldenbourg, Munich.

Bernasek, Richard (1934), 'Die Tragödie der österreichischen Sozialdemokratie', in Österreich, Brandherd Europas (1934).

Bindel, Jakob (Ed.) (1983), 75 Jahre Kinderfreunde 1908-1983. Skizzen-Erinnerungen-Berichte-Ausblicke, Jungbrunnen, Vienna.

Boll, Friedhelm (Ed.) (1986), Arbeiterkulturen zwischen Alltag und Politik. Beiträge zum europäischen Vergleich in der Zwischenkriegszeit, Europaverlag, Vienna.

Botz, Gerhard (1976), Gewalt in der Politik. Attentate, Zusammenstöße, Unruhen in Österreich 1918-1934, Oldenbourg, Munich.

Botz, Gerhard (1978), 'Streik in Österreich 1918 bis 1975. Probleme und Ergebnisse einer Quantitativen Analyse', in Botz, Hautmann, Konrad, Weidenholzer (1978).

Botz, Gerhard (1989), 'Der Mythos vom "Februaraufstand" und von Richard Bernaschek', in Internationale Tagung der Historiker der Arbeiterbewegung (1989).

Botz, Gerhard (1990a), '"Eine neue Welt, warum nicht eine neue Geschichte?" Österreichische Zeitgeschichte am Ende ihres Jahrhunderts, Teil I', Österreichische Zeitschrift für Geschichtswissenschaften, 1

Botz, Gerhard (1990b), 'Teil II: Die "Goldenen Jahre der Zeitgeschichte" und ihre Schattenseiten', Österreichische Zeitschrift für Geschichtswissenschaften, 1

Botz, Gerhard, Hautmann, Hans, Konrad, Helmut, Weidenholzer, Josef (Eds.) (1978), Bewegung und Klasse. Studien zur österreichischen Arbeitergeschichte, Europaverlag, Vienna.

Brandl, Manfred (1980), Neue Geschichte der Stadt Steyr. Vom Biedermeier bis heute, Ennsthaler, Steyr.

Bukey, Evan Burr (1986), Hitler's hometown. Linz, Austria 1908-1945, Indiana University Press, Bloomington.

Burgstaller, Hans, Lackner, Helmut (1984), Fohnsdorf. Erlebte Geschichte, Verlag Erich Mlakar, Judenburg.

Buttinger, Josef (1972), Das Ende der Massenpartei. Am Beispiel Österreichs, Verlag Neue Kritik, Frankfurt.

Carsten, Francis L. (1982), *Fascist movements in Austria*, Sage, London.
Clapham, Christopher (Ed.) (1982), *Private patronage and public power*, Pinter, London.
Cottrell, P.L., Teichova, A. (Eds.) (1983), *International business and Central Europe 1918-1939*, Leicester University Press, Leicester.
Crew, David F. (1979), *Town in the Ruhr. A social history of Bochum*, 1860-1914, Columbia University Press, New York.
Denkmaier, Christian, Janko, Siegbert (1988), 'Die Sozialdemokratie ist eine Kulturbewegung', in SPÖ-Bezirksorganisation Linz-Stadt (1988).
Dietrich, Elisabeth (1991), 'Feindbilder und Ausgrenzung als Fermente der politischen Radikalisierung in Tirol zwischen 1918 und 1923', in Konrad, Schmidlechner (1991).
Dreier, Werner (1984), 'Konjuntur der Hoffnung - Vorarlberger Arbeiterbewegung 1918-1934', in Greußing (1984).
Duczynska, Ilona (1975), *Der Demokratische Bolschewik. Zur Theorie und Praxis der Gewalt*, List, Munich.
Edmondson, C. Earl (1978), *The Heimwehr and Austrian politics, 1918-1936*, University of Georgia Press, Athens.
'Ein Oberösterreicher' (Ed.) (1928), *Oberösterreich und die Novemberrevolution*, Verlag der Linzer Volksbuchhandlung, Linz.
Eisenstadt, S.N., Lemarchand, René (Eds.) (1981), *Political clientelism, patronage and development*, Sage, Beverly Hills.
Ellmeier, Andrea, Singer-Meczes, Eva (1988-1989), 'Modellierung der sozialistischen Konsumentin. Konsumgenossenschaftliche (Frauen)-Politik in den zwanziger Jahren', *Zeitgeschichte*, **16**.
Ettl, Helmut (1988), 'Vorwärts und nicht vergessen. Die sozialistische Jugend in Linz', in SPÖ-Bezirksorganisation Linz-Stadt (1988).
Evans, Richard (1978), 'Introduction: Wilhelm II's Germany and the historians', in: Richard J. Evans (Ed.), *Society and politics in Wilhelmine Germany*, Croom Helm, London.
Evans, Richard J., Geary, Dick (Eds.) (1987), *The German unemployed. Experience and consequences of mass unemployment from the Weimar Republic to the Third Reich*, Croom Helm, London.
Feuerbestattungsverein 'Die Flamme' in Steyr (1927), *Festschrift zur Feier der Eröffnung der ersten Oberösterreichischen Feuerhalle in Steyr im Juni 1927*, Steyr.
Fiereder, Helmut (1979), 'Der Republikanische Schutzbund in Linz und die Kampfhandlungen im Februar 1934', in *Historisches Jahrbuch der Stadt Linz 1978*.
Filla, Wilhelm (1981), *Zwischen Integration und Klassenkampf. Sozialgeschichte der Betrieblichen Mitbestimmung in Österreich*, Europaverlag, Vienna.
Fischer, Conan J. (1986), 'Unemployment and left-wing radicalism in Weimar Germany, 1930-1933', in Stachura (1986).
Fischer, Ernst (1932), 'Österreich vor dem Bürgerkrieg', *Die Weltbühne*, 5-1-1932.
Fischer Ernst (1974), *An opposing man*, Allen Lane, London.
Fischer, P.G. (1983), 'The Österreichisch-Alpine Montangesellschaft, 1918-1938', in Cottrell, Teichova (1983).
Flanner, Karl (n.d.), *Geschichte der Wiener Neustädter Gewerkschaftsbewegung 1889-1945*, Volume 1, Gutenberg, Wiener Neustadt.

Flanner, Karl (1983), *Wiener Neustadt im Ständestaat. Arbeiteropposition 1933-1938*, Europaverlag, Vienna.

Fröschl, Erich, Mesner, Maria, Zoitl, Helge (Eds.) (1990), *Die Bewegung. Hundert Jahre Sozialdemokratie in Österreich*, Passagen, Vienna.

Gellner, Ernest, Waterbury, John (Eds.) (1977), *Patrons and clients in Mediterranean societies*, Duckworth, London.

Gerlich, Peter (1992) 'A farewell to corporatism', in Luther, Müller (1992).

Gerlich, Peter, Grande, E., Müller, W.C. (Eds.) (1985), *Sozialpartnerschaft in der Krise. Leistungen und Grenzen des Neokorporatismus in Österreich*, Böhlau, Vienna.

Glaser, Ernst (1990), 'Über die Organisationsstrukturen im sozialdemokratischen Lager', in Fröschl, Mesner, Zoitl (1990).

Grabner, Günther, Hangler, Reinhold, Hawle, Christian, Kammerstätter, Peter (1984), *"An die Wand mit ihnen". Zu den Ereignissen des Februar 1934 im Bezirk Vöcklabruck. Eine Dokumentation*, Selbstverlag, Vöcklabruck.

Greußing, Kurt (Ed.) (1984), *Im Prinzip: Hoffnung. Arbeiterbewegung in Vorarlberg 1870-1946*, Fink, Bregenz.

Greußing, Kurt (Ed.) (1989), *Die Roten am Lande. Arbeitsleben und Arbeiterbewegung im westlichen Österreich*, Museum Industrielle Arbeitswelt, Steyr.

Gruber, Helmut (1983), 'History of the Austrian working class: Unity of scholarship and practice', *International Labor and Working Class History*, No.24.

Gruber, Helmut (1985), 'Socialist Party culture and the realities of working class life in Red Vienna', in Rabinbach (1985).

Gruber, Helmut (1986), 'Working class women in Red Vienna: Socialist concepts of the "new woman" v. the reality of the triple burden', in Boll (1986).

Gruber, Helmut (1991), *Red Vienna. Experiment in working class culture 1919-1934*, Oxford University Press, New York and Oxford.

Gulick, Charles A. (1948), *Austria from Habsburg to Hitler*, 2 volumes, University of California Press, Berkeley and Los Angeles.

Gutkas, Karl (1983), 'Niederösterreich', in Weinzierl, Skalnik (1983).

Guttsman, W.L. (1981), *The German Social Democratic Party 1875-1933: from ghetto to government*, George Allen & Unwin, London.

Haas, Hans (1988), 'Es geht vorwärts. Die Salzburger Arbeiterbewegung von den Anfängen bis zum Ersten Weltkrieg', in Bauer (1988b).

Habe, Hans (1976), *Leben für den Journalismus. Band 1: Reportagen und Gespräche*, Knaur, Munich.

Halpern, S. (1987), 'The disorderly universe of consociational democracy', *West European Politics*, 10.

Hanisch, Ernst (1978), 'Die sozialdemokratische Fraktion im Salzburger Landtag, 1918-1934', in Botz, Hautmann, Konrad, Weidenholzer (1978).

Hanisch, Ernst (1983), 'Salzburg', in Weinzierl, Skalnik (1983).

Hanisch, Ernst (1990), 'Bäuerliches Milieu und Arbeitermilieu in den Alpengauen: ein historischer Vergleich', in Ardelt, Hautmann (1990).

Hautmann, Hans, and Kropf, Rudolf (1974), *Die Österreichische Arbeiterbewegung vom Vormärz bis 1945: Sozialökonomische Ursprünge ihrer Ideologie und Politik*, Europaverlag, Vienna.

Helmer, Oskar (1929), 'Wien und die Länder. Organisatorische Parteiprobleme', *Der Kampf*, 22.

Herlitzka, Ernst K. (1978), 'Josef Luitpold Stern (1886-1966). Versuch einer Würdigung', in Botz, Hautmann, Konrad, Weidenholzer (1978).

Hinteregger, Robert (1978), 'Die Steierische Arbeiterschaft zwischen Monarchie und Faschismus', in Botz, Hautmann, Konrad, Weidenholzer (1978).

Hinteregger, R., Müller, K., Staudinger, E. (Eds.) (1984), *Auf dem Weg in die Freiheit (Anstöße zu einer steirischen Zeitgeschichte)*, Leykam, Graz.

Hinteregger, R., Schmidlechner, K., Staudinger, E. (1984), 'Koloman Wallisch', in Hinteregger, Müller, Staudinger (1984).

Hummer, Hubert (1984), 'Der Widerstand auf dem Land', in Stadler (1984).

Hummer, Hubert (1989), '"Waun heit mei Vota aufstand, der sogat, ihr hoabts den Hümmi auf der Welt. Des haum mir erkämpft ..." Ein Bericht zur politischen Sozialisation im Kohlenbergbau-Revier', in Greußing (1989).

Hummer, Hubert, Kannonier, Reinhard, Kepplinger, Brigitte (Eds.) (1986), *Die Pflicht zum Widerstand. Festschrift Peter Kammerstätter zum 75. Geburtstag*, Europaverlag, Linz.

Hwaletz, Otto, et al. (1984), *Bergmann oder Werkssoldat. Eisenerz als Fallbeispiel industrieller Politik. Dokumente und Analysen über die Österreichisch-Alpine Montangesellschaft in der Zwischenkriegszeit*, Strahelm, Graz.

Hwaletz, Otto, Stocker, Karl (1984), 'Dokumente und Flugblätter zu den Gemeinderatswahlen in Eisenerz 1928 und 1932', in Hwaletz et al. (1984).

Iggers, George C. (1985), *New directions in European historiography*. Revised edition, Methuen, London.

Internationale Tagung der Historiker der Arbeiterbewegung (1983), *17. Linzer Konferenz 1981*, Europaverlag, Vienna.

Internationale Tagung der Historiker der Arbeiterbewegung (1989), *20. Linzer Konferenz 1984*, Europaverlag, Vienna.

Jäckel, Eberhard (1977), 'Rückblick auf die sog. Hitlerwelle', *Geschichte in Wissenschaft und Unterricht*, 28.

Jahoda, Maria, Lazarsfeld, Paul F., Zeisel, Hans (1960), *Die Arbeitslosen von Marienthal. Ein Soziographischer Versuch mit einem Anhang zur Geschichte der Soziographie*, Verlag für Demoskopie, Allensbach.

Jeffery, Charlie (1992a), 'Patronage, Macht und Ohnmacht: Die Sozialdemokraten in Steyr in der Ersten Republik', *Österreichische Zeitschrift für Politikwissenschaft*, 21.

Jeffery, Charlie (1992b), 'Konsens und Dissens im Dritten Reich. Mit einer Fallstudie über Oberösterreich', *Zeitgeschichte*, 19.

Jeffery, Charlie (1993), 'Beyond Red Vienna: new perspectives on Social Democracy in the Austrian First Republic', *German History*, 11.

Kammerstätter, Peter (1986), 'Antifaschismus, Berge, Heimat, Politik. Kristallisationspunkte einer oberösterreichischen Arbeiterbiographie', in Hummer, Kannonier, Kepplinger (1986).

Kannonier, Reinhard (1981), *Zwischen Beethoven und Eisler. Zur Arbeitermusikbewegung in Österreich*, Europaverlag, Vienna.

Kannonier, Reinhard (1987), 'Arbeitswelt und Kultur', in Kropf (1987).

Karny, Thomas (1990), *Lesebuch zur Geschichte der Oberösterreichischen Arbeiter*, Edition Geschichte der Heimat, Grünbach.

Kaut, Josef (1982), *Der steinige Weg. Geschichte der sozialistischen Bewegung im Lande Salzburg*, Graphia, Salzburg.

Kepplinger, Brigitte (Ed.) (1989), *Wohnen in Linz. Zur Geschichte des Linzer Arbeiterwohnbaus von den Anfängen bis 1945*, Böhlau, Vienna.

Kern, Felix (n.d.), *Der Oberösterreichische Bauern- und Kleinhäuslerbund.* Volume 2, Oberösterreichscher Landesverlag, Ried.

Kitchen, Martin (1980), *The coming of Austrian Fascism*, Croom Helm, London.

Klenner, Fritz (1951), *Die Österreichischen Gewerkschaften. Band 1*, Verlag des Österreichischen Gewerkschaftsbundes, Vienna.

Klenner, Fritz (1953), *Die Österreichischen Gewerkschaften. Band 2*, Verlag des Österreichischen Gewerkschaftsbundes, Vienna.

Kluge, Ulrich (1984), 'Krisenherde der Ersten Republik Österreich. Beiträge zur Früh- und Spätphase der innenpolitischen Entwicklung', *Neue Politische Literatur*, 29.

Knapp, Vincent J. (1980), *Austrian Social Democracy 1889-1914*, University Press of America, Washington DC.

Konrad, Helmut (1981), *Das Entstehen der Arbeiterklasse in Oberösterreich*, Europaverlag, Vienna.

Konrad, Helmut (1983a), *Geschichte als demokratischer Auftrag*, Europaverlag, Linz.

Konrad, Helmut (1983b), 'Arbeitergeschichte und Raum', in Konrad (1983a).

Konrad, Helmut (1983c), 'Zur Regionalgeschichtsschreibung der Arbeiterbewegung in Österreich', in Internationale Tagung der Historiker der Arbeiterbewegung, *17. Linzer Konferenz 1981*, Europaverlag, Vienna.

Konrad, Helmut (1986), 'Zur österreichischen Arbeiterkultur der Zwischenkriegszeit', in Boll (1986).

Konrad, Helmut (n.d.), 'Regionale Arbeitergeschichte in Österreich: Oberösterreichs Entwicklung und die Metallarbeiter Niederösterreichs als Beispiel', in Verein für Geschichte der Arbeiterbewegung (Ed.), *Feuer - nicht Asche. Festchrift zum 25-jährigen Bestehen des Vereins für Geschichte der Arbeiterbewegung*, Vorwärts, Vienna.

Konrad, Helmut, Schmidlechner, Karin (Eds.) (1991), *Revolutionäres Potential in Europa am Ende des Ersten Weltkrieges*, Böhlau, Vienna.

Konrad, Helmut, Maderthaner, Wolfgang (Eds.) (1984), *Neuere Studien zur Arbeitergeschichte. Zum 25jährigen Bestehen des Vereins für Geschichte der Arbeiterbewegung*, Europaverlag, Vienna.

Kotlan-Werner, Henrietta (1977), *Kunst und Volk. David Josef Bach, 1874-1947*, Europaverlag, Vienna.

Kotlan-Werner, Henriette (1982), *Otto-Felix Kanitz und der Schönbrunner Kreis. Die Arbeitsgemeinschaft sozialistischer Erzieher 1923-1934*, Europaverlag, Vienna.

Krammer, Reinhard (1981), *Arbeitersport in Österreich. Ein Beitrag zur Geschichte der Arbeiterkultur in Österreich*, Europaverlag, Vienna.

Kropf, Rudolf (Ed.) (1987), *Arbeit/Mensch/Maschine. Der Weg in die Industriegesellschaft*, Gutenberg, Linz.

Kulemann, Peter (1979), *Am Beispiel des Austromarxismus. Die Sozialdemokratische Arbeiterbewegung in Österreich von Hainfeld bis zur Dollfuß-Diktatur*, Junius, Hamburg.

Kutschera, Richard (1972), *Johannes Maria Gföllner. Bischof dreier Zeitenwenden*, Oberösterreichischer Landesverlag, Linz.

Langewiesche, Dieter (1979), *Zur Freizeit des Arbeiters. Bildungsbestrebungen und Freizeitgestaltung österreichscher Arbeiter im Kaiserreich und in der Ersten Republik*, Klett-Cotta, Stuttgart.

Langhof, Kordula (1983), *Mit uns zeht die Neue Zeit. Pädagogik und Arbeiterbewegung am Beispiel der österreichischen Kinderfreunde*, Geminal, Bochum.

Leichter, Otto (1964), *Glanz und Ende der Ersten Republik. Wie es zum österreichischen Bürgerkrieg kam*, Europaverlag, Vienna.

Leser, Norbert (1968), *Zwischen Reformismus und Bolschewismus. Der Austromarxismus als Theorie und Praxis*, Europaverlag, Vienna.

Lewis, Jill (1991), *Fascism and the working class in Austria. The failure of Austrian labour*, Berg, Oxford.

Lijphart, Arend (1968), 'Typologies of democratic systems', *Comparative Political Studies*, **1**.

Luther, Kurt Richard, Wolfgang C. Müller (Eds.) (1992a), *Politics in Austria. Still a case of consociationalism?*, Frank Cass, London.

Luther, Kurt Richard, Wolfgang C. Müller (1992b), 'Consociationalism and the Austrian political system', in Luther, Müller (1992a).

Mayr, Johann (1988), '100 Jahre - 10 Bürgermeister. Die Linzer vertrauen den Sozialisten', in SPÖ-Bezirksorganisation Linz-Stadt (1988).

Mayrhofer, Josef (n.d.), *Aus meinem Leben*, typewritten manuscript, Steyr.

McLoughlin, Barry (1983-1984), 'Die Organisation des Wiener Neustädter Schutzbundes', *Zeitgeschichte*, **11**.

Michels, Robert (1911), *Zur Soziologie des Parteiwesens in der modernen Demokratie*, Klinkhardt, Leipzig.

Michels, Robert (1959), *Political Parties. A Sociological Study of the Oligarchical Tendencies of Modern Democracy*, Dover, New York.

Mit uns zieht die neue Zeit': Arbeiterkultur in Österreich 1918-1934. Katalog zur Ausstellung (1981), Vienna.

Müller, Wolfgang C. (1988), 'Patronage im österreichischen Parteiensystem: Theoretische Überlegungen und empirische Befunde', in Pelinka, Plasser (Eds.) (1988).

Nasko, Siegrfried (1986), *Empor aus dumpfen Träumen. Arbeiterbewegung und Sozialdemokratie im St. Pöltener Raum*, SPÖ-Bezirksorganisation St. Pölten, St. Pölten.

Natter, Bernhard (1989), 'Ein "Schutzdamm gegen die Sturmesfluten des Sozialismus". Zur politischen Funktion der Bildungs- und Kulturarbeit der katholischen Arbeiterbewegung in Tirol vor 1934', in Greußing (1989).

Neugebauer, Wolfgang (1975), *Bauvolk der kommenden Welt. Geschichte der Sozialistischen Jugendbewegung in Österreich*, Europaverlag, Vienna.

Oberkofler, Gerhard (1982), *Der 15. Juli 1927 in Tirol. Regionale Bürokratie und Arbeiterbewegung*, Europaverlag, Vienna.

Oberkofler, Gerhard (1986), *Die Tiroler Arbeiterbewegung. Von den Anfängen bis zum Zweiten Weltkrieg*, Second Edition, Europaverlag, Vienna.

Österreich, Brandherd Europas (1934), Genossenschaft Universumsbücherei, Zurich.

Padgett, Stephen (1984), 'Social and cultural studies in mass politics: The German Social Democratic Party', *West European Politics*, **7**.

Panebianco, Angelo (1988), *Political parties: organisation and power*, Cambridge University Press, Cambridge.

Pauley, Bruce F. (1972), *Hahnenschwanz und Hakenkreuz. Steirischer Heimatschutz und österreichischer Nationalsozialismus 1918-1934*, Europaverlag, Vienna.

Perfahl, Brigitte (1984), 'Linz und Steyr - Zentren des Kampfes', in Stadler (1984).

Pelinka, Anton, Plasser, Franz (Eds.) (1988), *Das österreichische Parteiensystem*, Böhlau, Vienna.

Peukert, Detlev (1987), 'The lost generation: youth unemployment at the end of the Weimar Republic', in Evans, Geary (1987).

Pferschy, Gerhard (1983), 'Steiermark', in Weinzierl, Skalnik (1983).

Pfoser, Alfred (1980), *Literatur und Austromarxismus*, Löcker, Vienna.

Quatember, Wolfgang (1989), 'Generalstreik im Dorf. Der Aufstand des Republikanische Schutzbundes im Februar 1934 in Ebensee', in Greußing (1989).

Rabinbach, Anson G. (Ed.) (1985), *The Austrian Socialist experiment. Social Democracy and Austromarxism, 1918-1934*, Westview Press, Boulder, Colorado.

Rabinbach, Anson G. (1983), *The crisis of Austrian Socialism. From Red Vienna to civil war 1927-1934*, University of Chicago Press, London.

Radmoser, Walter (n.d.), *Der lange Weg. 100 Jahre Sozialdemokratie in Steyr*, Gutenberg, Linz.

Rásky, Béla (1992), *Arbeiterfesttage. Die Fest- und Feiernkultur der sozialdemokratischen Bewegung in der Ersten Republik Österreich 1918-1934*, Europaverlag, Vienna.

Resch, Andreas (1989), '"Rotes Gsott" und christlichsoziale Bauern. Der Steyrer Landarbeiterstreik im Jahre 1922', in Greußing (1989).

Riedmann, Josef (1983), 'Tirol', in Weinzierl, Skalnik (1983).

Rußmann, Julius (1928), 'Kann Steyr eine Stadt des Fremdenverkehrs werden?', in Stein (1928).

Salzer, Wilhelm (n.d.), *Geschichte der Christlichen Arbeiterbewegung Oberösterreichs*, Oberösterreichischer Landesverlag, Linz.

Schediwy, Robert (1990), 'Die Blütezeit des kommunalen Sozialismus', in Fröschl, Mesner, Zoitl (1990).

Scheu, Friedrich (1977), *Humor als Waffe. Politisches Kabarett in der Ersten Republik*, Europaverlag, Vienna.

Schiffer, Karl (1984), 'Die Linke in der steirischen Sozialdemokratie während der Ersten Republik. Ein autobiographischer Bericht', in Hinteregger, Müller, Staudinger.

Schindler, Gerd (1973-1974), 'Der 12. Februar in Kärnten', *Zeitgeschichte*, **1**.

Schlag, Gerald (1983), 'Burgenland', in Weinzierl, Skalnik (1983).

Schmidlechner, Karin-Maria (1991), 'Arbeiterbewegung und revolutionäres Potential in Europa am Ende des Ersten Weltkrieges: Die Situation in Österreich', in Konrad, Schmidlechner (1991).

Sechzig Briefe der Solidarität (1926), Jungbrunnen, Vienna.

Seibert, Franz (1978), *Die Konsumgenossenschaften in Österreich*, Europaverlag, Vienna.

Seper, Hans (1964), *100 Jahre Steyr-Daimler-Puch. Der Werdegang eines österreichischen Industrie-Unternehmens*, Mally & Co., Vienna.

Sichlrader, Franz (1930), 'Das Schicksal der Stadt Steyr', *Arbeit und Wirtschaft*, **8**.

Slapnicka, Harry (1974), *Von Hauser bis Eigruber. Eine Zeitgeschichte Oberösterreichs Band 1. 1918-1927*, Oberösterreichischer Landesverlag, Linz.

Slapnicka, Harry (1975), *Oberösterreich - Zwischen Bürgerkrieg und Anschluss (1927-1938)*, Oberösterreichischer Landesverlag, Linz.

Slapnicka, Harry (1983), 'Oberösterreich', in Weinzierl, Skalnik (1983).

Speiser, Wolfgang (1986), *Die sozialistischen Studenten Wiens 1927-1938*, Europaverlag, Vienna.

SPÖ-Bezirksorganisation Linz-Stadt (Ed.) (1988), *Die Bewegung lebt. 100 Jahre Linzer Sozialdemokratie*, Gutenberg, Linz.

SPÖ-Bezirksorganisation Vöcklabruck (Ed.) (1989), *Zeit und Zeugnis. Chronik der Sozialdemokratie im Bezirk Vöcklabruck*, Institut für Wissenschaft und Kunst Oberösterreich, Linz.

SPÖ Mauthausen (Ed.) (1989), *Der harte Weg. Die Geschichte der Arbeiterbewegung von Mauthausen*, Edition Geschichte der Heimat, Grünbach.

Stachura, Peter D. (Ed.) (1986), *Unemployment and the Great Depression in Weimar Germany*, Macmillan, London.

Stadler, Karl R. (Ed.) (1984), '*Es Wird Nicht Mehr Verhandelt ...' Der 12. Februar 1934 in Oberösterreich*, Gutenberg, Linz.

Starhemberg, Ernst Rüdiger (1971), *Memoiren*, Amalthea, Vienna.

Staudinger, Eduard G. (1985), '"Unabhängige Gewerkschaft" und Arbeiterschaft in der Steiermark 1927-1933', *Geschichte und Gegenwart*, **4**.

Stein, Erwin (Ed.) (1928), *Die Städte Deutschösterreichs. Band II. Steyr und Bad Hall*, Deutscher Kommunalverlag, Berlin.

Steinböck, Erwin (1983), 'Kärnten', in Weinzierl, Skalnik (1983).

Stiefel, Dieter (1979), *Arbeitslosigkeit. Soziale, politische und wirtschaftliche Auswirkungen am Beispiel Österreichs 1918-1938*, Duncker und Humblot, Berlin.

Stocker, Karl (1984), 'Akkumulationszwang und Arbeiterinteresse. Beiträge über die Umsetzung von Verwertungsinteressen in soziale Tatsachen am Beispiel der ÖAMG', in Hinteregger, Müller, Staudinger (1984).

Stocker, Karl (1991), '"Trotz völliger Lockerung der Mannszucht ..." Soziale Konflikte in der Österreichisch-Alpinen Montangesellschaft 1917-1919', in Konrad, Schmidlechner (1991).

Stockinger, Josef (1988), *Zeit, die prägt. Arbeiterbewegung in Steyr*, Gutenberg, Linz.

Stubenvoll, Karl (1984), 'Zur Genesis und Funktion des Anti-Terror-Gesetzes', in Konrad, Maderthaner (1984).

Sully, Melanie A. (1982), *Continuity and change in Austrian Socialism. The eternal quest for the third way*, Columbia University Press, New York.

Thurner, Erika (1989), 'Vom proletarischen Insel-Dasein zum Leben im "Roten Salzburg". Salzburger Impressionen nach dem Zweiten Weltkrieg', in Greußing (1989).

Treml, Erich, Hawle, Christian (1988), *Der Widerstand in Attnang-Puchheim 1934-1945. Eine Dokumentation*, Österreichischer Gewerkschaftsbund Bezirksbildungsausschuß Vöcklabruck, Timelkam.

Uitz, Helmut (1975), *Die österreichischen Kinderfreunde und Roten Falken 1908-1938. Beiträge zur sozialistischen Erziehung*, Geyer Edition, Salzburg.

Verein für Geschichte der Arbeiterbewegung (Ed.) (n.d.), *Feuer - nicht Asche. Festschrift zum 25jährigen Bestehen des Vereins für Geschichte der Arbeiterbewegung*, Vorwärts, Vienna.

Wadl, Wilhelm, Ogris, Alfred (1988), *Das Jahr 1938 in Kärnten und seine Vorgeschichte. Ereignisse - Dokumente - Bilder*, Verlag des Kärntner Landesarchivs, Klagenfurt.

Wandruszka, Adam, 'Österreichs politische Struktur. Die Entwicklung der Parteien und politischen Bewegungen', in Benedikt (1954).

Waterbury, John (1977), 'An attempt to put patrons and clients in their place', in Gellner, Waterbury (1977).

Wanner, Gerhard (1983), 'Vorarlberg', in Weinzierl, Skalnik (1983).

Weber-Felber, Ulrike (1990), *Wege aus der Krise: Freie Gewerkschaften und Wirtschaftspolitik in der Ersten Republik*, Europaverlag, Vienna and Zurich.

Weidenholzer, Josef (1981), *Auf dem Weg zum Neuen Menschen. Bildungs- und Kulturarbeit der österreichischen Sozialdemokratie in der Ersten Republik*, Europaverlag, Vienna.

Weidenholzer, Josef (1984), 'Bedeutung und Hintergrund des 12. Februar 1934', in Stadler (1984).

Weidenholzer, Josef, (1985) 'Red Vienna: a new Atlantis?', in Rabinbach (1985).

Weidenholzer, Josef (1988), 'Ein Jahrhundert Sozialdemokratie in Linz', in SPÖ-Bezirksorganisation Linz-Stadt (1988).

Weihsmann, Helmut (1985), *Das rote Wien. Sozialdemokratische Architektur und Kommunalpolitik*, Edition Spuren, Vienna.

Weinzierl, Erika, Skalnik, Kurt (1983), *Österreich 1918-1938. Geschichte der Ersten Republik*, Styria, Graz.

Weissel, Erwin (1976), *Die Ohnmacht des Sieges. Arbeiterschaft und Sozialisierung nach dem Ersten Weltkrieg in Österreich*, Europaverlag, Vienna.

Wilding, Peter (1990), " ... *Für Arbeit und Brot*" Arbeitslose in Bewegung. *Arbeitslosenpolitik und Arbeitslosenbewegung in Österreich*, Europaverlag, Vienna.

Witzany, Hans (1928), 'Kriegszeit und Revolution in Steyr', in 'Ein Oberösterreicher' (1928).

Zentralstelle des Fremdenverkehrs in Steyr und Umgebung (Ed.) (1930), *Stadt Steyr. Die Alte Eisenstadt in Oberösterreich. 980 bis 1930*, Steyr.

Zoitl, Helge (1992), *'Student kommt von Studieren!' Zur Geschichte der sozialistischen Studentenbewegung in Wien*, Europaverlag, Vienna.

Index